Green Park (Reading Business

Phase 2 Excavations 1995
Neolithic and Bronze Age Sites

by Adam Brossler, Robert Early and Carol Allen

with contributions by
Alistair Barclay, Paul Blinkhorn, Angela Boyle, Philippa Bradley, Gill Campbell,
Rowena Gale, Elaine Morris, Mark Robinson, Fiona Roe, Robert Scaife, Maisie Taylor,
David Williams, Bob Wilson

Illustrations by
Luke Adams and Mike Middleton

Oxford Archaeology

Thames Valley Landscapes Monograph No. 19

2004

The publication of this volume has been generously funded by Prudential Property Investment Managers Limited

Published for Oxford Archaeology by Oxford University School of Archaeology as part of the Thames Valley Landscapes Monograph series

Designed by Oxford Archaeology Graphics Office

Edited by Carol Allen and Angela Boyle

This book is part of a series of monographs about the Thames Valley Landscapes – which can be bought from all good bookshops and Internet Bookshops. For more information visit www.oxfordarch.co.uk

ISBN 0904220-33-8

Typeset and printed by the Dorset Press, Henry Ling Ltd

Contents

CHAPTER 1: INTRODUCTION *by Adam Brossler*

CHAPTER 2: EXCAVATIONS OF AREA 3017 *by Adam Brossler*

CHAPTER 3: EXCAVATIONS OF AREA 3000B *by Adam Brossler and Carol Allen*

CHAPTER 4: THE ARTEFACTS

CHAPTER 5: ENVIRONMENTAL EVIDENCE

CHAPTER 6: DISCUSSION AND CONCLUSIONS *by Adam Brossler and Carol Allen, with contributions by Angela Boyle*

Figures

Plates

Tables

Summary

In 1995 a second phase of excavations was undertaken by Oxford Archaeological Unit (OAU) at Reading Business Park in advance of development. Two areas, 3017 and 3000B, were investigated covering about 2.2 ha. Evidence of occupation in the Neolithic, Bronze Age and medieval periods was found.

In Area 3017 Neolithic features were uncovered, including an unusual segmented ring ditch, and a number of pits and postholes. The ring ditch was radiocarbon dated to the middle to late Neolithic, and an interesting flint assemblage from all features on the site was dated mainly to the later Neolithic. Numerous tree-throw holes also contained later Neolithic flint. Only two pits contained Neolithic pottery, one with Peterborough Ware and one with a Grooved Ware rim.

In the earlier phase of Area 3000B Deverel Rimbury pottery was deposited in pits, in one case with two cremations. Dating of associated charcoal gave a middle to late Bronze Age date, identical to the date from another pit containing late Bronze Age pottery. A field system, composed of rectangular boundary ditches, was laid out in the area prior to the establishment of a late Bronze Age settlement.

The late Bronze Age occupation area included five roundhouses, and a number of post-built structures. Waterholes, pits and postholes were also found, many of which contained late Bronze Age pottery. Some medieval activity was also present in this area.

The pottery assemblage of Area 3000B is unusual as it shows continuity from the Deverel Rimbury pottery types of the middle Bronze Age to the plainwares of the later Bronze Age. Little decorated pottery was found in Area 3000B, in contrast to the adjacent Area 3100 previously excavated, suggesting the settlement had shifted over time. Other artefacts found include a shale bracelet, worked wood, with one piece possibly from a cheese press, and a worked piece of human skull. Interesting comparisons are made between the flintworking, economic activities and environment of the Neolithic and Bronze Age farmers at this location. In the later Bronze Age numerous deposits of burnt flint were made in the north-east of Area 3000B, and these grew into a substantial and unusually large elongated burnt mound. The origin of the deposits is discussed together with the management of the landscape in the later Bronze Age.

Résumé

En 1995, une seconde phase de fouilles furent entreprises par l'*Oxford Archaeological Unit* (OAU) à *Reading Business Park*, en avance de la mise en exploitation. Deux zones, 3017 et 3000B, firent l'objet des recherches, couvrant un espace d'environ 2,2ha. Des preuves d'occupation du Néolithique à l'âge du Bronze et de la période médiévale furent découvertes.

Dans la zone 3017, des faits archéologiques du Néolithique furent mis au jour, y compris un *Ring ditch* segmenté inhabituel ainsi qu'un certain nombre de fosses et trous de poteaux. Le *ring ditch* fut daté par radiocarbone entre le milieu et la fin du Néolithique, tandis qu'un assemblage intéressant de silex taillés provenant des autres faits du site ont procuré une datation essentiellement du Néolithique tardif. De nombreux trous d'arrachement d'arbres contenaient également des silex de la fin du néolithique. Seulement deux fosses ont révélé de la poterie néolithique, l'une contenant le type *Peterborough* et l'autre avec un bord de type *Grooved Ware*.

Au cours de la phase la plus ancienne identifiée sur la zone 3000B, de la poterie de type *Deverel Rimbury* fut placé dans des fosses, dans un des cas accompagné de deux incinérations. La datation de charbon de bois associé a fourni une date du milieu à la fin de l'âge du Bronze, identique à la datation d'une autre fosse contenant de la poterie de la fin de l'âge du Bronze. Un système agraire, formé de fossés d'enceinte rectangulaire, fut établi dans cette zone antérieurement à la formation d'un site d'habitation de l'âge du Bronze tardif. La zone d'occupation de la fin de l'âge du Bronze comprenanit 5 maisons circulaires et un certain nombre de structures sur poteaux. Des points d'eau, fosses et poteaux furent également découverts, nombre d'entre eux contenaient de la poterie de l'âge du Bronze tardif.

Des activités liées à l'époque médiévale étaient également présentes dans cette zone.

L'assemblage de poterie de la zone 3000B est inhabituel étant donné qu'il montre une continuité depuis les poteries de type *Deverel Rimbury* du milieu de l'âge du Bronze jusqu'aux productions uniformes de l'âge du Bronze tardif. Peu de poterie décorée fut mise au jour dans la zone 3000B, en comparaison à la zone adjacente 3100, fouillée antérieurement, ce qui suggère un déplacement du site d'habitation au cours du temps.

Les autres objets découverts comprennent un bracelet d'argile schisteuse, du bois taillé, notamment une pièce provenant peut-être d'un pressoir à fromage et un fragment travaillé de crâne humain.

Des comparaisons intéressantes se posent en ce lieu entre le travail du silex, les activités économiques et l'environnement des fermiers du néolithique et de l'âge du Bronze.

Au cours de l'âge du Bronze tardif de nombreux dépôts de silex brûlés furent placés au nord-est de l'aire 3000B. Ces derniers se développèrent en un *burnt mound* (tertre de pierres brûlées) substantiel, de taille inhabituellement large et de forme allongée. L'origine de ces dépôts fait l'objet d'une discussion en même temps que l'exploitation du paysage vers la fin de l'âge du Bronze.

Zusammenfassung

1995 führte die Oxford Archaeological Unit (OAU) im Reading Business Park vor Beginn der Erschließungsarbeiten eine zweite Grabungsphase durch. Untersucht wurden zwei Areale, 3017 und 3000B, die eine Fläche von etwa 2,2 Hektar umfassen. Dabei wurden neolithische, bronzezeitliche und mittelalterliche Siedlungshinweise gefunden.

In Areal 3017 kamen neolithische Spuren zum Vorschein, unter anderem ein ungewöhnlich segmentierter Kreisgraben sowie mehrere Gruben und Pfostenlöcher. Der Kreisgraben konnte mithilfe von Radiokarbonmessungen auf das mittlere bis späte Neolithikum datiert werden, eine interessante Feuersteinsammlung von allen Fundstätten des Areals stammte vornehmlich aus dem späten Neolithikum. Auch zahlreiche durch Baumwurf verursachte Löcher enthielten spätneolithischen Feuerstein. Nur zwei Gruben zeigten neolithische Keramik, eine davon »Peterborough Ware«, die andere einen »Grooved Ware«-Rand.

In der Frühzeit von Areal 3000B wurde »Deverel Rimbury«-Keramik in Gruben eingelagert, in einem Fall zusammen mit zwei Brandbestattungen. Die Datierung von zugehörigen Holzkohleresten verwies auf die mittlere bis späte Bronzezeit. Dies stimmte mit dem Datum einer anderen Grube überein, die Keramik aus der späten Bronzezeit enthielt. Schon vor der spätbronzezeitlichen Besiedlung wurde in dem Gebiet ein Flursystem mit rechteckigen Begrenzungsgräben angelegt. Das Siedlungsareal aus der späten Bronzezeit zeigte fünf Rundhütten und mehrere Pfostenbauten. Darüber hinaus wurden Wasserlöcher, Gruben und Pfostenlöcher gefunden, viele mit spätbronzezeitlicher Keramik. Dieses Areal enthielt außerdem Hinweise auf mittelalterliche Aktivitäten.

Die Keramiksammlung aus Areal 3000B ist ungewöhnlich, da sie auf eine Kontinuität von der Keramik des »Deverel Rimbury«-Typs aus der mittleren Bronzezeit bis zur einfachen Keramik der späten Bronzezeit hinweist. Im Gegensatz zum angrenzenden Areal 3100, das schon vorher ausgegraben worden war, fand sich in Areal 3000B kaum verzierte Keramik, was darauf schließen lässt, dass sich die Besiedlung mit der Zeit verlagerte. Zu den sonstigen Funden zählten ein Schieferarmband, bearbeitete Holzteile, darunter eines, das möglicherweise von einer Käsepresse stammte, und ein menschliches Schädelfragment, das Bearbeitungsspuren aufwies. Es werden interessante Vergleiche zwischen der Flintbearbeitung, den wirtschaftlichen Aktivitäten und der Umwelt der neolithischen und bronzezeitlichen Bauern, die diesen Ort besiedelten, angestellt.

In der späten Bronzezeit wurden zahlreiche Feuersteine mit Brandspuren im Nordosten von Areal 3000B abgelagert, die schließlich einen ungewöhnlich großen, lang gestreckten Brandhaufen bildeten. Der Ursprung dieser Ablagerungen wird in Zusammenhang mit der Landnutzung in der späten Bronzezeit diskutiert.

Acknowledgements

Oxford Archaeology gratefully acknowledges the funding of Prudential Property Investment Managers Ltd for both the excavations and publication of this second phase of excavations at Green Park (formerly called Reading Business Park). We would also like to thank Paul Chadwick and Pete Fasham (Berkshire County Council and Babtie, respectively) for their advice and assistance. We are grateful to Lee Montague of Caversham Project Management for his assistance with the smooth running of the project. The OAU project director was Rob Early, and the site supervisor was Richard Brown. Thanks are due to all the specialists who contributed their reports, and to those who provided additional information, particularly Philippa Bradley and Elaine Morris, and to Oxford Archaeology North staff Joanne Cook and Erika Guttmann for assistance. The report was initially written by Adam Brossler and edited by Angela Boyle and it was completed and finally edited by Carol Allen. Wendy Sherlock was the copy editor and the translations were undertaken by Valerie Diez and Gerlinde Krug. The illustrations were compiled by Mike Middleton, Luke Adams and Lesley Collett.

Location of the project archive

The archive of the Reading Business Park excavations will be deposited with Reading Museum, Berkshire under accession code 1996.193.

A copy of the archive will also be deposited with the National Monuments Record Centre, Swindon.

Chapter 1:   Introduction

by Adam Brossler

Location

The site of Reading Business Park is being developed over an area of approximately 80 ha just to the south-west of Reading at Small Mead Farm (Fig. 1.1). The site lies 3.5 km from the centre of Reading and just to the north of the M4 (SU 470170). The River Kennet runs approximately 1 km to the north and a tributary, Foundry Brook, flows from north-east to south-west through the area.

Background to the excavations

This is an area of high archaeological potential and has been the subject of a number of archaeological investigations. All these, summarised below, confirmed the presence of extensive archaeological remains (Moore and Jennings 1992, 2–3).

A field walking programme, undertaken in 1983 and 1984 as part of the Kennet Valley Survey, funded by English Heritage, produced finds from a number of locations in the development area. Following this in 1985, the Trust for Wessex

Archaeology (TWA) carried out an archaeological evaluation based on excavation of a series of test-holes and mechanically excavated trenches (see Fig. 1.2).

First phase of excavations 1987–8

Oxford Archaeological Unit (OAU) carried out further evaluation and subsequently excavated Areas 5 and 2000 in 1987. Flooding temporarily halted excavations in Area 3100 in 1987, and excavations in Areas 4000, 5000 and 6000 were completed (Fig. 1.2). Excavations of Area 3100 were finished in August 1988, and the results of all these excavations were then published (Moore and Jennings 1992). The work carried out by OAU in 1987 and 1988 was the first full phase of investigations prior to development of the Reading Business Park and in this report are referred to as the RBP1 excavations. The first stage of work was funded by Bucknall Brothers (Holdings) Limited and Sheraton Securities International plc.

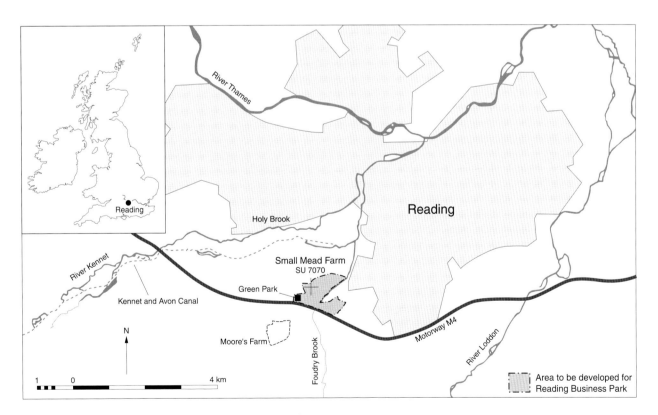

Figure 1.1   Location of Reading Business Park development

1

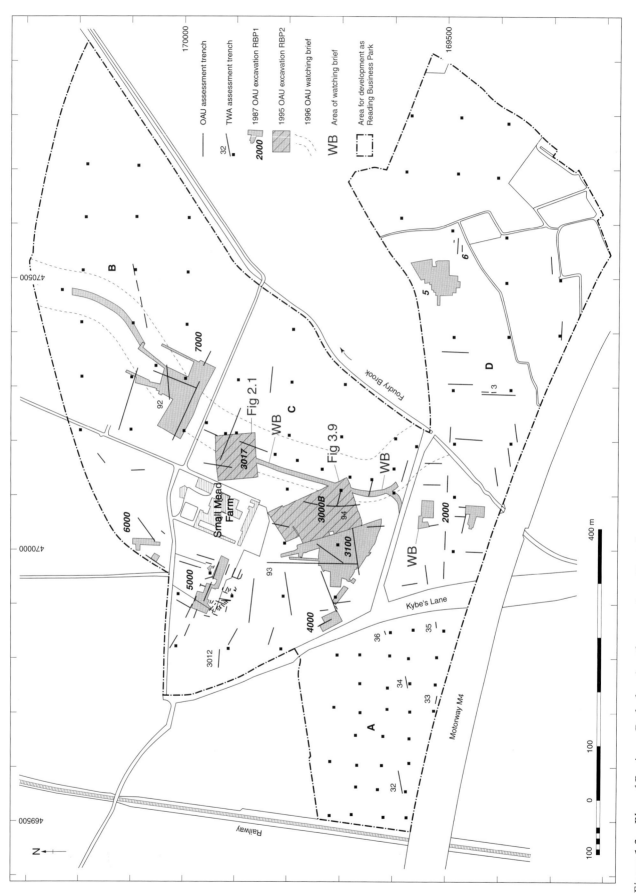

Figure 1.2   Plan of Business Park showing the areas investigated

2

Second phase of excavations 1995

The second phase of the excavations at Reading Business Park took place in 1995 when Areas 3017 and 3000B were investigated (Fig. 1.2). The results of these excavations (RBP2) are the subject of this report, and this volume also presents the results of the watching brief undertaken in 1996. Area 3017 lay on an island of gravel just to the south-west of Area 7000 and Area 3000B was an eastwards continuation of Area 3100 excavated in the first stage, where extensive archaeological remains were found (ibid.). Prudential Portfolio Managers funded this phase of the excavations.

Structure of this report

This chapter summarises the results of the Phase 1 excavations, and subsequent chapters report the results of the 1995 excavations, commencing with the Neolithic activity in Area 3017 in Chapter 2. A small amount of Bronze Age and medieval remains were also apparent in this area. The main location of intensive late Bronze Age occupation was found in Area 3000B, which is presented in Chapter 3. The artefactual evidence forms Chapter 4, and Chapter 5 presents results of the environmental analysis. Discussion of the features and artefacts for each period is covered in Chapter 6. Reference is made throughout the report to the earlier excavations on this site and to other nearby sites of similar date, in order to compare and interpret the current material. This is particularly relevant to the important assemblage of late Bronze Age pottery found in both the RBP1 and RBP2 stages of excavations.

No attempt is made in this report to present an overview of the current state of knowledge in this locality during the prehistoric periods, particularly of the late Bronze Age. Excavations at Green Park in the west of the Reading Business Park development area continued between October 2000 and May 2001, and excavation has also taken place in advance of a planning application for gravel extraction, at Moore's Farm, Burghfield, to the south of Reading Business Park in the summer of 1999 (see Fig. 1.1). At both locations late Bronze Age features were found and the results of all these investigations will be considered together in a later volume.

Summary of first phase of excavations

The first phase of excavations, carried out by OAU between 1987 and 1988, examined seven Areas, 5, 2000, 3100, 4000, 5000, 6000 and 7000. The two sites of particular relevance to the 1995 excavations were Area 3100, adjacent to Area 3000B, and Area 7000, which was located to the north of Area 3017. Substantial evidence of prehistoric activity was found, particularly of Neolithic and late Bronze Age date.

Area 3100

Excavations identified five phases of field boundary ditches considered to be of Bronze Age date, and aerial photographs indicate that these rectilinear ditches run across the entire development area (Moore and Jennings 1992, 1). Extensive late Bronze Age settlement was also identified, and a palaeo-channel lay to the north of the occupied area. The archaeological features uncovered comprised 928 postholes, 95 pits and an undated inhumation, and these were seen to form 10 roundhouses, 1 oval structure, 23 6–post and 4–post structures, and 38 2–post structures. The 95 pits were divided into two typologies, scoops and basin-shaped profiles, and it was suggested that the basin-shaped pits were primarily used for grain storage and were reused as rubbish pits. The function of the scoop-profiled pits was unclear. An east-west aligned row of pits, south of the main settlement, was interpreted as an area for flax retting and this was supported by the environmental evidence (ibid., 39–42).

Area 7000

Features of Neolithic, late Bronze Age and Roman date were revealed. A total of 118 pits, one of which held a cattle burial, and 34 postholes of Neolithic date were identified. Flints found dated the Neolithic activity and it was thought that the material had a possible date in the 3rd millennium BC (Bradley and Brown 1992, 89–90). The Neolithic pits, the main features identified during the excavation, formed a broad band orientated approximately north-west to south-east. It is possible therefore that this represented an area of special activity employing the flint assemblage (Moore and Jennings 1992, 6–13).

Areas 5, 2000, 4000, 5000 and 6000

Excavations of Area 5 revealed late Bronze Age activity, including a settlement of 20 circular structures, several 6–post and 4–post structures, and at least 33 2–post structures. Trial trenching around the area indicated that the settlement was associated with a Bronze Age field system (ibid., 14). In Area 2000 a total of 49 ditches, 70 pits, 62 postholes and 18 gullies ranging in date from the 1st to the 4th centuries AD were uncovered (ibid., 58).

Within Area 4000, to the west of Area 3100, two definite and two possible postholes, three pits and six scoops were found. Four features contained late Bronze Age worked flint, and a pit contained one sherd of Roman pottery (ibid., 48). Three different types of field boundary were revealed in Area 5000, pit alignments, segmented ditches and continuous ditches. A number of pits and postholes were scattered across the excavation area. No dating evidence was recovered from any of these features but it was assumed that they were contemporary with the prehistoric field boundaries (ibid., 55–6)

Within Area 6000 the excavated ditches were undated but it was suggested that these were Bronze Age. A small number of pits and scoops were found in the area, and these may have been of the same date. A number of intercutting ditches, thought to represent part of a post-medieval boundary, were found in Area 7000 (ibid., 56–7).

Excavation methodology

The RBP2 site was excavated in accordance with the agreed scheme for the development area (Moore and Miles 1988). The Areas 3000B and 3017 were machine-stripped to the first archaeological horizon or, in its absence, to the natural subsoil. The areas were cleaned and the features were hand excavated with OAU's single context recording scheme being used (Wilkinson 1992). A sampling strategy was designed based on the information from the results of the phase one excavations (Moore and Jennings 1992, 2 and 4). It was intended that approximately 50% of all pits and postholes should be sectioned, with the features chosen on the basis of spatial distribution, character and potential relationships with other features, particularly structures. In the event on Area 3017, 100% of features, with the exception of tree-throw holes were excavated. Ditches were sectioned at points where they shared a relationship with other features, and also along their lengths to establish their character. The burnt mound was divided into three areas and the two opposing quadrants of each area were fully excavated. The two quadrants of the burnt mound were environmentally sampled using a metre square grid, with alternate squares being 100% sampled.

The general environmental strategy was to target features that were likely to produce good material. Pits represented the main priority, while postholes were only sampled if they were part of a structure or contained artefactual material. Separate samples of 10 litres were taken from waterlogged deposits, and monoliths were taken from the palaeochannel and waterlogged pits.

A watching brief was maintained throughout the project in order to identify and sample archaeological deposits identified outside of the excavation areas.

Geology

The site is located on the valley gravel (Geological Survey Map, sheet 268) and Area 3000B was located on the first gravel terrace and Area 3017 on the second terrace. The gravel is overlain by poorly drained gley soils developed in light grey, non-calcareous clayey alluvium derived from London clay (Jarvis 1968, 67–9). At present the site is fairly level at 38 m OD and slopes gently from east to west. Slight variations in the underlying gravel have been covered by alluvium and disturbed by intensive modern ploughing and the construction of a Victorian sewage works. Further details on the soils, sediments and hydrology were provided in the first stage of the excavations (Moore and Jennings 1992, 4–5).

Chapter 2:   Excavations of Area 3017

by Adam Brossler

Introduction

Neolithic activity was identified within a ring ditch, tree-throw holes, pits and postholes in this area during the 1995 excavations. There was also evidence for a number of late Bronze Age pits and some medieval agricultural activity. Excavations uncovered an area of approximately 0.64 ha.

Neolithic

The segmented ring ditch

A ring ditch, composed of at least two semi-circular ditches, lay in the east of this area (Fig. 2.1, Plate 2.1), and a small oval pit lay between the north-eastern terminals of the two ditches (Fig. 2.2). The two main segments and the central area of the ditch were heavily truncated by modern land drains, ploughing and also by a medieval field boundary.

Ten sections were excavated through the ring ditch, examining approximately 90% of the surviving archaeology. The external diameter of the ditch was approximately 10 m, the width was between 0.80 and 1.60 m and the depth varied from 0.22 m to 0.62 m. The angle of the sides sloped from 45–60° down to a rounded or flat base. The base was irregular and undulating which resulted in the varying depths of the ditch sections shown on Figure 2.3. It was not clear from the excavated evidence whether the ring ditches had been deliberately or naturally backfilled although the two north-eastern terminals and the more westerly of the south-westerly terminals appeared to have been recut at some time.

No features were found within the central area of the ring ditch nor was there any evidence for the presence of either an outer bank or an internal mound, although the interior had been severely disturbed as described above. A ploughsoil (5001) of uncertain date covered the ring ditch, which cut into the natural loess (5002).

The lower ditch fills of the two main ditch segments (Fig. 2.2) were a brown-yellow silty sand (5074, 5077, 5100), and the upper fills (5073, 5076, 5092, 5095, 5112, 5114) were a darker silty sand with 1% charcoal flecks. Fills 5076 and 5092 each

Plate 2.1   Area 3017: segmented ring ditch, from the north

5

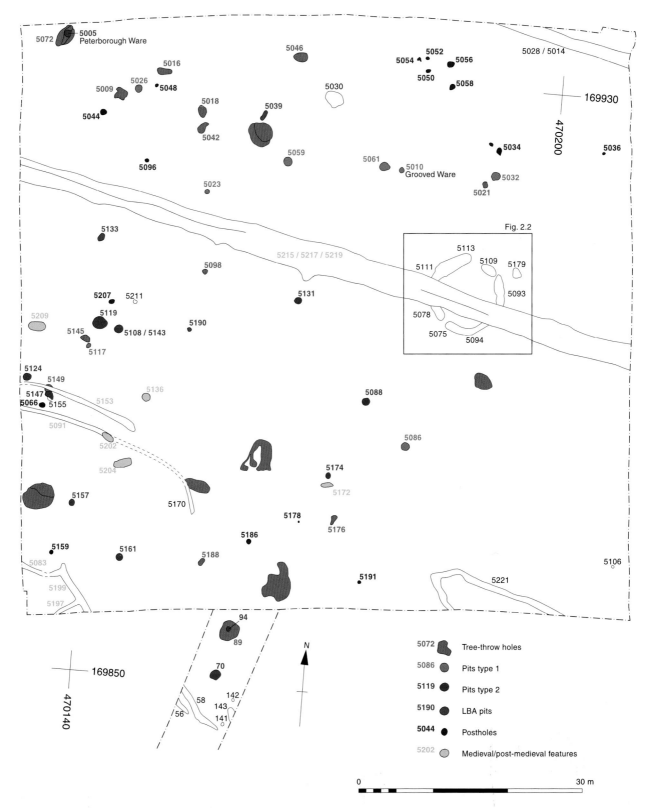

Figure 2.1   Plan of Area 3017 showing excavated features

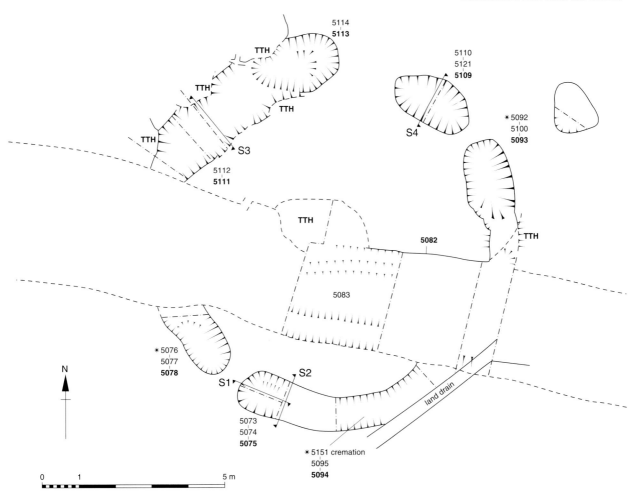

Figure 2.2   Plan of the Neolithic segmented ring ditch

contained worked flint and animal bone, together with one sherd of late Bronze Age pottery. This suggests that there was some disturbance of the upper part of the ditch in the late Bronze Age. Antler was also found in 5092, and worked flint in 5073, 5074, 5095 and 5100. Animal bone from 5076 was radiocarbon dated to 2900–2580 cal BC (95.4% confidence NZA9411, Table A1.1). A fragment of antler from 5092 gave a date of 2920–2620 cal BC (95.4% confidence NZA 9478, Table A1.1), suggesting that the ring ditch was of late Neolithic date. The flint found within the ditch fills also falls within this date (Bradley, Chapter 4).

In the southern part of the ditch the upper fill 5095 (of cut 5094) contained animal bone and one sherd of late Bronze Age pottery. In addition, an uncontained human adult female cremation (5151) was excavated from within this fill of the ditch (Boyle, Chapter 5). A sample of animal bone from 5095 was dated to 1700–1440 cal BC (95.4% confidence NZA 9508, Table

A1.1). This is only a single date but suggests that the cremation may have been cut into the ring ditch, and that the ditch was still visible during the middle Bronze Age, possibly a thousand years after it originated. No further burials were located within the ditch or the area it enclosed.

The oval pit 5109 between the terminals measured 2.10 × 1.14 m and was up to 0.45 m deep, with sides sloping at 70° down to a rounded base (Fig. 2.3). The fills were very similar to the main ditches and the upper fill 5110 contained flint.

Tree-throw holes

Twenty-eight tree-throw holes were excavated in Area 3017, and worked flint of later Neolithic date was found in eight of these (Table 4.3: 5009, 5016, 5021, 5042, 5046, 5072, 5145 and 5149).

The cuts of the tree-throw holes were irregular in shape, with a varying angle of slope of the sides, as

Table 2.1   Pits (Area 3017)

Date	Type 1	Type 2	Irrregular	Total no.	Context nos
Neolithic Pits	8			8	5010, 5023, 5026, 5032, 5059, 5061, 5086, 5117
		11		11	5005, 5088, 5108, 5119, 5124, 5131, 5143, 5147, 5157, 5161, 5174
Late Bronze Age		2		2	5133, 5190
			1	1	5039
Medieval		5		5	5136, 5172, 5202, 5204, 5209
Total	8	13	6	27	

Section 1

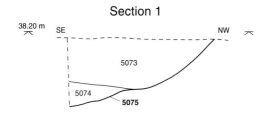

Section 2

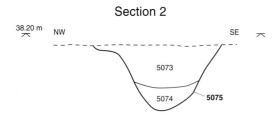

Section 3

Section 4

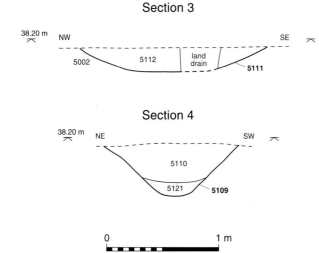

Figure 2.3   1–4: sections through ring ditch: for locations see Figure 2.2

seen in the sections in Figure 2.4. Fills, usually a silty loam, varied from grey-brown to red-brown. Fill 5148 (of 5149), was a loess sand, and fills of 5145, 5176, 5188 were also dark black-brown loess sand with a 10–25% charcoal content.

The trees fell to the north and east similar to most of those seen on Area 3100 of RBP1, whilst on Area 7000 trees had fallen in all directions (Moore and Jennings 1992, 47 and 13). Five sections indicated which way the trees had fallen in Area 3017, and three of these are illustrated (Fig. 2.4: 5016, 5018 and 5072). Three trees, shown by tree-throw holes 5009, 5072 and 5098, fell to the north and two, 5016 and 5018, fell to the east. There was no evidence for the deliberate burning of the trees, or for tree clearance.

Pits

Nineteen pits considered to be of Neolithic date were identified in this area (Table 2.1). There were two major types, pits circular or oval in plan with scooped sides and a round base (type 1), and those which were circular with a more rectangular profile and flat base (type 2). The pits were cut into the natural loess (5002) and were covered by the ploughsoil (5001). These are very similar to the two types found in the Neolithic Area 7000, which lay just to the north-east of Area 3017 (ibid., fig. 3).

Eight were circular or oval type 1 pits with scoop sides and round bases (5010, 5023, 5026, 5032, 5059, 5061, 5086, 5117). The angle of slope of the sides was fairly uniform varying little between 40–50°, although the diameter varied considerably from 0.50 m to 1.15 m. Two pits (5059, 5117) were more oval, measuring 0.40–0.90 m in diameter and 0.14–0.41 m in depth, and 5117 also truncated a tree-throw hole. Almost all the pit fills contained a low frequency of charcoal (1–5%).

Two pits of type 1 (5010, 5061) contained more than one fill, with two of the pits having a primary fill of yellow-brown sandy silt and an upper fill of dark brown clay silt. Pit 5010 contained three fills

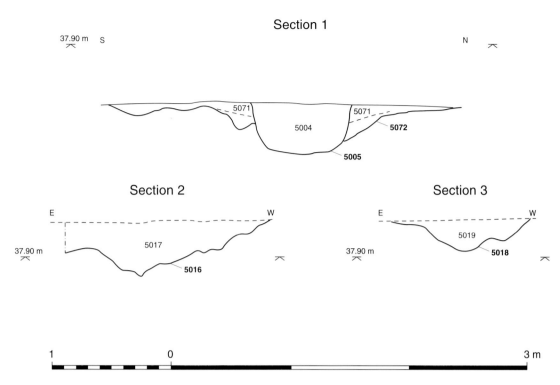

Figure 2.4 *Sections through tree-throw holes 5016, 5018 and 5072, and pit 5005*

Table 2.2 *Dimensions of postholes (Area 3017)*

Posthole no.	Shape	Dimensions m	Depth m
5034	oval	0.35 × 0.3	0.11
5036	circular	0.31 × 0.31	0.11
5044	circular	0.4 × 0.4	0.2
5048	circular	0.4 × 0.4	0.1
5050	oval	0.7 × 0.45	0.2
5052	circular	0.32 × 0.32	0.17
5054	circular	0.2 × 0.2	0.1
5058	circular	0.1 × 0.1	0.1
5066	circular	0.56 × 0.56	0.17
5096	circular	0.48 × 0.48	0.14
5159	circular	0.5 × 0.5	0.16
5178	circular	0.12 × 0.12	0.10
5186	circular	0.52 × 0.52	0.11
5191	circular	0.2 × 0.2	0.27
5207	oval	0.75 × 0.5	0.34

(Fig. 2.5.1), and one sherd of Grooved Ware pottery was found within the primary fill (5011) (Barclay, Chapter 4). The upper fill (5013) contained one sherd of pottery of indeterminate early prehistoric date. The secondary fill (5062) of pit 5061 (Fig. 2.5.2) contained five sherds of Iron Age pottery which was considered to be intrusive as there was no other Iron Age activity recorded on the site.

Eleven were circular type 2 pits, with a slightly more rectangular profile and flat base (5005, 5088, 5108, 5119, 5124, 5131, 5143, 5147, 5157, 5161, 5174).

The angles of slope of the sides varied between 45° and 85°, the depths varied from 0.14 m to 0.57 m and the diameters from 0.70 m to 1.37 m.

Two of the type 2 pits had been truncated, 5143 (Fig. 2.5.3) and 5147, and two others, 5005 (Fig. 2.4) and 5161 (Fig. 2.5.4) were dug into tree-throw holes. Pit 5108 had been dug into another of similar shape, 5143 (Fig. 2.5.3). An undated but later, and possibly medieval, ditch 5153 cut through tree-throw hole 5149 which truncated pit 5147. Fill 5150 of pit 5147 contained one sherd of medieval pottery which was most likely to be intrusive. A number of pits contained more than one fill, and in four of these the lower fills (5120, 5122, 5150 and 5164) contained both gravel in varying quantities (1–20%) and charcoal (4–25%). The upper fills were mainly a grey to mid-brown loess sand, containing a low frequency (1–5%) of charcoal. Fill 5164 of pit 5161 contained three sherds of pottery of an early prehistoric type.

Pit 5005 (Fig. 2.4.1) contained the highest concentration of worked flint recovered from Area 3017. The pit was about 0.86 m in diameter and 0.36 m deep, with a fill (5004) of brown-grey silty loam which contained some charcoal. A total of 845 pieces of worked flint was recovered from this feature, along with two sherds of Peterborough Ware (Barclay, Chapter 4), cattle bones and pig teeth. Pit 5005 cut tree-throw hole 5072, which contained eight pieces of flint. A sherd of late Bronze Age pottery was also found in 5004 suggesting some later disturbance of the pit.

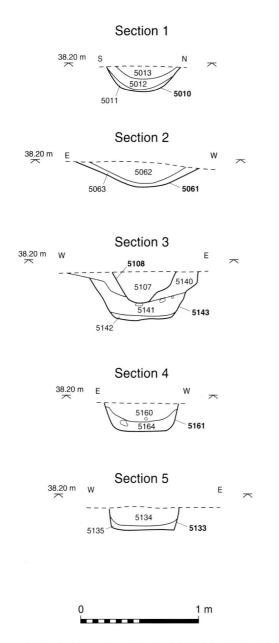

Figure 2.5 Sections through pits: Neolithic 1. 5010, 2. 5061, 3. 5143 and 5108, 4. 5161, and late Bronze Age 5. 5133

Postholes

A total of 15 postholes were half-sectioned and recorded (Table 2.2), and small clusters of these could suggest some structures had been present. Only one posthole (5066) contained two fills and no post-pipes were evident.

Some of the postholes located seem to have similar characteristics and may have formed small groups as parts of structures, as with postholes 5044, 5048 and 5096, lying in the north-western corner of the excavation. A small cluster of postholes, 5050, 5052, 5054, 5056 and 5058, may

have been connected although their dimensions are not uniform. Flint of Neolithic date was found in a number of these postholes spread across the site, including a core fragment from 5058 and a notched and serrated flake from 5207 (Bradley, Chapter 4).

Late Bronze Age

Pits

Three pits considered to be of late Bronze Age date were found in this area (5133, 5190, 5039) (Table 2.1). Pits 5133 and 5190 were located in the western part of Area 3017. Both were circular in plan and had a rectangular profile with a flat base (as type 2) (Fig. 2.5.5). These pits were 0.60–0.77 m in diameter and 0.22–0.25 m deep. The primary fill 5135, of pit 5133, was light brown clay with 15% gravel. The secondary fill 5134 was red-brown sandy clay with 1% charcoal and a single sherd of late Bronze Age pottery. Fill 5189 of pit 5190, was mid-brown loess sand, with 5% charcoal which contained one sherd of late Bronze Age pottery.

A figure-of-eight-shaped pit 5039 lay towards the north of the area and was 1.40 m long, 0.50 m wide and 0.30 m deep with vertical sides and a rounded base. The pit contained one fill 5038, a grey-brown silty loam, with 1% gravel and two sherds of late Bronze Age pottery.

Medieval and post-medieval

Pits

Four pits considered to be of medieval date were identified in this area (5172, 5202, 5204 and 5209). The primary fill 5139, of pit 5136 was a mottled-orange-grey silty clay, with a secondary layer 5138 of grey-black clay with charcoal, and this fill contained 17 sherds of pottery of medieval date. The upper fill 5137 was a grey-brown sandy clay. The second and upper fills both contained some flint and bone.

One pit of rectangular plan (5172) was partially excavated but severe tree disturbance did not permit full investigation. Three other pits similarly rectangular in plan were also noted (5202, 5204, 5209). The upper fill 5203 of pit (5204) contained four sherds of medieval pottery (Blinkhorn, Chapter 4).

Ditches

Eleven ditches were identified during the excavation, listed in Table 2.3. In the south-west corner of the excavation the three ditches had sloping sides and flat (5083, Fig. 2.6.1, and 5197) or rounded bases (5199). The conjoined ditches 5083, 5197 and 5199 were seen to form part of an apparent field system seen in aerial photographs prior to excavation. Pottery of 11th-12th century date found within the ditches indicates that these were medieval boundaries.

Table 2.3   Ditches (Area 3017)

Ditch no.	Location	Length m	Width m	Depth m	Slope	Base degrees	Fills	Type of fill	Finds
5014/5028	NE	19.0	0.9–1.14	0.22–0.24	N 60–70 S 35–70	flat	5015, 5029	mid-brown clay silt	–
5083	SW	4.2	1.10	0.34	45	flat	5083	grey brown silty sand	29 sherds medieval pottery
5197	SW	3.8	0.72	0.13	30	flat	5198	brown sandy clay 15% stone & charcoal	15 sherds medieval pottery
5199	SW	7.0	0.25	0.09	45	round	5200	brown sand clay & 5% flint	–
5153	W	17.0	0.60	0.30	65	flat	5152	grey-brown loess sand & 5% charcoal	–
5091	W	12.0	0.35	0.13	35	flat	5090	grey-brown silty sand & 5% charcoal	10 sherds medieval pottery
5170	W	3.6	0.35	0.13	45	flat	5169	as 5090	–
5221	SE	12.0	0.83	0.28	60	flat	5222	as 5090	–
5215	SE-NW	86.0	0.71	0.44	30	rounded	–	–	–
5217	SE-NW	86.0	2.00	0.52	irregular	flat	–	–	–
5219	SE-NW	86.0	1.35	0.40	30	flat	–	–	–

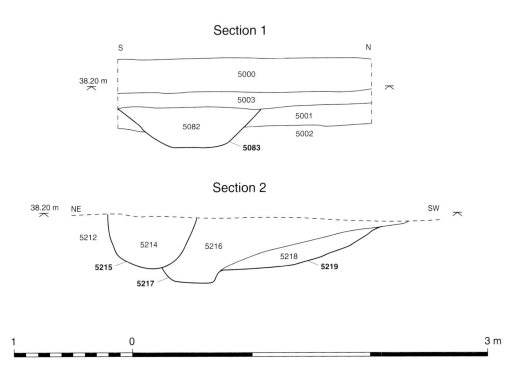

Figure 2.6   Sections through ditches: medieval 1. 5083 and post-medieval 2. 5215, 5217 and 5219

In the west of the site parallel ditches 5153 and 5091 were separated by a gap of about 2.00 m. Pottery of 11th-12th century date was found in 5091, indicating that these ditches probably represent the boundary of a medieval trackway cutting across the area. Ditch 5221 running towards the south-east of the area may also be part of the trackway boundary.

The ditches running from south-east to north-west across the site, 5215, 5217, 5219, cut across the segmented ring ditch, and may represent part of a field boundary system. The initial ditch was recut (Fig. 2.6.2), and could have been a hollow-way (5219, 5217) eventually recut as a boundary ditch (5215). These ditches are undated but are most likely to be post-medieval.

Results of the 1996 watching brief

Late Bronze Age

In the watching brief a small number of features were noted to the south of Area 3017 (Fig. 2.1). A tree-throw hole (89) contained six pieces of worked flint and ten sherds of late Bronze Age pottery. This was cut by pit 94, of type 2, which contained two pieces of worked flint. Another type 2 pit, 70, contained ten pieces of worked flint within the three fills. No finds were recovered from the other features recorded.

Medieval

Two ditches, 56 and 58, were identified during the 1996 watching brief (Fig. 2.1), and could be extensions of the medieval field system identified just to the north in Area 3017. The northern ditch was about 7 m long, 0.70 m wide and 0.18 m deep with a rounded base. The fill, grey silty clay, contained one sherd of late Bronze Age pottery, assumed to be residual. The southern ditch was 2.10 m long, 0.93 m wide and 0.26 m deep with a flat base. There were no finds.

Chapter 3:   Excavations of Area 3000B

by Adam Brossler and Carol Allen

Introduction

Excavations in Area 3000B were situated to the east of the earlier 1987 excavation (RBP1, Area 3100: Moore and Jennings 1992, chapter 4) and uncovered approximately 1.53 ha, as shown on Figure 3.1. The 1995 (RBP2) excavations in Area 3000B uncovered evidence for Bronze Age use of the area. An extension of the field systems previously uncovered in Area 3100 was found together with some pits, a waterhole and a human cremation in a Deverel Rimbury pot. The field system went out of use and evidence for subsequent late Bronze Age occupation of the area included a number of post-built round-

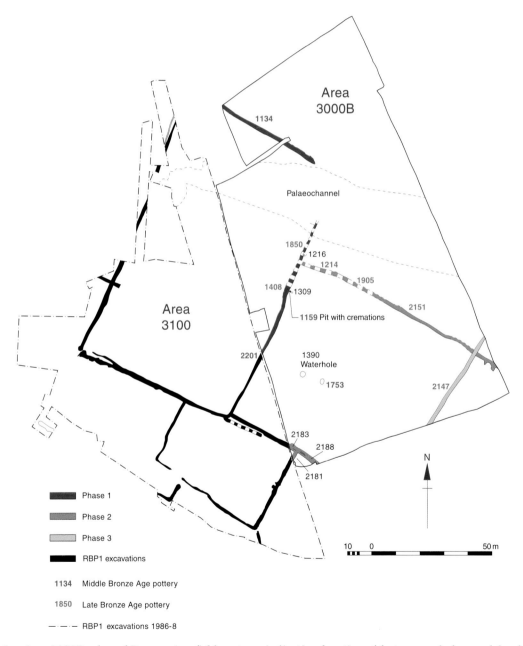

Figure 3.1   Area 3000B, plan of Bronze Age field systems indicating location of features and phases of development

Table 3.1 Middle Bronze Age ditches of pre-settlement field system (Area 3000B)

Ditch no.	Location 3000B and Fig.	Orientation	Length × width × depth m	Slope degrees	Base	Fill (1 = primary etc)	Comments Finds (sherds no.)
2181	SW Fig. 3.2.1	NE-SW	3.7 × 1.6 × 0.32	60	flat	2180 brown-grey silt clay & 40% gravel	terminus of RBP1 field boundary
2183	SW Fig. 3.2.2	NW-SE	2.0 × 0.6 × 0.18	45	flat	2182 dark grey silt clay & 5% gravel	as above, 0.2 m gap between ends
2188	SW Figs 3.2.2	NW-SE	c 14 × 1.2 × 0.4	60	flat	2187(1) grey clay & 1% gravel: 2186(2) silt sand & mainly gravel: 2185(3) grey silt clay & 20% gravel: 2184(4) grey silt clay & 5% gravel	cuts 2183 and makes continuation of ditch 2183, with 3.5 m slot cut into ditch
1214	SE Figs 3.2.3 and 3.3.2	NW-SE	11 × 1.25 × 0.54	70	round	1299(1) grey clay silt & 5% gravel: 1215(2) grey silt clay, flint (some burnt)	relationship with ditch 1408 not established: *1215 LBA pottery (12)*
1905	SE Fig. 3.1	NW-SE	1 × 1.2 × 0.4	70	round	1904(1) mid-grey sand slumped: 1903(2) mid-grey silt clay & gravel: 1902(3) orange loam, sand & gravel: 1901(4) orange loam, sand & burnt flint: 1900(5) grey sandy clay, sand & gravel: 1899(6) black clay loam & gravel: 1898(7) black silty loam & gravel	1901 slumped from S edge silting of second phase, possibly related to burnt mound *1898 upper fill LBA pottery (5)*
2151	SE Fig. 3.2.4	NW-SE	1 m (not fully excavated) × 1.2 × 0.45	85	flat	2150(1) grey clay & 3% gravel: 2149(2) grey silt clay & 1% gravel: 2148(3) brown clay, 5% gravel & some charcoal	2151 cut by ditch 2147 *upper fill 2148 LBA pottery (3)*
2147	SE Fig. 3.2.4	NE-SW	43 × 1.3 × 0.55	30–80	flat	2146(1) light grey clay 1% gravel: 2145(2) light grey clay, 20% gravel & 1% burnt flint: 2144(3) grey clay & 3% gravel	2147 cut 2151 and was overlain by burnt mound *2145 LBA pottery (7) 2144 LBA pottery (7)*
1134	NW Fig. 3.3.1	NW-SE	40 × 3.59 × 0.62	25	round	1132(1) dark grey clay & 1% gravel: 1133(2) dark grey clay & 1% organic: 1131(3) mid-grey clay: 1130(4) grey-yellow clay & 1% gravel: 1129(5) brown sandy silt & 1% gravel	ditch cut a tree-throw hole *1130 MBA pottery (19)*
2201	centre Fig. 3.3.4	NE-SW	20 × 1.8 × 0.42	45–80	flat	2200(1) brown clay sand & gravel: 2199(2) grey silt clay & 30% gravel	*2199 middle BA pottery (4)*
1408	centre Fig. 3.3.5	NE-SW	4 × 1.4 × 0.5	60	flat	1410(1) brown clay silt & 2% gravel: 1409(2) orange sand, silt & gravel	relationship with 1214 not established: 1408 cut pit 1216: 1519 possible recut of 1408, sealed by burnt mound *1409 LBA pottery (12)*
1850	centre Fig. 3.3.3	NE-SW	4 × 0.9 × 0.5	60	flat	1849(1) brown clay, some organic: 1848(2) light grey clay, 30% gravel & 2% charcoal	*1848 LBA pottery (2)*

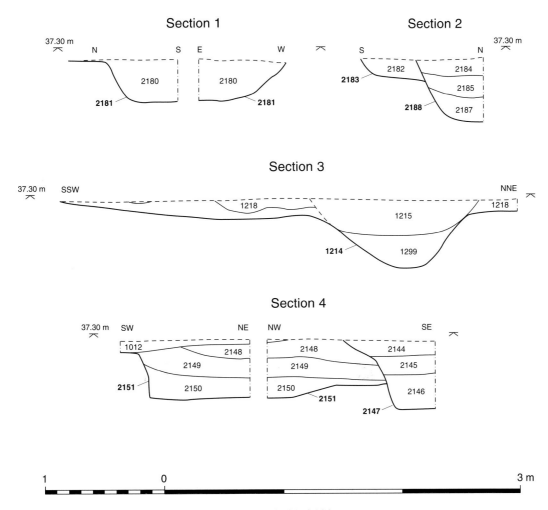

Figure 3.2 Bronze Age ditch sections 1214, 2147, 2151, 2181, 2188

houses and other post structures, together with evidence of waterholes, pits and a burnt mound.

Middle to late Bronze Age

Pre-settlement field system

A number of ditches of a field system were uncovered in Area 3000B during the RBP2 excavations (Fig. 3.1). These were clearly a continuation of boundary ditches from the RBP1 excavations of the adjacent Area 3100 to the west. The presence of such field systems had also been established within Areas 5000 and 6000 of the RBP1 excavations. The ditches of Area 3100 (Moore and Jennings 1992, fig. 18) were thought to continue southwards through Area 2000, and were a feature established prior to the late Bronze Age settlement *(ibid., 120)*. The ditches found in the RBP2 1995 excavations are detailed on Table 3.1, and the sections are illustrated in Figures 3.2 and 3.3.

A number of different phases were recognised in RBP1 Area 3100 ditches (ibid., fig. 18). In these excavations, RBP2, it was considered that three

phases of ditches could be clearly identified (Fig. 3.1) based on stratigraphic relationships. Ditch 2188 cut 2183 (Fig. 3.2.2), and also ditch 2147 cut 2151 (Fig. 3.2.4); the burnt mound feature overlay ditch 2147. These three phases may equate to phases one, three and five respectively of the RBP1 excavations (ibid., fig. 18). In the earlier excavations it was noted that deeper cuts of ditches had replaced shallow cuts thereby making the interpretation of the phases problematical. In the later excavations too it was not always possible to establish the relationship of conjoining ditches, such as 1214 and 1408 (Fig. 3.3.2).

Late Bronze Age pottery was found in the upper fills of the excavated sections of ditches 1214, 1905, 2151, 2147, 1408 and 1850, and also in the middle fill of 2147. Such ditches may have been recut as suggested above and could have been open for some time. Pottery of middle Bronze Age type was found in the fourth fill (of five) of ditch 1134 and in the upper fill of 2201.

The field system indicates a deliberate division of the landscape into a number of fields and as indicated by the pottery these could be of middle to late Bronze Age date. Comparable fields of these

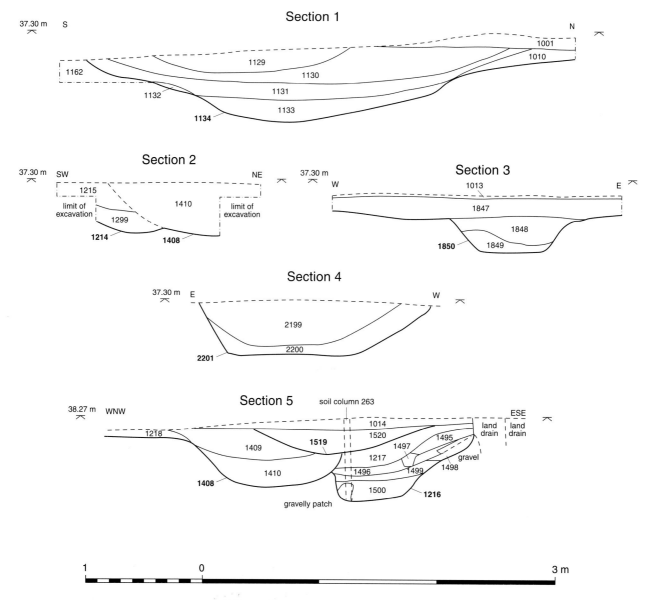

Figure 3.3   Bronze Age ditch sections 1134, 1214/1408, 1850, 2201, 1408 and pit 1216

periods have been identified in the Middle Thames Valley, and are also known at Knight's Farm, Burghfield (Bradley *et al.* 1980), Weir Bank Stud Farm, Berkshire (Barnes and Cleal 1995), Marsh Lane and Lake End Road West (Foreman and Bradley 1998).

Cremation

A middle Bronze Age Deverel Rimbury bucket urn (Fig. 4.7.1: 1160, Morris, Chapter 4) containing cremated human bone was found in pit 1159. The pit was located on the western side of a large square field (Fig. 3.1). The vessel was lifted and subsequently excavated under controlled conditions (Boyle, Chapter 5). The pit was circular in plan, 0.60 m diameter and 0.15 m deep, with

gently sloping sides and a flat base (Fig. 3.4, Plate 3.1).

A radiocarbon date was obtained from charcoal (Gale, Chapter 5) associated with this vessel and gave a date of 1220–890 cal BC (92.0% confidence NZA 9422, Table A1.1). This is quite a late date for this type of pottery and is identical to the date obtained for animal bone associated with late Bronze Age pottery in pit 1518 on this site (see Table A1.1 and late Bronze Age type 4 pits, below). The cremation found in pit 1159 very close to the ditch could suggest that the field systems and the burial are very likely of similar middle to late Bronze Age date.

Just to the south-east (Fig. 3.1), pit 1753 was oval in plan, 0.55 m long, 0.45 m wide and 0.25 m deep, with a flat base and steep sides. The fill (1754, grey clay silt with 20% gravel) contained 264 sherds of

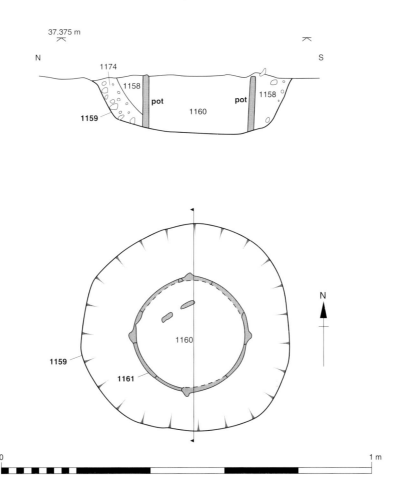

Figure 3.4   Middle Bronze Age cremation in pit 1159, plan and section

Plate 3.1   Area 3000B: excavation of bucket urn 1160

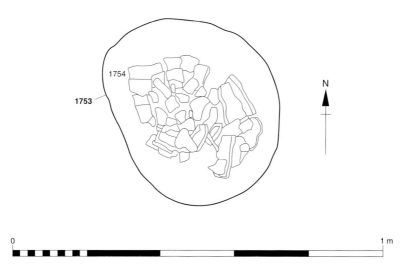

Figure 3.5   Plan of fragmented middle Bronze Age vessel in pit 1753

Plate 3.2   Area 3000B: crushed bucket urn 1754

Deverel Rimbury pottery (Fig. 3.5, Plate 3.2), including a fragmentary, but almost complete, pot (Fig. 4.7.2). No cremation deposit was associated with this vessel.

Pit 1216

Pit 1216 was cut by ditch 1408 (Fig. 3.3.5). The ditch cut was probably of middle to late Bronze Age date, as discussed above, and the upper fill contained late Bronze Age pottery.

Pit 1216 was oval in plan, 1.50 m long, 0.90 m wide and 0.60 m deep, with sides of varying slope and a flat base. The pit had seven fills, from dark brown and grey silty loam with some gravel in the lower fills (1500, 1499) to grey sand (1498) and red-brown silty clay (1497). This was followed by grey-brown sandy silt (1495) and the upper fill (1217) was also red-brown silty clay. No other finds were recovered.

Waterhole 1390

Waterhole 1390 was circular in plan, with variable sloping sides and a rounded base (Fig. 3.6). The feature was 2.14 m wide and 0.64 m deep, with nine fills. The primary fill (1411) was a gravel layer, possibly resulting from natural erosion of the sides. The following fills (1392, 1382, 1353, 1391, 1398) were all waterlogged silt or clay deposits. The upper three fills each contained sherds of middle Bronze Age pottery; fill 1318 had eight sherds, and 1334 had four sherds and 1317 one sherd.

Late Bronze Age

Structures

Five roundhouse structures (RH1–RH5), one 6-post structure (SP6), thirteen 4-post structures (FP7–FP18, FP19 is a possible 4-post structure) and ten 2-post structures (TP20–TP29) were positively identified. The chronological sequence of the building of the roundhouses and other post-built structures was not easily determined. The level of truncation resulting from modern ploughing was not known, but as no clear occupation layers were identified substantial disturbance must have taken place.

In one case, two of the roundhouses (RH1 and RH2) overlapped, but as there was no stratigraphic relationship it was not possible to distinguish which was the earliest. In addition, some of the postholes of the 4-post structures appeared to be shared with the roundhouses. Therefore, although the sequence of use could not be accurately determined, it was clear that at least two phases of structural activity must be represented on the site.

Measurements of the buildings were taken from the centre of postholes and across the widest area, and distances between postholes were taken from posthole centres. All postholes cut natural (1009) and were overlain by an alluvial deposit (1021).

Roundhouses

Five roundhouses were identified in the RBP2 excavations; RH1–RH5. These are shown together with the RBP1 roundhouses in Figure 3.7; Figures 3.8 and 3.9 show the two adjacent areas at a greater scale. The number of postholes making up the houses varied from 8 to 15 per structure. However, the postholes identified were not always spaced at regular intervals, and sometimes were not uniform in size and depth (Table 3.2). This may indicate that alterations were made to the structures or that episodes of rebuilding or repair took place within each house. The diameters of the features defined by the post-settings, ranging from 8.00–9.00 m, were quite similar to those seen in the RBP1 roundhouses of the previous excavations (Moore and Jennings 1992, table 1, Area 5 and table 6, Area 3100). It was supposed that the post-rings were roof supports with walls lying outside them. There was no evidence for the walls themselves, which may have been of wattle and daub (Avery and Close-Brooks 1969, 347).

Porches were clearly seen on RH3 and RH4 and there may have been posthole remains of porches on RH1 and RH2. The sizes varied slightly but the porches measured approximately 1.30–1.70 m × 1.50 m. In the previous excavations the porches were seen to be facing in a broadly south-easterly direction, but the four porches of these excavations are not so consistent. The porch of RH1 may have faced south-east, but the porch of RH2 faced north-north-west, RH3 looked to the east and RH4 porch faced south-south-east. Only one roundhouse, RH4, had a central posthole.

Where porches were apparent or suspected the wall diameter of the house could be estimated, and these were: RH1 12.4 m, RH2 11.00 m, RH3 12.00 m and RH4 11.60 m. These wall diameters are comparable with those of RBP1 Area 3100 (Moore and Jennings 1992, table 6) lying at the upper end of the size range previously recognised.

Late Bronze Age pottery was found within postholes in all of the roundhouses and was particularly common in RH3 and RH4 as detailed on Table 3.2. Burnt flint was found in postholes of RH5, which lay close to the burnt mound.

Roundhouse 1

RH1 had eight posts, which were mainly circular in plan, and the profile of the postholes varied from shallow scoops to holes with vertical sides and a flat base; the postholes formed a circle 8.75 m in diameter (Fig. 3.10, Table 3.2). If the unexcavated posthole 2369 did represent part of a porch, the wall diameter of the house would have been 12.40 m, and the porch faced south-east.

Within RH1 pit 2115 and a number of other postholes were found (Fig. 3.10). The postholes may have formed part of internal structures or may

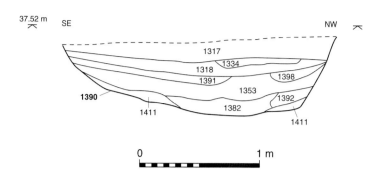

Figure 3.6   Section of Bronze Age waterhole 1390

Table 3.2   Late Bronze Age roundhouses (Area 3000B)

Round-house Fig no.	Postring diam m *No. of posts* Wall diam m	Posthole measurements *Diameter m* Depth m	Distance between postholes m *Entrance*	Porch & central post (CP)	Posthole Fills	Finds (sherds no.)	Postholes
RH1 Fig. 3.10	8.75 m *8 posts & poss porch* c 12.4 m	*0.25–0.40* 0.08–0.25	1.5–4.5 *south-east*	Porch poss 2369, not excavated No CP	brown silty clays with gravel	LBA pot: 1871 (3) & 1881 (1)	1560, 1564, 1866, 1871, 1881, 1988, 2122, 2128
RH2 Fig. 3.10	9.0 m *11 post & poss porch* c 11 m	*0.25–0.52* 0.08–0.24	1.6–4.0 *north-north-west*	Porch 2142 & 2315 but uncertain No CP	clay silt with gravel, clay in 2137 & 2139	LBA pot: 1442 (18) & 1889 (2)	1442, 1572, 1889, 2047, 2126, 2130, 2132, 2134, 2136, 2138, 2140
RH3 Fig. 3.11	8.7 m *15 posts & 4 of porch* 12 m	*0.30–0.45* 0.06–0.30	1.2–5.0 *east*	Porch 2077/75, 1652, 1293, 1441 No CP	dark grey-black silty loam & clay silts with some gravel	LBA pot: 1227(2), 1229(2), 1233(6), 1235(2), 1652(7), 1342(8), 1344((7)	1225, 1227, 1229, 1233, 1235, 1285, 1291, 1293, 1340, 1342, 1344, 1348, 1441, 1614, 1950
RH4 Fig. 3.11	8.0 m *11 pots & 4 of porch* 11.6 m	*0.30–0.54* 0.10–0.30	0.7–3.4 *south-south-east*	Porch 1670, 1671, 2242, 1730 CP 2346	grey-black silty clay and sandy loam 1451 & 1733 had postpipes	LBA pot: 1277(1), 1403(16), 405(3), 1452(1), 1668(2), 1670(7), 1730(8), 1735(21), 2342(4)	1277, 1403, 1452, 1664, 1666, 1735, 2235, 2334, 2335, 2340, 2342
RH5 Fig. 3.12	8.3 m *12 posts*	*0.23–0.45* 0.07–0.22	1.5–3.2	No porch No CP	grey-black/ brown sandy silts and loam, some flint & gravel	LBA pot: 1183(1), 1191(4) Burnt flint: 1175, 1191	1175, 1178, 1183, 1185, 1191, 2154/57, 2158/59, 2165, 2192, 2198, 2259, 2264

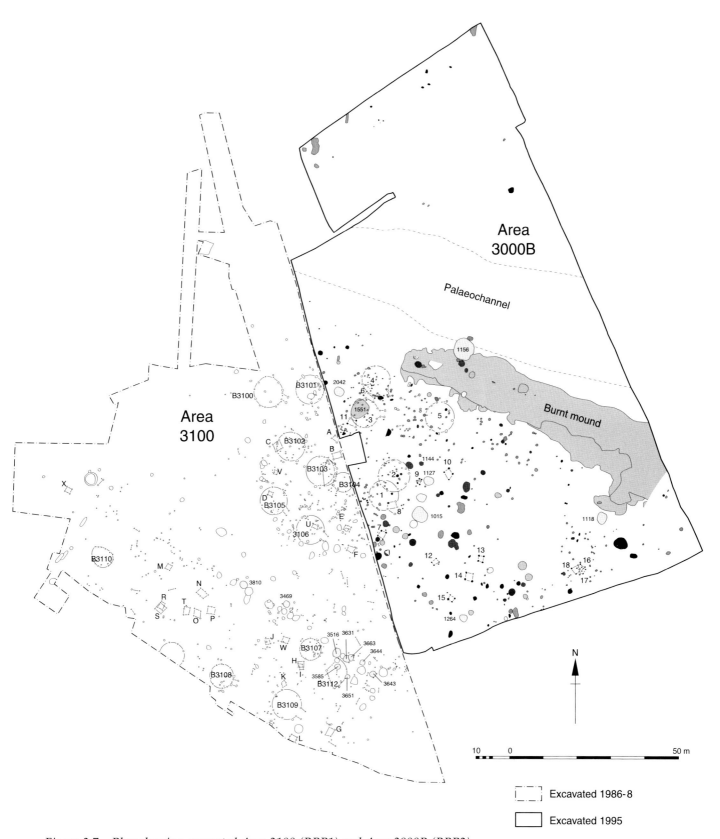

Figure 3.7   Plan showing excavated Area 3100 (RBP1) and Area 3000B (RBP2)

represent other phases of building. Postholes 2126 and 2047 in the north-east of the structure were part of RH2, and postholes 1444 and 1522, together with 1564 and 1560, formed part of 4-post structure FP8. Both of these structures, RH2 and FP8, had to either predate or post-date RH1.

Roundhouse 2

RH2 had 11 posts forming a circle 9.00 m in diameter (Fig. 3.10, Plate 3.3). Two postholes, 2142 and 2315, may have been part of a porch lying on the north-north-west of the house, thus indicating a

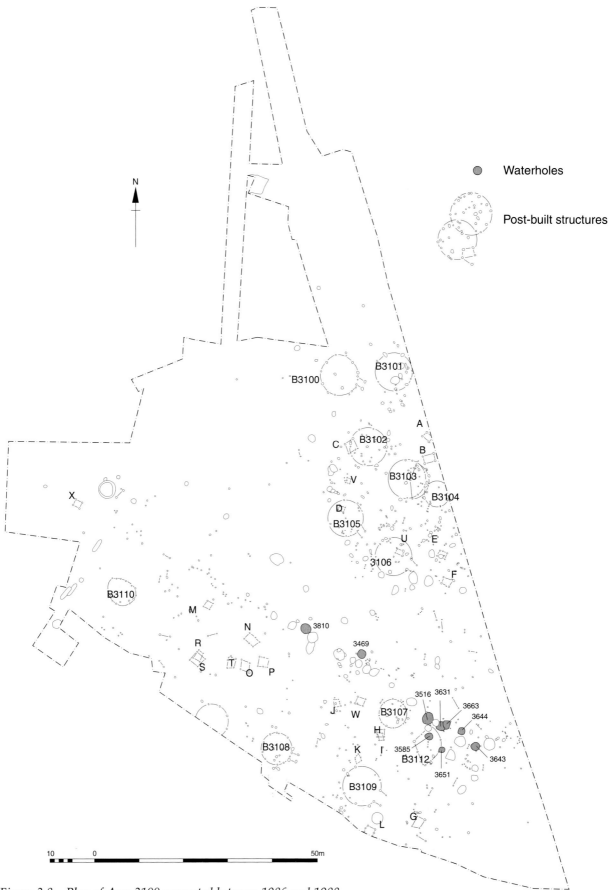

Figure 3.8   Plan of Area 3100 excavated between 1986 and 1988

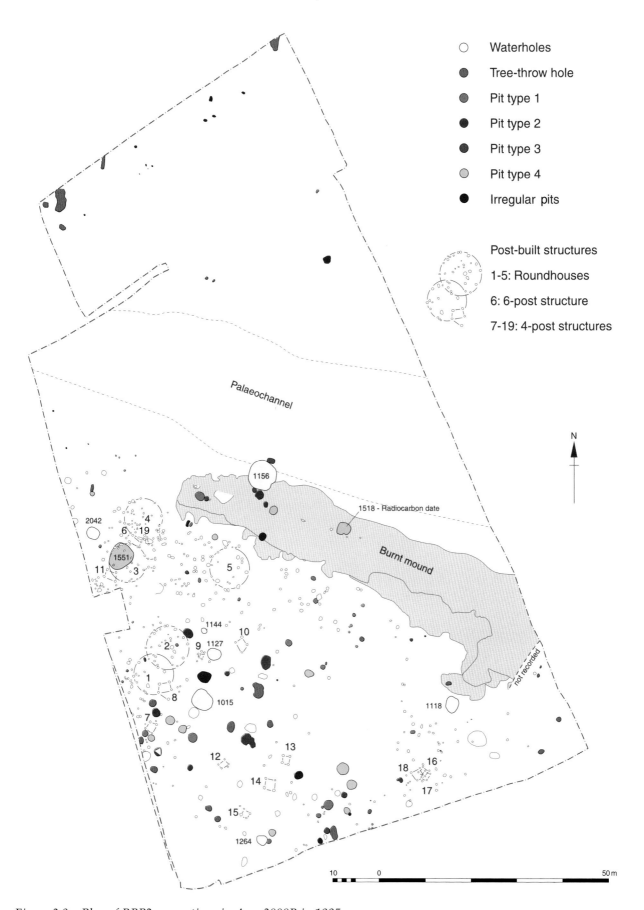

Waterholes ○
Tree-throw hole ●
Pit type 1 ●
Pit type 2 ●
Pit type 3 ●
Pit type 4 ●
Irregular pits ●

Post-built structures

1-5: Roundhouses

6: 6-post structure

7-19: 4-post structures

Palaeochannel

1156

1518 - Radiocarbon date

Burnt mound

2042

4

6 19

1551

11 3

5

1144

10

2 9 1127

1 8

1015

7

12 13

14

18 16

17

15

1264

1118

not recorded

N

10   0   50 m

Figure 3.9   Plan of RBP2 excavations in Area 3000B in 1995

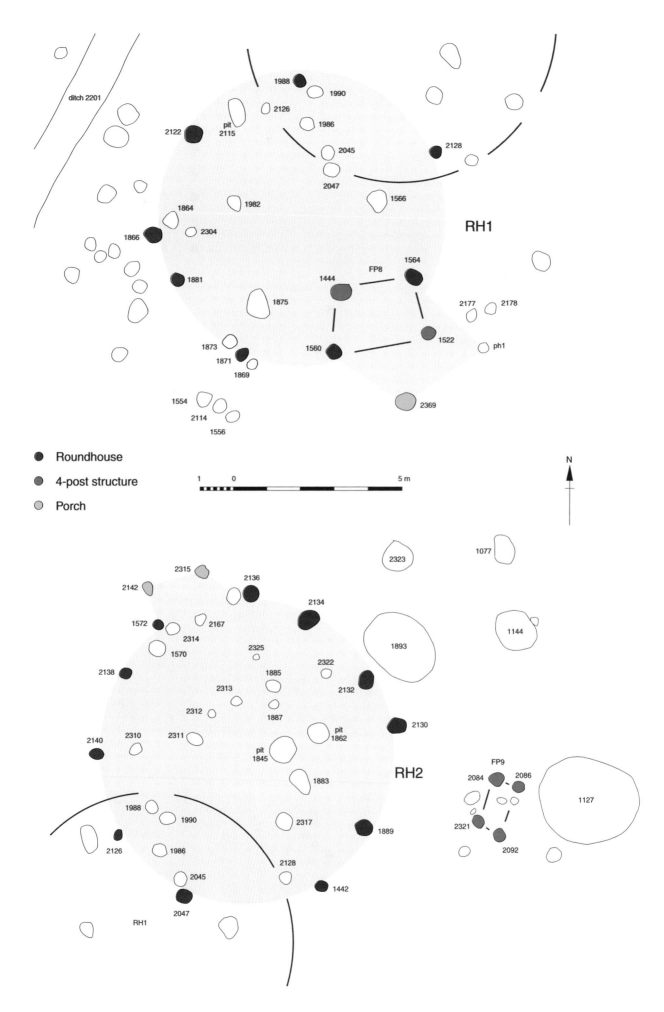

Figure 3.10   Plan of roundhouses RH1 and RH2

Figure 3.11   Plan of roundhouses RH3 and RH4

Plate 3.3   Roundhouse RH2

Plate 3.4   Roundhouse RH3 and pit 1551

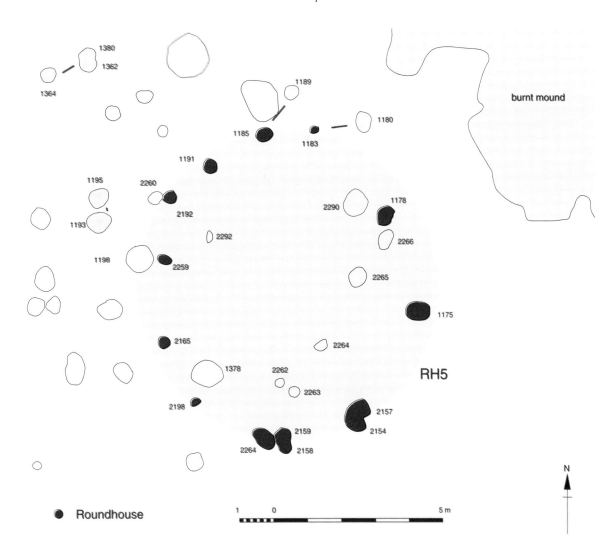

Figure 3.12   Plan of roundhouse RH5

wall diameter of 11.00 m. However, the two posts lie at an angle to the main structure and this is an unusual orientation for a porch. Most of the posts of RH2 were equally spaced at 2.25–2.70 m with a larger gap of 4.00 m on the south side which might represent an entrance into the building.

A number of postholes were excavated within RH2 and a further seven postholes were identified but not excavated. The function of these postholes within RH2 was unclear, but they may have been part of internal structures. Two pits, 1862 (type 1) and 1845 (type 3), were found within RH2. Seventy-seven sherds of late Bronze Age pottery were found in pit 1862 together with fragments of animal bone (Wilson, Chapter 5) and a fragment of fired clay. In pit 1845, 76 sherds of late Bronze Age pottery and fragments of animal bone were found. It seems unlikely that these pits were in use within the roundhouse and they may be rubbish pits of the adjacent RH1.

Roundhouse 3

RH3 had 15 posts making a roughly circular structure 8.70 m in diameter (Fig. 3.11, Plate 3.4). Four posts, 2075/77 (intercutting postholes), 1652, 1293 and 1441, formed a porch about 1.4 × 1.60 m on the east side of the house and, based on the location of the porch, the wall diameter of the roundhouse was 12.00 m. Most of the posts of the roundhouse structure were spaced equally about 2.00 m apart.

Seven excavated and four unexcavated postholes were also identified in the interior of RH3. Posthole 1231 in the southern part of the roundhouse, together with 1612, 1348 and 1614, formed 4-post structure FP11. Two postholes of this roundhouse, 1235 and 1340, and two postholes of RH4, 1277 and 2342, together with postholes 1275 and 1674, formed 6-post structure SP6. The remaining post-holes did not seem to form any coherent pattern. Two sherds of middle Bronze Age pottery were

Table 3.3   Six-, four- and two-post structures (Area 3000B)

Structures	Location Fig. no.	Length × width m Area m²	Postholes	Finds	Posthole size and shape diameter m, *depth m* shape
Six-post structure					
SP6	between RH 3 and RH4 Figs 3.10 & 3.12	3.2 × 1.4 *4.48*	1235, 1275, 1277, 1340, 1674, 2342	LBA pot: 1235 (2), 1275 (1)	0.28–0.40, *0.09–0.21* scoops and steep sides with flat base
Four-post structures					
FP7	south of RH1 Fig. 3.10	2.1 × 2.0 *4.2*	1524, 1526, 1528, 1558	–	0.3–0.45, *0.26 - 0.32* scoops
FP8	porch area of RH1 Figs 3.10 & 3.11	2.8 × 1.7 *4.76*	1444, 1522, 1560, 1564	–	0.35–0.52, *0.10–0.38* scoops and u-shaped profiles
FP9	east of RH2 Figs 3.10 & 3.11	1.5 × 0.7 *1.05*	2084, 2086, 2092, 2321	–	0.30, *0.13–0.26* scoops and u-shaped profiles
FP10	east of RH2 and FP9 Fig. 3.10	2.5 × 2.0 *5.00*	1352, 1699, 1701, 1703	–	0.22–0.54, *0.10–0.26* scoops and steep sides
FP11	within east side of RH3 Figs 3.10 & 3.12	2.5 × 1.8 *4.50*	1231, 1348, 1612	–	0.30–0.40, *0.14–0.20* scoops
FP12	south of area in cluster of four-post structures Fig. 3.10	1.75 × 1.3 *2.28*	1838, 1840, 1842, 1844	LBA pot: 1840(8), 1842(1)	0.25–0.32, *0.06–0.18* scoops and steep-sided profiles
FP13	south of area east of FP12 Fig. 3.10	1.7 × 1.4 *2.38*	1801, 1803, 1805, 1807	LBA pot: 1801(11), 1805(10), 1807(2)	0.26–0.48, *0.1–0.2* scoops
FP14	south of FP13 not excavated Fig. 3.10	2.15 × 2.1 *4.52*	1956, 2053, 2054, 2061	–	not excavated
FP15	south of FP12 Fig. 3.10	1.65 × 1.45 *2.39*	1655, 1657, 1659, 1661	–	0.20–0.35, *0.16–0.20* sloping sides, flat base
FP16	south-east of area sharing postholes with 17 & 18 Fig. 3.10	1.65 1.5 *2.48*	1502, 1504, 1506, 1589	LBA pot: 1504(1) burnt flint: 1502, 1504	0.24–0.32, *0.17–0.20* steep sides, flat or round base
FP17	south east of area Fig. 3.10	1.5 × 1.3 *1.95*	1585, 1587, 1600, 1602	LBA pot: 1585(1), 1600(1)	0.21–0.30, *0.18–0.20* steep sides and flat base
FP18	south east of area Fig. 3.10	2.0 × 2.0 *4.0*	1510, 1589, 1678, 1680	–	0.22–0.30, *0.10–0.14* steep sides, flat or round base
FP19	within RH4 Fig. 3.12	0.9 × 0.6 *0.54*	2337, 2338, 2339 truncated by modern pipe trench	LBA pot: 2337(13), 2338(1), 2339(71)	0.25–0.30, *0.20–0.25* sloping sides and round base
Two-post structures		**Length m**			
TP20	west of FP11 east-west	1.3	1606, 1610	–	0.4, *0.14–0.18* sloping sides, flat or round base
TP21	east of RH4	1.3	1208, 1210	–	0.35–0.43, *0.10* sloping sides, flat or round base
TP22	east of FP11	1.3	1364, 1362/1380	LBA pot: 1364(3)	0.24–0.37, *0.24–0.26* sloping sides, flat or round base
TP23	north of RH5	1.5	1185, 1189	Worked flint & burnt stone 1189	0.3–0.4, *0.14–0.20* sloping sides, uneven round base
TP24	north of RH5	1.5	1180, 1183	LBA pot: 1180(6), 1183(1)	0.3–0.5, *0.08–0.25* sloping sides, v-shaped or rounded base
TP25	east of RH3	1.65	1049, 1061	LBA pot: 1049(4) burnt flints: 1061	0.32, *0.10–0.22* sloping sides, flat or uneven base
TP26	south of RH5 truncated by land drain	1.65	2194, 2198	–	0.23–0.52, *0.07–0.17* gently sloping sides, round base
TP27	west of FP18	1.3	1510, 1767	–	0.22, *0.10–0.14* sloping sides, round base

found in posthole 1727 in the north of RH3, and 16 sherds of the same date in 1283, and this pottery seems likely to have been redeposited. A later feature, a large pit 1551, cut into the roundhouse structure (Plate 3.4).

Roundhouse 4

RH4 had 11 postholes forming a circle 8.00 m in diameter (Fig. 3.11). Four postholes, 1670, 1671, 1668 and 1730, formed a porch 1.50 m square which faced south-south-east. The diameter of the wall of the roundhouse was therefore 11.6 m, and this was set around a central post. This central posthole, 2346, was excavated but could not be recorded due to flooding.

Another 13 postholes were excavated in the interior of RH4 and 14 unexcavated postholes were also identified. Late Bronze Age pottery was recovered from 1401, 2338 and 2339. Posthole 1405 contained a possible post-pipe and postholes 2337, 2338 and 2339 formed part of a possible 4-post structure FP19, described in more detail below. The chronological relationship of RH4 to FP19 or to SP6 was unfortunately not clarified by excavation, but at least two phases of construction were indicated. The remaining postholes did not form any recognisable pattern.

Roundhouse 5

RH5 was composed of a circle of 12 postholes 8.30 m in diameter (Fig. 3.12). No porch or central posthole was apparent. Only two of the postholes were circular in plan and the profiles were mainly scoop shapes. The relationship between the intercutting postholes 2158 and 2159 and 2154 and 2157 and their function was not clear from excavation, although they may have represented repairs to the roundhouse.

A number of postholes were found in the interior of RH5, and only one, 1378, was excavated. None of the postholes appeared to form an internal structure.

Six-, four- and two-post structures

One 6-post structure, SP6, thirteen 4-post structures, FP7–FP19, and eight 2-post structures, TP20–TP27, were identified within Area 3000B. The details of the postholes, which were judged, from their location, size and fill, to comprise each structure are given in Table 3.3. The fills of the postholes varied a little but were mainly dark grey to grey-black in colour, with occasional orange sandy fills. Most fills were clay loam, silty loam or silty sands with 10–40% gravel inclusions. All the postholes cut into the gravel (1009) and were overlain by the alluvial deposit (1021). The locations of the structures are shown on Figure 3.9. Late Bronze Age pottery was found in postholes of many of the structures as indicated in Table 3.3.

In some cases the postholes of these structures were shared with the postholes of the roundhouses. Four-post structure FP8 shared postholes with RH1 (Fig. 3.10), FP11 shared postholes with RH3 (Fig. 3.11), and 6-post structure SP6 shared postholes with RH3 and RH4 (Fig. 3.11). However, in each case the chronological sequence of the construction and use of the posthole structures could not be defined. In addition, three 4-post structures, FP8, FP11 and FP19 lay partly or wholly within a roundhouse and another, FP9, lay just outside but very close to RH2 (Fig. 3.9). Both the apparent sharing of postholes and the location of these latter structures indicates that at least two stages of construction are represented, as in each case the structures could not have been in use at the same time. Three 4-post structures, FP16, FP17 and FP18, appeared to overlap, suggesting several phases of use (Plate 3.5).

Apart from FP18 which was 2.00 m square, the remaining 4-post structures were rectangular, varying from the smallest at 0.9 × 0.6 m in size to the largest at 2.8 × 1.7 m. The size of each structure is detailed in Table 3.3. Apart from the smallest 4-post structure, FP19, which was truncated, the sizes of the structures defined were similar in area to those noted in the RBP1 excavations of the adjacent area 3100 (Moore and Jennings 1992, table 7). In the earlier excavations the area of the 4- and 6-post structures varied from 1.15 m^2 to 5.52 m^2, and in these RBP2 excavations the areas varied from 1.05 m^2 to 5.00 m^2 (Table 3.3). This suggests different functions for structures of apparently similar layout. The 2-post structures were noted where two similar postholes lay about 1.30–1.65 m apart. The construction, possible appearance and function of the 6-post, 4-post and 2-post structures are discussed in Chapter 6.

Postholes

Area 3000B contained 289 postholes and stakeholes, of which 125 were assigned to structures, 66 to roundhouses and an additional 59 to the 6-post, 4-post and 2-post structures found on the site. A further 164 postholes were identified during the excavation and assigned a number, but these were not excavated. These postholes were scattered across the site and must represent other phases of construction. However, no other discernible buildings or structures were apparent due to the random nature of the spacing of the features.

Waterholes

Seven features, 1015, 1118, 1127, 1144, 1156, 1264, 2042, located on Figure 3.9, were identified as waterholes and each was found to contain either waterlogged wooden objects and/or unusual small finds. All cut the natural (1009) and were overlain by the alluvial layer (1021).

Plate 3.5   4-post structures FP16, FP17 and FP18

These features were up to 1 m deep and initially were cut below the likely water level. When no longer in use as waterholes these silted up and in their final stage often became rubbish pits, as indicated by the high frequency of domestic refuse found in the upper fills (Figs 3.13–3.16). This suggests that the use of parts of the settlement, including these waterholes, changed over time. Details of the dimensions of the waterholes, their fills and finds are given in Table 3.4.

Waterhole 1015 (Fig. 3.13) shows this sequence of events as there was evidence of silting and then slumping on the north-west side. In the lower fills wooden objects and a fragment of a disc from a human skull were found. This was followed again by silting and then sandy silt upper fills containing large quantities of pottery together with a smoothed sarsen fragment and pieces of loomweight.

All the waterholes contained late Bronze Age pottery. In some, 1015, 1118 and 1144, the pottery was found in lower fills, and all the waterholes except 1264 (Fig. 3.16) had larger numbers of late Bronze Age pottery sherds in the upper fills, as shown in Table 3.4. Waterhole 1127 contained 182 sherds in the upper fill (Plate 3.6). A hammerstone and a burnt stone rubber were also found in waterhole 1144. Worked wood was found in the

second fill of 2042 and in the sixth fill of 1156. The burnt mound overlay waterhole 1156.

Three of the waterholes, 1118, 1144 and 2042, contained 97% of the F4 ceramic material found on the site. This material was unlike the late Bronze Age pottery examined and was considered most likely to represent clay lining for the waterholes (Morris, Chapter 4). However, the other waterholes showed little or no material of this type and could indicate a slight difference in function or period of use. The relationship of the waterholes to the round-houses and their use within the occupation area is discussed in Chapter 6.

Pits

A total of 72 pits were excavated and fully recorded in this area. Of these 3 were dated to the middle Bronze Age, 68 to the late Bronze Age, summarised in Table 3.5, and one was considered to be of the post-medieval period. Four main types of pits were recognised as described below which accounted for 59 of the late Bronze Age pits, and all were circular or oval in plan. A further nine late Bronze Age pits of irregular plan and section were uncovered. The pits were cut into the natural (1009) and sealed by the alluvial deposit (1021). The location of all the

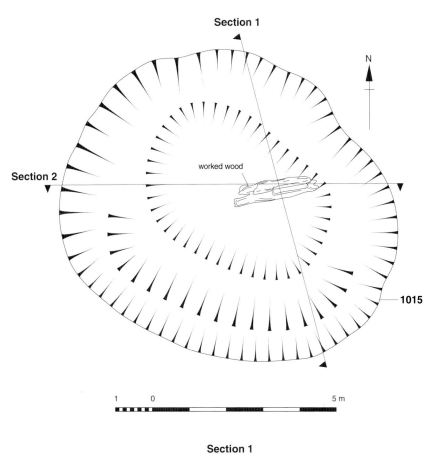

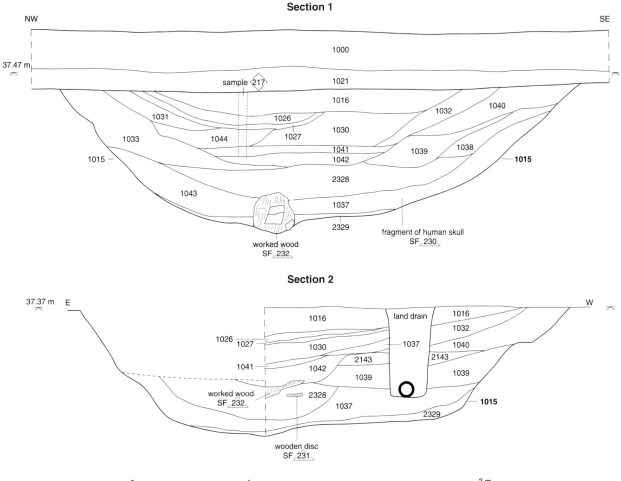

Figure 3.13   Waterhole 1015 plan and section showing worked wood and human skull fragment

31

Table 3.4   Details of waterholes (Area 3000B)

Cut no.	Fig. no.	Length × width × depth m	Fills: total no. Type from primary to upper	Fills with finds (sherds, no. of pieces) Comments
1015	3.13	4.4 × 4.0 × 1.08	18: 2329, 1037, 1043, 2328, 1033, 1038, 1039, 2143, 1042, 1041, 1040, 1032, 1030, 1044, 1031, 1027, 1026, 1016 silts, gravels, silts, sands & gravel, silts & charcoal flecks in upper fills	LBA pot, 2329(1), 1037(4), 2143(1), 1040(10), 1032(2), 1030(36), 1031(33), 1027(115), 1016(396) Partial disc of human skull 1037(4) Wooden disc and jointed piece 2328 Smoothed sarsen fragment 1026 loomweight pieces (12), clay(5) 1016
1118	3.14	2.95 × 2.6 × 0.7	6: 1065, 1064, 1063, 1055, 1054, 1053 clay, organic & gravel, silty clay gravel & charcoal, silty sands & gravel, upper fill 30% gravel	LBA pot, 1065(6), 1064(36), 1063(11), 1055(22), 1054(308), 1053(69) burnt flint 1063, 1054, 1053 oven plate fragments 1054 F4 clay lining (70)
1127	3.14	3.0 × 3.0 × 1.0	8: 1282, 1281, 1141, 1280, 1139, 1140, 1142, 1128 waterlogged silty clay & gravel, silty sand gravel, silty clay & gravel, sandy silt, dumped burnt sand(1142), black silt with gravel (1128)	LBA pot, 1139(13), 1140(185), 1141(118), 1128(182)
1144	3.9	1.27 × 0.9 × 0.51	5: 1145, 1173, 1146/1060, 1143, 1147 dark grey silty clay with burnt flint, gravel & charcoal	LBA pot, 1173(7), 1146(138), 1060(20), 1143(31), 1147(72) Burnt stone rubber & burnt hammerstone 1173 F4 clay lining (225)
1156	3.15	6.0 × 6.0 × 0.8	10: 1619, 1618, 1155, 1154, 1617, 1153, 1152, 1151, 1616, 1150 loose gravel (1619), grey clay gravel, burnt flint (1618/1155), sand (1617) followed by lay organic material & burnt flint	LBA pot, 1153(27), 1616(13), 1150(6) Worked wood 1153 1156 cut pits 1623 & 1690 and was overlain by burnt mound 1014
1264	3.16	1.9 × 1.9 × 0.64	8: 1263, 1260, 1261, 1262, 1259, 1258, 1257, 1256 clay silt with 40% gravel, silty loam with gravel & charcoal, sandy silts, loam (backfill) & silty sands gravel & iron pan (1259), clay silts & gravel	LBA pot, 1262(2), 1257(3) 1264 cut pit 1266
2042	3.16	2.5 × 2.5 × 0.65	5: 2041, 2040, 2039, 2038, 2024 sand, clay & gravel, clay & gravel, silty clay with gravel, burnt flint & charcoal	LBA pot, 2038(78), 2024(379) F4 clay lining (349) Worked wood 2040

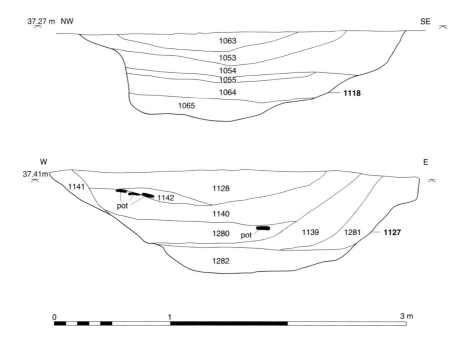

Figure 3.14   Sections of waterholes 1118 and 1127

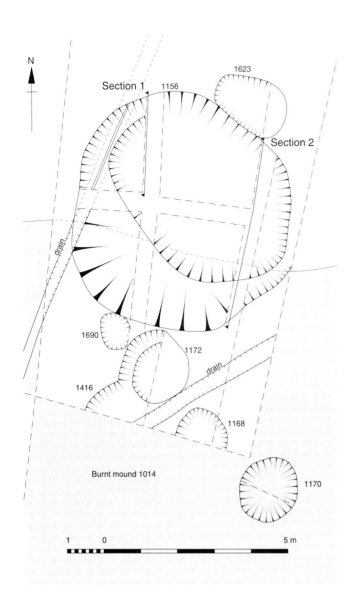

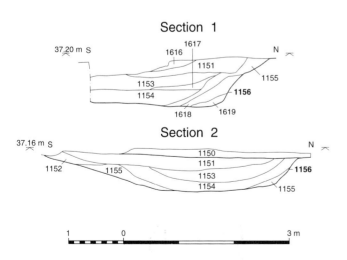

Figure 3.15 Waterhole 1156 overlain by burnt mound, plan and section

pits is indicated in Figure 3.9. The pits may have been created by gravel extraction, or have been used for processing and storage of cereals or other produce, but many seem to have eventually functioned as rubbish pits. The use of the pits and their spatial distribution and relationship to other structures within the occupation area, such as the round-houses, is considered below and in Chapter 6.

Type 1 pits

Twenty-three pits of this description were found, detailed in Table 3.5. The pits were oval or circular in plan, showing a shallow scoop in section and a rounded base. In profile these pits are very similar to those identified as scoops in the RBP1 Area 3100 excavations (Moore and Jennings 1992, 39). Three pits typical of this type are illustrated (Fig. 3.17). Eleven of the pits were oval in plan and twelve were circular. The dimensions of the pits were not uniform and are summarised on Table 3.5.

Five pits (1266, 1250, 1640, 1823, 2011) were truncated, either by other pits, or by a waterhole or a tree-throw hole. Six of these pits (1300, 1305, 1376, 1710, 1862, 2011) contained late Bronze Age pottery (totalling 137 sherds, 1233 g) as detailed in Table 4.17, and pit 1892 contained part of a saddle quern. The number of fills varied, from only one in some pits (1438, Fig. 3.17) to seven in other pits (1305, Fig. 3.17). Fills varied from grey silty sands with 5–40% gravel inclusions to silty loams with flint and gravel inclusions.

Type 2 pits

Fifteen of these pits were found and their dimensions are summarised in Table 3.5. These pits were either oval or circular in plan and had a rectangular or sub-rectangular profile with a flat base. Sections of three typical pits are illustrated on Figure 3.18. In the RBP1 excavations a number of similar pits were recognised, and described as basin-like features with steep sides (ibid., 40: fig. 28, 3475). Two of the pits in the current excavations were truncated, as a land drain cut pit 1387 and pit 1818 cut 1821. Pit 1168 cut into the buried soil and was overlain by the burnt mound deposit. Late Bronze Age pottery (totalling 210 sherds, 2762 g) was found in ten of the pits (1114, 1168, 1172, 1269, 1387, 1403, 1723, 1752, 1770 and 1967), as detailed in Table 4.17. Pit 1114 contained 127 sherds of pottery (Plate 3.7). Pit 1168 contained a number of pieces of worked wood.

These pits contained between one and seven fills, and 12 contained two or more fills (see 1114, 1893 and 2009, Fig. 3.18). The primary fills of the pits varied but were mainly silty clays with up to 30% gravel inclusions. Subsequent fills were dark brown silty loam with some charcoal and 10% gravel. Upper fills were mainly sandy silts with 5–10% gravel inclusions. Pit 1752 showed signs of slumping, with some cess-like organic fill.

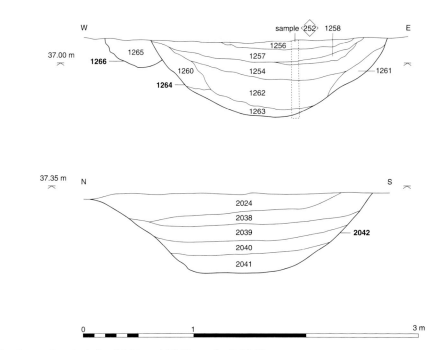

Figure 3.16   Sections of waterholes 1264 and 2042, and pit 1266

Plate 3.6   Pottery in fills of waterhole 1127

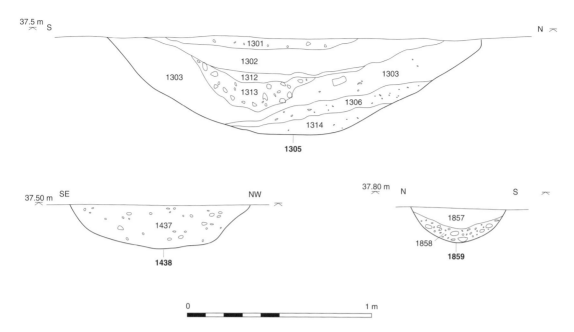

Figure 3.17   Sections of type 1 pits 1305, 1438 and 1859

Table 3.5   Late Bronze Age pits (Area 3000B)

Type no.	Shape in plan and no.	Length/ diameter m	Width m	Depth m	Profile	Pit nos	Fig. no.
Type 1 23	Oval 11	0.39–2.05	0.3–2.0	0.07–0.55	45–60°	1071, 1087, 1248, 1250, 1266, 1273, 1300, 1305, 1376, 1438, 1640, 1710,	1305, 1438, 1859 Fig. 3.17
	Circular 12	0.3–1.9	–	0.12–0.52	45–60°	1785, 1823, 1859, 1862, 1892, 2011, 2027, 2043, 2049, 2190, 2327	
Type 2 15	Oval 6	0.55–2.7	0.45–2.70	0.25–0.93	70–90°	1114, 1168, 1172, 1269, 1309, 1387, 1403, 1723,	1114, 1893, 2009
	Circular 9	0.48–1.75	–	0.2–0.78	70–90°	1752, 1770, 1821, 1893, 1967, 2009, 2032	Fig. 3.18
Type 3 7	Oval 5	0.65–2.0	0.55–1.60	0.3–0.55	60–70°	1290, 1338, 1623, 1628, 1690, 1845, 2115	1290, 1338, 1623
	Circular 2	0.65–2.0	–	0.3–0.5	60–70°		Fig. 3.19
Type 4 14	Oval 4	1.3–2.0	1.2–1.7	0.42–0.8	40–45°	1023, 1170, 1389, 1420, 1480, 1518, 1550, 1551,	1170, 1389, 1518, 1927
	Circular 10	0.9–2.5	–	0.4–0.7	40–45°	1599, 1704, 1745, 1818, 1927, 2018	Fig. 3.20 radio-carbon date pit 1518
Irregular 9	Table 3.6 for details	–	–	–	–	1245, 1255, 1416, 1490, 1638, 1691, 1810, 2271, 2289	1416, 1691 Fig. 3.21

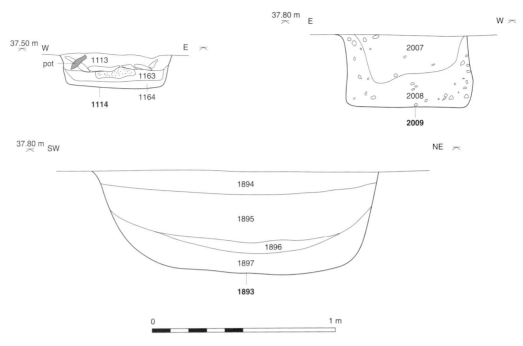

Figure 3.18   Sections of type 2 pits 1114, 1893 and 2009

Plate 3.7   Pottery in upper fill of pit 1114

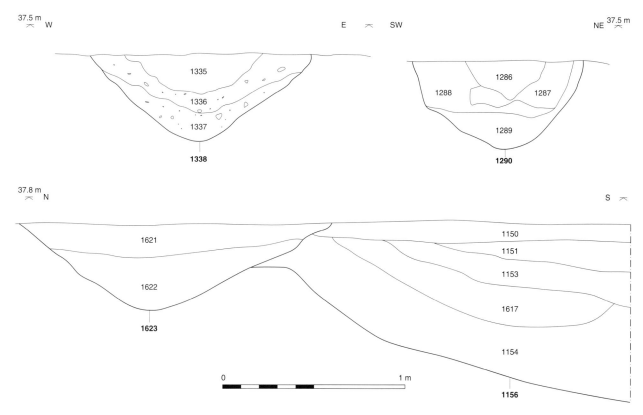

Figure 3.19   Sections of type 3 pits 1156, 1290, 1338 and 1623

Type 3 pits

These seven pits were oval or circular in plan with a v-shaped profile, and contained between one and four fills (Fig. 3.19). Primary fills varied from light grey clays with 10% gravel inclusions to sandy silts. Subsequent fills were mainly sandy loams with 5–10% gravel. Pit 1623 was overlain by palaeo-channel deposit 1013. Waterhole 1156 overlay pit 1690 and was cut by 1623 (Fig. 3.15). Only a few pits of similar type were identified in the RBP1 excavations, for example, 3508 (ibid., fig. 30). Late Bronze Age pottery (73 sherds, 820 g) was recovered from pit 1845. Pit 1628 did not contain any pottery and was overlain by a buried soil (see below) and could be earlier in date.

Type 4 pits

These 14 pits are similar to type 1 with scooped sides and round base, but are deeper (Fig. 3.20) and resemble some of the larger scoop type pits of RBP1 such as 3469 (ibid., fig. 29). In plan the pits were oval or circular and the dimensions are summarised on Table 3.5.

All of the pits contained at least two fills. Lower pit fills varied from dark grey silty clays to light grey sand or silty sand. The majority of the upper pit fills composed a silty or clay loam. Late Bronze Age pottery (totalling 219 sherds, 1219 g) was recovered from seven pits of this type (1389, 1480, 1550, 1551, 1599, 1704 and 1927). Pit 1518 contained eight fills (Fig. 3.20); the third fill, 1695, contained two sherds and a later fill, 1516, contained one sherd of late Bronze Age pottery. An animal bone found in context 1695 was radiocarbon dated to 1220–890 cal BC (93.0% confidence NZA 9412, Table A1.1). This date is comparable to others obtained elsewhere for associations with late Bronze Age pottery as discussed in Chapters 4 and 6. Part of a possible quernstone was also recovered from 1695. Pit 1551 cut into the postholes of roundhouse RH3 and contained 52 sherds of late Bronze Age pottery. The fragment of a possible rubber stone was recovered from the upper fill 1552. A type 1 pit 1823 cut pit 1818, and was itself cut by a type 2 pit 1821. A burnt mound deposit 1448 sealed the pit 1518.

Irregular pits

Nine excavated pits were of a more irregular shape and did not fall within the typologies described above. These pits are summarised in Table 3.6, and three, 1416, 1691 and 1810, are illustrated in Figure 3.21. This shows their irregular form and the likelihood that these were backfilled. Pit 1691 cut into pit 1810 (Fig. 3.21, Plate 3.8). All the pits cut into the natural 1009 and were overlain by the alluvial deposit 1021. Pit 1638 was overlain by a buried soil (see below) and could be earlier in date.

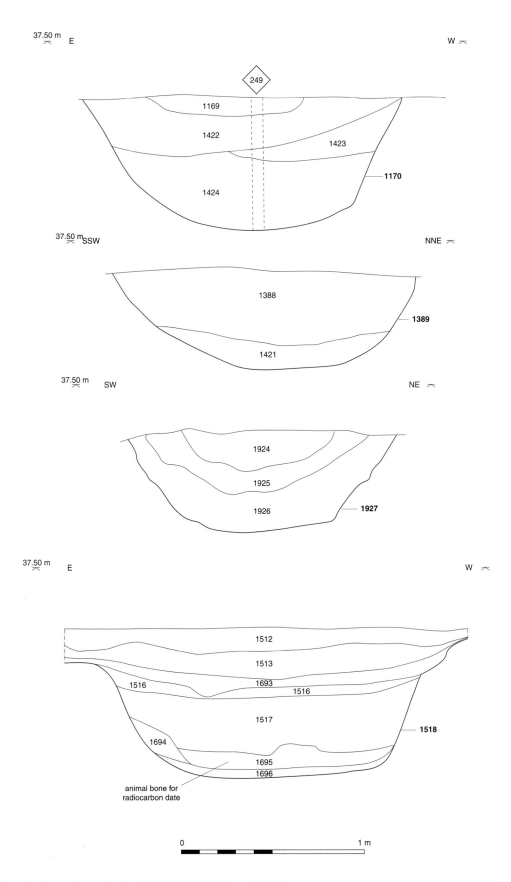

Figure 3.20   Sections of type 4 pits 1170, 1389, 1518 and 1927

Table 3.6   Irregular pits (Area 3000B)

Pit no.	Shape in plan	Length × width × depth m	Slope of sides ° Base	Fills nos	Fills type	Finds	Comments Fig. no.
1245	sub-rectangular	1.90 × 1.05 × 0.48	45–80 round	1238, 1239, 1240, 1241, 1242, 1243, 1244	silty & sandy	none clays, some charcoal in 1240	–
1255	circular	0.85 × 0.85 × 0.42	70 flat	1251, 1252, 1253, 1254	sandy silts & 40% gravel	none	–
1416	sub-circular	1.4 × 1.3 × 0.3	40–60 undulating	1413, 1414, 1415	red-brown silty clay & gravel	none	cut by pit 1172 Fig. 3.21
1490	oval	0.90 × 0.95 × 0.11	30–45 concave	1491, 1492, 1493	green-brown sandy silt	none	–
1638	sub-rectangular	0.66 × 0.37 × 0.11	variable uneven	1639	grey-brown clay silt, 3% gravel	none	–
1691	sub-circular	1.4 × 1.4 × 0.9	55–85 flooded	1692, 1808, 1809	silty clays, up to 40% gravel	upper fill 1692, 56 sherds of LBA pottery	cut pit 1810 Fig. 3.21
1810	sub-circular	1.5 × 1.5 × 0.9	70 unclear	1811, 1812, 1813, 1814, 1815, 1816, 1817	sandy gravels slumped from west	bone no pottery	cut by 1691 may be naturally silted Fig. 3.21
2271	circular	1.6 × 1.6 × 0.55	60–80 flat	2267, 2268, 2269, 2270	sandy clays & gravel	none	–
2289	sub-rectangular	0.6 × 0.38 × 0.04	varying slope: base disturbed by tree-throw hole	2288	sandy clays	none	–

Burnt mound

The burnt mound deposits, 1012/1014/1448/1466, were located to the south of the palaeochannel (Fig. 3.22). The mound deposits within the excavated site covered an area approximately 85 m long, 25 m wide and up to 0.20 m deep (Plate 3.9). However, it was clear that the mound had been disturbed and truncated by modern ploughing, and it was not possible to excavate the south-eastern end of the mound due to disturbance and flooding. Two quadrants and six slots were excavated across the mound, which comprised 70% burnt flint in a black burnt silt and sand soil containing up to 10% gravel inclusions and high frequencies of charcoal (Plate 3.10).

The mound was dated to the late Bronze Age period by the 259 sherds (1846 g) of pottery found in the deposit. Eight sherds came from layer 1012, and deposit 1014 contained 180 sherds together with a fragment of a shale bracelet, animal bone fragments and two joining pieces of a quernstone. Layer 1448 contained 30 late Bronze Age sherds and animal bone, and layer 1406 contained 41 late Bronze Age sherds. An alluvial deposit 1021 lay over the burnt mound and the mound itself sealed a number of features including four pits (1300 type 1, 1623 and 1172 type 2 and 1518 type 4), three postholes (1457, 1459, 1461) and a waterhole (1156). The burnt mound also sealed the buried land surface discussed below.

The size of the burnt mound suggests that it is likely that the deposit represents numerous episodes of activity, and the mound seems to be a series of depositions of burnt materials. The burnt flint may be the result of some industrial process taking place on the site in this period, and its function and chronological place within the occupation area is discussed further in Chapter 6. The environmental evidence indicates that oak was the major fuel source, and that in some cases this wood had been exposed to temperatures of up to 800°C (Gale, Chapter 5).

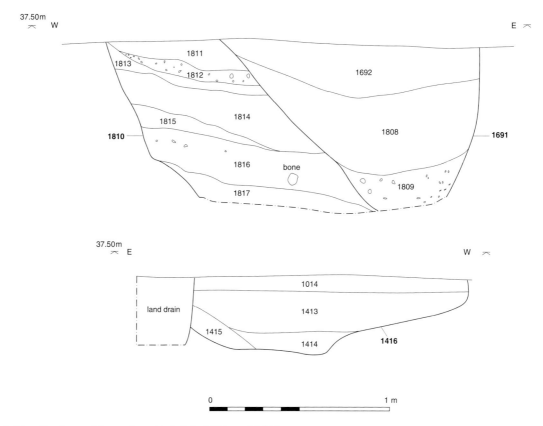

Figure 3.21   Sections of irregular pits 1416, 1691 and 1810

Plate 3.8   Intercutting irregular pits 1691 and 1810

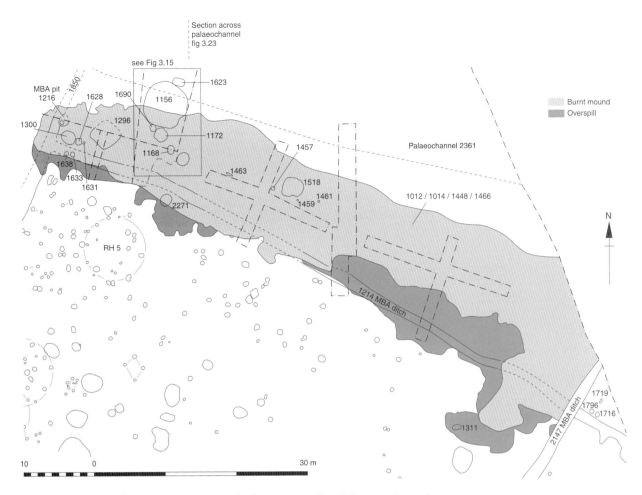

Figure 3.22   Plan showing the extent of the burnt mound and features located

Plate 3.9   View of burnt mound deposits in Area 3000B

41

Plate 3.10   Sections through the burnt mound deposits

Other prehistoric features

Buried land surface

A buried soil horizon, 1157/1218/1456/2348, was located beneath the late Bronze Age burnt mound and was excavated within the same quadrants. The deposit was up to 0.25 m deep, and comprised red-brown silty clay, containing up to 15% gravel inclusions. Layer 1456 contained three sherds of late Bronze Age pottery.

All these deposits were truncated (Fig. 3.22) by middle Bronze Age ditch 1214 and middle Bronze Age pit 1216, and also by late Bronze Age features including five pits (1300 type 1, 1168 and 1172 type 2, 1690 type 3, 1518 type 4) and three postholes (1457, 1459, 1461). The buried soil appeared to overlay a posthole (1631), two pits (1628 type 3, and 1638 an irregular pit), and a tree-throw hole (1633). Layer 1157 contained a polished stone axe which could be dated to the Bronze Age or Neolithic period (Roe, Chapter 4). The buried soil therefore could be of middle Bronze Age date suggesting that posthole 1631 and pits 1628 and 1638 may be of similar date.

Palaeochannel

The palaeochannel (2361) lay to the north of the burnt mound (Fig. 3.22) and was stratigraphically earlier. It was aligned north-west to south-east and part of the channel was excavated, measuring 120 m long by up to 17 m wide and a maximum of 1.10 m deep. The angle of slope of the sides was 5–30°, but the base was not fully excavated due to flooding. The channel 2361 was cut by the middle to late Bronze Age ditches and contained 13 fills which are recorded in Table 3.7 and Figure 3.23. The soils, sediments, hydrology and possible chronology of use of the palaeochannel are described elsewhere (Robinson, Chapter 5). It is suggested here that the channel could have provided a winter source of water for the burnt mound activity. Charcoal and burnt stone from the late Bronze Age burnt mound situated to the south extended out into the channel.

Results of watching briefs

A number of features were identified in the area directly south of 3000B (Fig. 1.2). These comprised one unexcavated pit, and four excavated and five unexcavated postholes. The features did not appear to form structures, but may have represented fence lines. A number of tree-throw holes were also identified but only a small number were excavated.

An area just to the north-east of Area 2000 (Fig. 1.2), which had been excavated in 1988, was recorded during a watching brief in 1996. Two possible 4-post structures were identified in this area, along with a number of excavated and

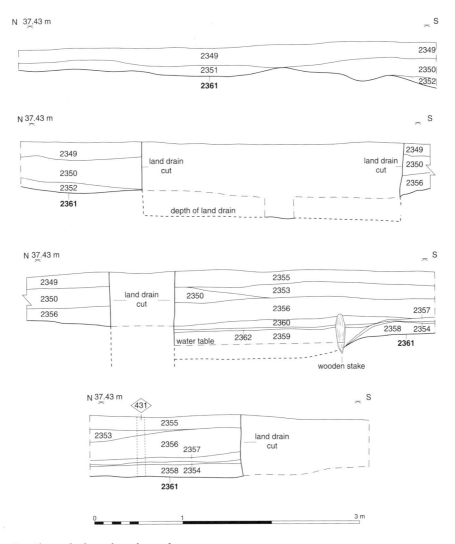

Figure 3.23 Section through the palaeochannel

Table 3.7 Fills of palaeochannel (Area 3000B)

Context	Colour	Type	Inclusions	Location
2351	dark grey-brown	silty clay	40% gravel	upper edge of northern slope
2352	dark grey-black	silty gravel	5% roots	below 2351 on northern slope
2358	creamy white	silt	1% gravel	southern side of palaeochannel
2354	grey-black	sandy clay	burnt flint	slumping of burnt mound
2357	grey-brown	clay silt	occasional gravel	seals 2354
2359	brown	silty peat	30% roots & gravel	deposit sealing a wooden stake of unknown function
2362	grey-white	sand	gravel	layer
2357/2362	grey	sandy clay	gravel & stones	layer
2356	grey	silty clay	15% gravel	layer
2353	red-brown	clay peat	grit & stones	2349 & 2355 cut by land drain
2349/2355	grey-brown	clay	10% gravel	2353 layer

unexcavated postholes. The sizes of structures (132 and 133) fell within the same dimensions and have similar postholes to those of the 4-post structures identified in Area 3000B. One of the two 4-post structures, 132, was excavated. Three of the post-holes contained burnt flint and two of these also contained some charcoal. Late Bronze Age pottery was recovered from the fills of two of the postholes. A number of other postholes were noted to the west and north of the structures 132 and 133 which may have been part of fences, and late Bronze Age pottery was recovered from four of the postholes.

During a watching brief in 1996, some overheated late Bronze Age pottery (see Morris, Chapter 4) was recovered from a deposit (67) which overlay the burnt mound. The deposit was a blue-grey silty clay, with shell, grit, gravel and burnt flint inclusions, and may have been a result of alluvial action. The presence of the deposit suggests seasonal flooding, possibly at the end of the Bronze Age or later, which eroded the sides of the burnt mound and resulted in the burnt flint inclusions in the deposit.

Post-medieval pit

Pit 1048, located in the north-eastern corner of the site, was sub-rectangular in plan, measuring 0.80 m in length, 0.60 m in width and 0.08 m in depth. The pit was not fully excavated as lime was discovered in the fill, and it was concluded that it had been dug for a pig burial.

Chapter 4:   The Artefacts

Worked flint

by Philippa Bradley

Introduction

An assemblage of 2148 pieces of worked flint and 1503 pieces of hand-retrieved burnt, unworked flint, weighing 7.8 kg, was recovered from the excavations. In addition 46.13 kg of burnt, unworked flint was recovered from soil samples taken mainly from the burnt mound; this material has not been included in the summary tables. The flint came from two main areas of activity, Area 3017, which was mainly Neolithic in date, and Area 3000B which was part of a late Bronze Age settlement. A small quan-

tity of flint was also recovered during the watching brief. However, as the material from the two areas is spatially as well as chronologically distinct, it is discussed separately. The material is compared with the assemblage found in the previous excavations (Bradley and Brown 1992) and placed in its local context. The assemblages are summarised in Table 4.1; selected pieces are described in the catalogue and illustrated in Figures 4.1–4.4.

Raw materials and condition of flint

The majority of the flint is dark brown to black in colour with lighter mottles; some cherty and crystalline inclusions were also noted. In addition some

Table 4.1   Summary of flint assemblage

Context type	Flakes*	Blades, blade-like flakes	Chips	Irregular waste	Cores, core fragments	Retouched forms	Total	Burnt, unworked flint	
								no.	g
Area 3017									
Segmented ring ditch	98	2	7	1	5	3	116	50	236
Pits	1460	28	151	18	41	53	1751	60	1033
Postholes	15	–	6	–	1	–	22	6	20
Tree-throw holes	49	3	1	–	3	3	59	12	50
Medieval features	11	–	–	–	–	2	13	–	–
Other	15	–	–	1	–	–	16	31	33
Total	1648	33	165	20	50	61	1977	159	1372
Area 3000B									
Pits	23	–	2	–	5	1	31	585**	4167
Waterholes	57	1	2	2	5	3	70	445	1429
Postholes	19	–	–	–	–	–	19	17	159
Burnt mound and associated contexts	7	–	–	–	–	2	9	295**	662
Palaeochannel deposits	3	1	–	–	–	1	5	–**	–
Later contexts	8	–	–	–	–	–	8	–	–
Other	2	–	–	–	–	–	2	1 (7)**	7
Watching brief	21	1	–	–	–	5	27	1 (7)	7
Total	140	3	4	2	10	12	171	1344	6431
Overall total	1788	36	169	22	60	73	2148	1503	7803

* including core rejuvenation flakes and flakes from polished implements;

** burnt, unworked flint from samples not included in these totals pieces of mid-brown, yellow-brown and honey-coloured flint were present. The cortex is very thin, either grey, buff or white, and is usually worn. Cortication, where recorded, is generally light to medium, but occasionally very heavy cortication was noted. Although this flint is mostly good quality it is almost certainly from a derived source and may have been available locally within river gravel or superficial deposits. A few pieces of Bullhead flint (Shepherd 1972, 114) were noted. This material would also have been available locally and was presumably chosen for its distinctive appearance. A single piece of green chert was recovered (context 5156, fill of pit 5157). The flakes from polished implements are grey in colour; one piece (context 5160, pit 5161) has a contrasting darker grey band. The polished implement from context 5004 (fill of tree-throw hole 5005) is a creamy-yellow colour. It is likely that the polished implements were made from non-local flint as it is of higher quality. Much of the flint from Area 3017 is very fresh with sharp edges and there appeared to be very little post-depositional damage on this material. However, some of the flint from Area 3000B is worn and abraded. It was noticeable that the flint from Area 3000B was also of poorer quality to that used on the earlier Neolithic site. The burnt, unworked flint is generally very heavily calcined and is a dark grey to white colour with intense cracking and crazing.

Area 3017 – Neolithic

Flint was recovered from the segmented ring ditch, pits, postholes, tree-throw holes and a range of later contexts. The single largest deposit of flint came from the fill of pit 5005 that was cut into the top of a tree-throw hole (5072) and several other pits also produced substantial assemblages (Table 4.1). The segmented ring ditch also produced a small but significant quantity of flintwork.

Flintworking

The assemblage is a flake-based one; specific blank types such as blades and blade-like flakes, for example, were not produced in any quantity as these form just less than 2% of the struck flint. However, blades and blade-like flakes seem to have been selected as blanks for some of the serrated and retouched flakes (Fig. 4.3.18). Fairly large and thick flakes were frequently chosen as blanks for scrapers and these often tended to be preparation flakes or trimming flakes, presumably because in the reduction sequence these are obviously among the largest (for example, Fig. 4.3.17). This particular example has notches along both edges perhaps indicating that it had originally been hafted. Another example that may have been hafted is illustrated (Fig. 4.2.6) as it has been made on a long blank with a suitable tang-like projection.

The incidence of keeled and discoidal cores is of some interest (Fig. 4.1.1, 4.1.4–5); the latter have been associated with the production of blanks for transverse arrowheads (Green 1980, 38). Discoidal cores are a common type in pit 5005 (context 5004) and a complete chisel arrowhead and a possible unfinished example were also recovered from this context (see below).

The material has generally been quite carefully knapped with some evidence for platform edge abrasion and rejuvenation of exhausted platforms. Rejuvenation was achieved by removing unworkable core faces or the top of the core. The former being the most common method of rejuvenation with 14 face/edge flakes recovered, only a single core tablet was found in this area. Of the complete cores, multi-platform flake types were the most commonly recovered, although keeled and levallois examples are also well represented. Two single platform flake cores, three tested nodules and 21 core fragments were also recovered. The cores have been well reduced; the largest assemblages from the pits have an average core weight of 48.6 g and the single example from a tree-throw hole weighs 53 g.

Segmented ring ditch

A relatively small but significant quantity (116 pieces) of flint was recovered from the segmented ring ditch. This material is summarised by context in Table 4.2. Although the ring ditch had been truncated and disturbed by later activity, it can be seen that its lower fills were relatively clean, with only a few flakes and chips being recovered. There seem to have originally been some spatial differences in the deposition of the material. The ditch was about 90% excavated, but no flint was recovered from the north-western part and there were concentrations of material in the ditch terminals, although it is possible that subsequent disturbance affected the distribution. A single flake was recovered from the post-medieval ditch (context 5083, fill of 5082) which cut the segmented ring ditch.

No diagnostic retouched pieces were recovered from the ring ditch, but a keeled core (Fig. 4.1.1) was found in an upper fill of the ditch (context 5095, fill of 5094). This type of core is more common within the later Neolithic (Healy 1985) and other examples have been recovered from tree-throw holes and pits (Tables 4.4 and 4.7). The general character of the flint is closely comparable with that from the pits and the tree-throw holes. Given the similarity of this material with the rest of the assemblage, the presence of the keeled core and its provenance within a later Neolithic segmented ring ditch, its dating is quite secure.

Tree-throw holes

Table 4.3 shows the composition of the assemblages from the tree-throw holes. The material is spread

Table 4.2   Summary of flint from segmented ring ditch (Area 3017)

Context	Flakes	Blade-like flakes	Chips	Irregular waste	Cores, core fragments	Retouched forms	Total	Burnt, unworked flint no.	g
Upper fills of ring ditch									
5073	10	1	2	–	–	–	13	14	50
5076	6	1	–	–	(tested nodule)	–	8	2	27
5092	56*	–	1	-	3 (1 multi-platform, 2 core fragments)	3 (1 retouched flake, 2 miscellaneous retouch)	63	9	71
5095	6	–	–	1	1 (keeled)	–	8	2	9
5110 upper fill of pit	4	–	1	–	–	–	5	–	–
Lower fills of ring ditch									
5074	10	–	3	–	–	–	13	21	37
5100	6	–	–	–	–	–	6	2	42
Total	98	2	7	1	5	3	116	50	236

* including one core tablet

Table 4.3   Summary of flint from tree-throw holes (Area 3017)

Context	Cut no.	Flakes	Blade-like flakes	Chips	Cores, core fragments	Retouched forms	Total	Burnt unworked flint no.	g
5008	5009	2	–	–	–	–	2	1	5
5017	5016	8	–	–	—	1	9	6	30
5019, 5020	5021	15	2	–	3	1	21	3	12
5040	5042	13	–	–	–	–	13	2	3
5045	5046	–	–	–	–	1	1	–	–
5071	5072	7	–	1	–	–	8	–	–
5144	5145	3	–	–	–	–	3	–	–
5148	5149	1	1	–	–	–	2	–	–
Total		49	3	1	3	3	59	12	50

very thinly across the contexts and consists largely of debitage with flakes clearly dominating. Three cores were found in tree-throw hole 5018, comprising a tested nodule and a discoidal core (5019) and a core fragment (5020) as shown in Table 4.4. Few retouched forms were recovered from the tree-throw holes. These are summarised in Table 4.5. A fabricator was recovered from context 5045 (fill of 5046) and is the only example from the site (Fig. 4.2.13). A rod or fabricator-like implement (Fig. 4.3.16) was recovered from context 5160 (upper fill of pit 5161), with only slight wear at its distal end and this may have been used for a different function. Fabricators have been found in association with Grooved Ware (Wainwright and Longworth 1971, 176, 177, fig. 77, F82–3, 256, 260) and in other later Neolithic assemblages, for example, at Dorchester-on-Thames (Atkinson *et al.* 1951, 114, fig. 31, nos 144, 147, 199; 115). The flint from the tree-throw holes appears to be of a consistent later Neolithic date and can be compared typologically and technologically to the much larger assemblages from the pits.

Pits

Fifteen pits produced worked flint but of these only nine contained any quantity of material (Table 4.6). Generally these features contained only one fill, but five pits which produced flint had more than one fill and these are amongst the largest of the assemblages. However, pit 5005 which cut into the top of

Table 4.4   Core types from tree-throw holes (Area 3017)

Context	Keeled and discoidal	Core fragments	Tested nodule	Total
5019, 5020	1	1	1	3

Table 4.5   Retouched forms from tree-throw holes (Area 3017)

Context	Fabricator	Denticulate, piercer	Total
5016, 5017	–	1	1
5019, 5020	–	1	1
5045	1	–	1
Total	1	2	3

tree-throw hole 5072, produced the single largest flint assemblage from the site and contained only one fill.

Context 5004 (pit 5005) contained 845 pieces of worked flint and 14 pieces of burnt, unworked flint. The group is summarised in Table 4.6 and selected pieces are illustrated (Fig. 4.1.3–5 and Fig. 4.2.6–12). The assemblage is dominated by debitage, but it is noticeable that there are very few pieces of irregular waste (8 pieces or 0.9% of the total assemblage) perhaps suggesting that the contents were deliberately selected for deposition with the more irregular pieces of the reduction sequence largely being excluded. Keeled and discoidal cores dominate (Table 4.7), but a range of other types was also recovered (for example, Fig. 4.1.2 and 4.1.3). The dominance of keeled and discoidal cores is typical of later Neolithic assemblages (Healy 1985, 192–3)

Table 4.6   Summary of flint from pits (Area 3017)

Context	Flakes*	Blade-like flakes	Chips	Irregular waste	Cores, core fragments	Retouched forms	Total	Burnt, un-worked flint no.	g
5004	712*	2	86	8	18	19	845	14	110
5011, 5012, 5013	84	8	5	–	1	4	102	1	12
5038	4	–	–	–	–	–	4	7	36
5060	139	–	51	1	2	3	196	6	27
5062	67	2	–	–	2	5	76	8	43
5107	2	–	–	–	–	1	3	–	–
5118, 5120, 5122	63	–	2	–	6	3	74	1	10
5125	8	–	–	–	–	1	9	–	–
5134	–	–	–	1	–	–	1	1	29
5137, 5138	180	6	5	3	9	6	209	12	708
5141	9	1	–	–	–	–	10	–	–
5146, 5150	56	2	–	–	1	5	64	–	–
5156	56*	6	–	2	–	–	64	–	–
5160, 5164	76*	1	2	3	2	6	90	10	58
5189	1	–	–	–	–	–	1	–	–
Total	1457	28	151	18	41	53	1748	60	1033

* includes core rejuvenation flakes and flakes from polished implements

Table 4.7   Core types from pits (Area 3017)

Context	Single platform	Multi-platform	Keeled and discoidal	Core fragments	Tested nodule	Total
5004	2	3	5	7	1	18
5010	–	1	–	–	–	1
5060	–	1	–	1	–	2
5062	–	1	–	1	–	2
5118, 5122	–	3	–	3	–	6
5137, 5138	–	3	1	5	–	9
5150	–	–	–	1	–	1
5160, 5164	–	1	–	1	–	2
Total	2	13	6	19	1	41

Table 4.8 Retouched forms from pits (Area 3017)

Context	Scrapers	Retouched flakes	Serrated flakes	Piercer, awl	Arrowheads	Axe/pick	Miscellaneous retouch	Total
5004	8 (7 end and side, 1 end scraper)	2	1	–	2 (1 chisel, 1 unfinished, possible chisel)	–	6	19
5013	–	3	–	–	–	–	1	4
5060	2 (1 end, 1 end and side)	–	–	–	–	–	1	3
5062	1 (end)	2	2	–	–	–	–	5
5107	1 (end)	–	–	–	–	–	–	1
5120, 5122	–	–	–	1 (piercer)	1 (chisel)	1 (pick fragment?)	–	3
5125	1 (end and side)	–	–	–	–	–	–	1
5137, 5138	–	–	1	1 (piercer)	–	1 (pick)	3	6
5146, 5150	2 (1 end and side, 1 end)	1	1	–	–	–	1	5
5160, 5164	–	1	1	1 (awl)	2 (chisel)	–	1	6
Total	15	9	6	2	5	2	13	53

and it is possible that discoidal cores were used to strike blanks for transverse arrowheads (Green 1980, 38). Some of the chisel arrowheads have certainly been struck from discoidal cores (for example, Fig. 4.3.19) and, interestingly, context 5004 produced both discoidal cores and chisel arrowheads (Tables 4.7–4.8, Figs 4.1.4–5, and 4.2.11–12).

The retouched forms recovered from context 5004 are quite limited in type and are dominated by scrapers (Table 4.8), although it is the largest retouched component from a single feature on the site (Fig. 4.2.6–12). The miscellaneous retouched forms include a polished implement (Fig. 4.2.10) with polishing along three edges, two broken scrapers and three flakes with areas of retouch along their edges. The broken scrapers are either end forms or end-and-side forms. The other retouched forms present include cutting tools (retouched and serrated flakes), a chisel arrowhead and another probable unfinished or symbolic chisel arrowhead. This arrowhead (Fig. 4.2.12) may be compared with some of those found at the Wyke Down henge (Brown 1991, 119, fig. 6.5 f–h).

Debitage clearly dominates the assemblages from the pits (Table 4.6) and interestingly there is a higher number of blades and blade-like flakes compared with the tree-throw holes (Tables 4.6 and 4.3), but this may simply reflect the higher numbers of pits that were excavated compared with tree-throw holes. Otherwise the composition of these two groups is very similar, although the pits have a slightly higher quantity of retouched pieces and burnt, unworked flint. The cores from the pits are mostly multi-platform types; keeled and discoidal

cores were recovered from contexts 5004 and 5137; core fragments are also well represented (Table 4.7). This contrasts markedly with the paucity of cores from the tree-throw holes (Table 4.4).

The range of retouched types is much wider from the pits than from the tree-throw holes (Tables 4.8, 4.5, Fig. 4.2.13–14 and Fig. 4.3.15–20) with scrapers, serrated flakes and retouched flakes dominating. One difference that is very striking is the lack of serrated and retouched flakes from the tree-throw holes when compared with the pit deposits (Tables 4.5 and 4.8, Fig. 4.3.18). This may be a functional difference between the assemblages as it is unlikely to have been caused by post-depositional factors. Alternatively it may reflect the much smaller assemblages recovered from these features compared with the pits.

The average core weight for the pits at 48.6 g can be compared with the single complete core weight from the tree-throw holes at 53 g and the average weight of 51.92 g for all of the complete cores from Area 3017. Interestingly the cores from the pit deposits have a higher flake to core ratio; 70.85 flakes per core, compared with 53.5 flakes per core for the whole assemblage. This indicates that the cores deposited within the pits were more extensively worked than those from other contexts. However, within these averages there is quite a wide range of weights and numbers of removals indicating a more complicated picture.

The distribution of flint within pits that had more than one fill is of some interest; the majority of the flint from these features was concentrated in the upper fills but in one, feature 5147, the situation was reversed. Here the upper fill contained 7 flakes and a scraper whilst the primary fill produced 56 pieces of flint including flakes, 2 blade-like flakes, a core fragment and 4 retouched pieces. Overall the composition of the assemblages from these features is similar. Two pick-like implements, one fragmentary, were recovered from the fills of pits 5119 and 5136 (Fig. 4.3.20), which might suggest a specialised aspect to some of these pit deposits. However, pit 5136 also contained medieval pottery suggesting substantial medieval disturbance.

There are three possible pairs of pits (5010 and 5061, 5124 and 5147, 5143 and 5119). The composition of these pit groups was studied in order to look for any differences between the flints. The first pair of pits, 5010 and 5061, produced quite large flint assemblages (contexts 5011–5013 and 5062) with fairly comparable compositions (Tables 4.6–4.8). The assemblages from another possible pair of pits, however, provide a contrast, with pit 5124 (context 5125) producing only eight flakes and a scraper, whilst pit 5147 (contexts 5146 and 5150) contained much more flint (Tables 4.6–4.8). The third pair of pits includes 5119 with a large assemblage (contexts 5118, 5120, 5122) and one that contained a very small quantity of debitage (context 5141, Table 4.6). The assemblage from pit 5119 was dominated by debitage, including three multi-platform flake cores (Tables 4.6–4.7). The three retouched pieces from this feature include a pick, a piercer and a chisel arrowhead (Fig. 4.3.19, Table 4.8).

Pit 5005 was located towards the north-west of the excavated area, a little way away from most of the other flint-rich contexts. The contents of this pit stand out from the others, in terms of the overall size of the assemblage and its composition (Tables 4.1 and 4.6). The material seems to have been fairly extensively worked, but the differences in composition and range of artefacts together with the location of the pit may suggest that the flintwork was formally deposited, rather than merely disposed of as rubbish.

Of the remaining pits that produced flint, the assemblages were limited in character and dominated by debitage (for example, contexts 5038, 5107, 5125 and 5134 (Table 4.6)). Only two retouched pieces were recovered from these contexts, both of which are scrapers (Table 4.8). It seems likely, given its low density, that the material in some of these contexts was not included deliberately.

Postholes and other contexts

A small quantity of flint was recovered from postholes, medieval features and other contexts (Table 4.1). The flint from the postholes consisted of debitage and was spread over a number of contexts. A single core fragment was recovered from context 5057, the fill of posthole 5058. The medieval and later contexts again largely produced debitage (Table 4.1) but a notched and a serrated flake came

from 5206, fill of posthole 5207. In general this material was very similar in character to the rest of the assemblage from the same area; the two retouched pieces compare well with other examples recovered. It is likely that this material is contemporaneous with the activity on the site; the flint from the medieval and later contexts simply being redeposited within those features.

Area 3000B

This area produced a small assemblage of worked flint comprising 171 pieces (including 27 from the watching brief), and 6.43 kg of hand-retrieved, burnt, unworked flint was also recovered. All this material is summarised in Table 4.1. In addition a large quantity of burnt, unworked flint (approximately 46 kg) was recovered from soil samples taken from the burnt mound and other deposits, and this material has not been included in the tables.

Flintworking

The flintwork from this area largely consists of debitage and the flint is of poorer quality than that used in Area 3017. The incidence of blades and blade-like flakes is much lower than in Area 3017 and only two core rejuvenation flakes (a core tablet and a face/edge flake) were recovered from context 1406. Hard hammer percussors dominate and the flakes from this area tend to be smaller and less well knapped than the material from the other area. Thus flakes frequently have very prominent bulbs of percussion and butts tend to be wide. Flaking angles of around 120° are not uncommon. Hinge fractures and other accidents of knapping are commonly recorded amongst this material, as also are incipient cones of percussion. All of these traits indicate general loss of control during knapping and show that less care was being exercised than in earlier periods.

The core types recovered are very limited; a single multi-platform flake core (Fig. 4.3.21) is the only formally worked example and the remainder are core fragments with a single tested nodule. The retouched forms are similarly limited and consist of piercing tools, a single scraper and cutting tools (Fig. 4.4.22–5). These have mostly been minimally retouched and are fairly typical of the sort of tools present in later Bronze Age flint assemblages (cf. Ford *et al.* 1984). They are similar to the finds from RBP1 excavations (Brown 1992, 92).

Pits and waterholes

Only 31 pieces of worked flint were recovered from pits within the area (Table 4.1). The material is spread very thinly across 21 pits, the largest assemblage being 7 flakes, a chip and 269 pieces of burnt, unworked from pit 1704. Flakes dominate the assemblages from the pits. Three core fragments and two tested nodules were recovered, together with two chips and a retouched flake. The incidence of burnt, unworked flint is more numerous but it is again spread quite thinly across the contexts with only a couple of pits producing any weight of this material, for example, 1144 (1492 g) and 1770 (584 g).

The waterholes produced slightly larger groups of material (70 pieces in total) and these were again dominated by debitage (Table 4.1). Four waterholes produced flint (1015, 1118, 1264 and 2042). Waterhole 2042 also produced a single piece of burnt, unworked flint weighing 5 g, which may not have been deliberately included in the fill. Waterhole 1015 produced the largest assemblage, 52 pieces of worked flint. This material consisted of flakes, two pieces of irregular waste, four core fragments, a multi-platform core (Fig. 4.3.21) and three retouched pieces. The retouched pieces are all minimally retouched and consist of a side scraper (Fig. 4.4.22), a piercer (Fig. 4.4.23) and a retouched flake. This material was dispersed between six layers in the upper part of the waterhole, but no burnt, unworked flint was recovered from this feature. However, waterhole 1118 produced only eight flakes but a considerable quantity of burnt, unworked flint (*c* 1.2 kg). The fourth waterhole that produced flint contained seven flakes, a blade-like flake, two chips and twelve pieces of burnt, unworked flint (119 g).

Burnt mound and associated contexts

Very little worked flint was recovered from the burnt mound (Table 4.1). The two retouched pieces are a small, worn piercer (Fig. 4.4.24) from the upper layer of the mound and a retouched flake from the layer below the mound. Neither of these pieces can provide any reliable dating evidence but are probably later Bronze Age in date on technological grounds.

Postholes and other contexts

Thirty-four pieces of worked flint and 18 pieces of burnt, unworked flint were recovered from postholes, the palaeochannel, a middle Bronze Age ditch and later contexts (Table 4.1). Seventeen flakes and two core rejuvenation flakes (one face/edge and one tablet) together with 17 pieces of burnt, unworked flint (159 g) were recovered from the postholes. This was again spread very thinly across a number of contexts. The middle Bronze Age ditch produced a single small piece of burnt, unworked flint whilst the palaeochannel produced three flakes, a bladelet and a denticulate (Fig. 4.4.25). Alluvial and plough-soil contexts produced eight flakes.

Discussion

Area 3017 produced the largest quantity of flint from the excavations (Table 4.1). Without exception

the flint from this area is later Neolithic in date with typologically and technologically good assemblages being recovered from some of the pits and tree-throw holes (Tables 4.1, 4.3–4.8). Less diagnostic material was also recovered from the segmented ring ditch and other contexts (Table 4.2). The flint from this area indicates that a wide range of activities, including knapping, hide preparation, possibly woodworking and food processing, was occurring on site. This range of activities is consistent with the date of the assemblage and the context of deposition of the material. Two small sherds of Neolithic Peterborough Ware were recovered from context 5004 – the fill of pit 5005, cut into the top of a tree-throw hole – which also produced the single largest flint assemblage (Table 4.6). Context 5011, a fill of pit 5010, produced a rim of later Neolithic Woodlands style Grooved Ware (Barclay, this Chapter), although it is possible that the pottery may be redeposited. Chisel arrowheads tend to be associated with the Woodlands substyle of Grooved Ware (Green 1980, 108) and this type was found exclusively on the site.

The deposition of material within Neolithic pits has been discussed (Thomas 1991, 59–64; Brown 1991; Barclay and Halpin 1999). No direct evidence for the structuring of the deposits was encountered at this site but a comparison of the material from the pits provided some tentative evidence, as discussed above. A complete pick and another fragmentary example were also deposited within two of the pits, one of which was recovered from the primary fill. The very large assemblage of flint from pit 5005 produced a wide range of artefact types and the cores seem to have been quite extensively worked. There is also a suggestion that the pit was spatially separate from the other contemporaneous activity.

In comparison, at Radley, Oxfordshire, Grooved Ware pits sited within a Neolithic and Bronze Age barrow cemetery produced cores that had not been worked to their full potential (Bradley 1999). These cores could be compared with others at Radley from a series of pits where the cores were more reduced, and therefore seemed to be much less formally selected for deposition in the pits (ibid.). At Radley too there was more obvious evidence for structuring of the deposits (Barclay and Halpin 1999). The deposition of burnt, broken, used and seemingly unused artefacts can also be identified at a number of other sites (Thomas 1991, 60; Bradley 1999).

Some similarities have already been drawn between the flintwork previously published from the earlier RBP1 excavations and the present assemblage. In general terms similar types of artefacts were recovered and they seem to have been worked using comparable methods (Bradley 1992). It is likely therefore that this flintwork represented the same activity, although there was also a possible earlier element to the flintwork previously found

(Bradley 1992, 90). The reuse of broken polished implements was also a feature of the RBP1 assemblage (Bradley 1992, 90–1). However, the diagnostic retouched forms from the earlier excavations can be paralleled in the present RBP2 collection, for example, the transverse arrowheads, polished implements and discoidal cores (ibid.). A chisel fragment (Bradley 1992, 91, fig. 53, 7309) of late Neolithic date is one of the few objects that is not seen in the present RBP2 assemblage, although the broken polished implement (Fig. 4.2.10) could be an unfinished example.

The flint assemblage from the Green Park excavations at Reading Business Park can be compared with flintwork from other similar sites in the area. At Thames Valley Park, Reading, a pit containing worked and burnt flint, together with Peterborough Ware pottery, was found during excavations (Butterworth and Hawkes 1997, 83; Seager Smith and Cleal 1997, 89). A series of pits that produced Peterborough Ware, fairly substantial assemblages of worked flint and charred plant remains was also excavated at Lake End Road West as part of the Maidenhead-Slough (Berks and Bucks) Flood Alleviation Scheme (Lamdin-Whymark in prep.). Other later Neolithic flintwork in the vicinity includes an assemblage from a ring ditch at Engelfield near Theale (Healy 1991–3, 15). At Engelfield the assemblage included a *petit tranchet* derivative and two chisel arrowheads (Healy 1991–3, 15, 17, table 3) and some of the assemblage was associated with Peterborough Ware. Smaller quantities of Neolithic flintwork have been recovered at a number of sites including Field Farm, Burghfield (Harding 1992a, 38–9), Anslow's Cottages, Burghfield (Harding 1992b, 106), Weir Bank Stud Farm, Bray (Montague 1995, 21) and Wickhams Field, Reading (Harding 1996, 142).

The assemblages from these excavations provide an opportunity to contrast later Neolithic and later Bronze Age flintworking practices. A simple study of the component parts of each of the assemblages indicates that striking differences emerge. The Neolithic assemblage is composed of a mixture of debitage with a wide variety of retouched forms and in contrast the Bronze Age assemblage is dominated by debitage with a very limited number of formally retouched tools. There are also differences in the use of raw materials, with generally better quality flint being used on the later Neolithic site, with gravel flint of poorer quality tending to dominate the later Bronze Age assemblage.

Core types are also limited from the late Bronze Age Area 3000B but there is a wide variety of types present in the assemblage from the Neolithic Area 3017. The cores from each area have been very differently worked, those from 3017 have been prepared and maintained to some extent but those from Area 3000B have been very roughly worked. Indeed there is only one formally classifiable core

from the latter area, the others are core fragments and tested nodules. This is also borne out by the incidence of rejuvenation flakes from the two areas.

During the later Neolithic there is still some concern for using particular types of blank for artefacts such as serrated and retouched flakes and chisel arrowheads. To this end there is some predetermination to the reduction sequence. In the later Bronze Age, however, the aim of reduction is to produce a useable piece of flint of any form. Retouch is used on the later Neolithic artefacts not only to shape them but also to enhance their appearance; much larger areas are often retouched than would be needed for purely functional needs. Retouch in the later Bronze Age is used in a very different way merely for functional purposes and little excess retouching can be noted.

These differences reflect the differing attitudes to flintworking from the later Neolithic to the later Bronze Age. Later Bronze Age flintworking practices have begun to receive more attention (for example, Fasham and Ross 1978; Healy 1981; Ford *et al.* 1984; Brown 1992; Bradley 1994, 1997; Montague 1995; Brown and Bradley forthcoming), and a number of patterns are emerging:

1. Expedient knapping strategies were employed.
2. Production concentrated on a limited number of retouched forms (scrapers, piercing tools and cutting tools) but usewear analyses have shown that much of the unretouched component was indeed used (Brown 1992; Brown and Bradley forthcoming).
3. Little concern with the selection of raw materials, anything that could be flaked was used.
4. Little concern with the production and maintenance of regular cores.
5. Little concern with initial preparation or the finishing of products.

The retouched tools that were produced were presumably still used as they functioned better than their metal counterparts. The elaborately retouched items produced during the Neolithic were no longer required as metal was now used for display purposes; flint was therefore left for the mundane domestic tasks only.

There is considerable evidence locally for later Bronze Age activity (see for example, Butterworth and Lobb 1992; Barnes *et al.* 1995; Johnston 1983–5; Moore and Jennings 1992). At many of these sites lithic assemblages have been recovered and it can be seen that characteristics of the small later Bronze Age element of the present assemblage can be paralleled in these large assemblages from these sites. The flint from the present excavations can be seen as part of the same assemblage recovered from the earlier excavations (Brown 1992). There are no real differences in terms of raw material type, artefacts present or reduction strategies. What is surprising is the much smaller quantity of material recovered in 1995.

Catalogue of illustrated flint

The catalogue is arranged in the following order: brief description of the object, raw material and condition, weight (cores only), context number and small find number (if any).

Area 3017
Figure 4.1

1. Keeled core with several hinge fractures, good quality flint, medium to heavy cortication, 35 g, 5095 (fill of segmented ring ditch).
2. Single platform flake core, with some platform edge abrasion, very cherty flint, medium cortication, 77 g, 5004 (fill of pit 5005).
3. Multi-platform flake core, small very well reduced example with some platform edge abrasion, heavily corticated, some large cherty and crystalline inclusions, 34 g, 5004.
4. Discoidal core, fairly crude example with flakes removed from one side only, vesicular cortex, medium to heavy cortication, 37 g, 5004.
5. Discoidal core, neatly worked example with flakes removed from one side, other side partially prepared, good quality flint with a very small area of cortex surviving, heavily corticated, 61 g, 5004.

Figure 4.2

6. End and side scraper on a side-trimming flake, possibly originally hafted, long tang-like projection may have allowed a haft to be attached, large cherty inclusions, lightly corticated, scraping angle 60–70°, 5004.
7. End and side scraper on a trimming flake, damaged and worn scraping edge, probably occurred during use and was not subsequently resharpened, heavily corticated, scraping angle 50–65°, 5004.
8. End scraper, small patch of surviving cortex, cherty flint, medium cortication, scraping angle 55–60°, 5004.
9. Serrated flake on a trimming flake, upper right hand side and distal end coarsely serrated almost notched retouch, lightly corticated, 3 serrations per 10 mm, 5004.
10. Polished implement, broken, rod-like implement with slightly curved profile and square section. The object has been extensively flaked and has been polished on at least three sides, possibly an unfinished chisel, creamy flint with cherty patches, 5004.
11. Chisel arrowhead, slight break to left hand side, medium cortication, 5004.
12. Possibly unfinished or symbolic chisel arrowhead, flake with thinned butt and minimal retouching to dorsal surface, overall shape suggests chisel arrowhead, very light cortication, 5004.

13. Fabricator with marked plano-convex section with some surviving cortex, steeply retouched along both edges, slightly invasive in some areas, worn at distal and proximal ends, lightly corticated, 5045 (fill of tree-throw hole 5046).
14. Chisel arrowhead, slight break to upper left hand side, steeply retouched edges, lightly corticated, 5164 (primary fill of pit 5161).

Figure 4.3

15. Awl on side trimming flake, with quite a long, neatly worked point, some wear to point, very lightly corticated, 5160 (upper fill of pit 5161).
16. Rod/fabricator, oval blank with reduced butt and retouched along right hand side, cortical backing left hand side, denticulated retouch to right hand side, some wear and battering to distal end, very lightly corticated, 5160.
17. End and side scraper on a large, slightly irregular preparation flake, notches on both edges suggest that it may have originally been hafted, scraping angle 60–75°, lightly corticated, 5146 (upper fill of pit 5147).
18. Serrated flake, on slightly blade-like blank, left hand side serrated, 12 serrations per 10 mm, heavily corticated, small area of cortex at distal end, 5062 (fill of pit 5061).
19. Chisel arrowhead on a flake from a discoidal core, steeply retouched on a fairly thick blank, wide cutting edge, lightly corticated, 5120 (fill of pit 5119).
20. Pick, with bulbous base with slightly sinuous profile and alternate flaking along edges, cherty flint stained yellow, heavily corticated, 5138 (fill pit 5136).

Area 3000B

21. Multi-platform flake core, irregularly worked with one keeled platform and many hinge fractures on flaking faces, small example made on a gravel pebble, uncorticated, 38 g, 1027 (fill of waterhole 1015).

Figure 4.4

22. Side scraper with denticulated edge, some incipient cones of percussion, brown uncorticated flint, 1030 (fill of waterhole 1015).
23. Piercer on a thick, partly cortical flake, irregularly worked with a small point, gravel flint with cherty inclusions, uncorticated, 1030 (fill of waterhole 1015).
24. Piercer on a thick blank with hinge fracture, small, worn point worked to the upper left hand side, minimal retouching, gravel flint, very light cortication and some orange staining, 1014 (burnt mound) SF2.
25. Denticulate made on the bulbar face of a thick non-cortical flake with areas of fine retouch, some of which might have been formed by use, rather than by formal retouch, mid-brown flint with orange mottles and large cherty inclusions, uncorticated, 1013 (fill of palaeochannel) SF163.

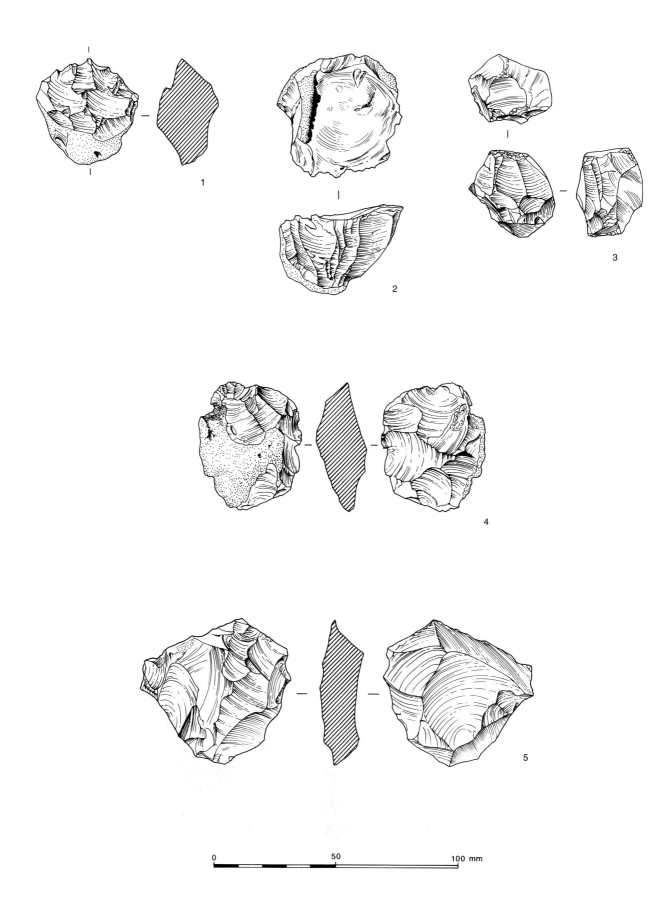

Figure 4.1   Flints: 1–5. Area 3017

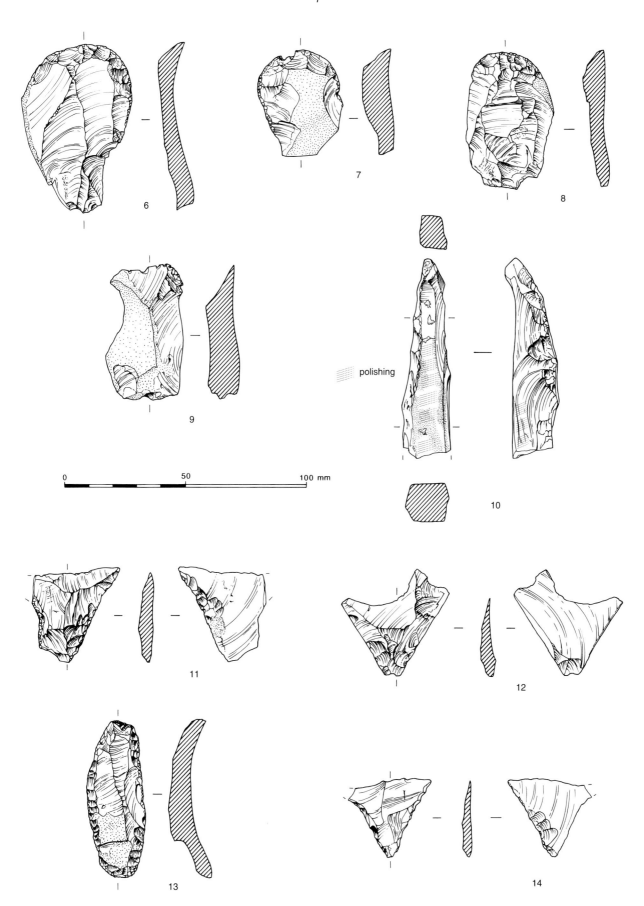

polishing

0   50   100 mm

Figure 4.2   Flints: 6–14. Area 3017

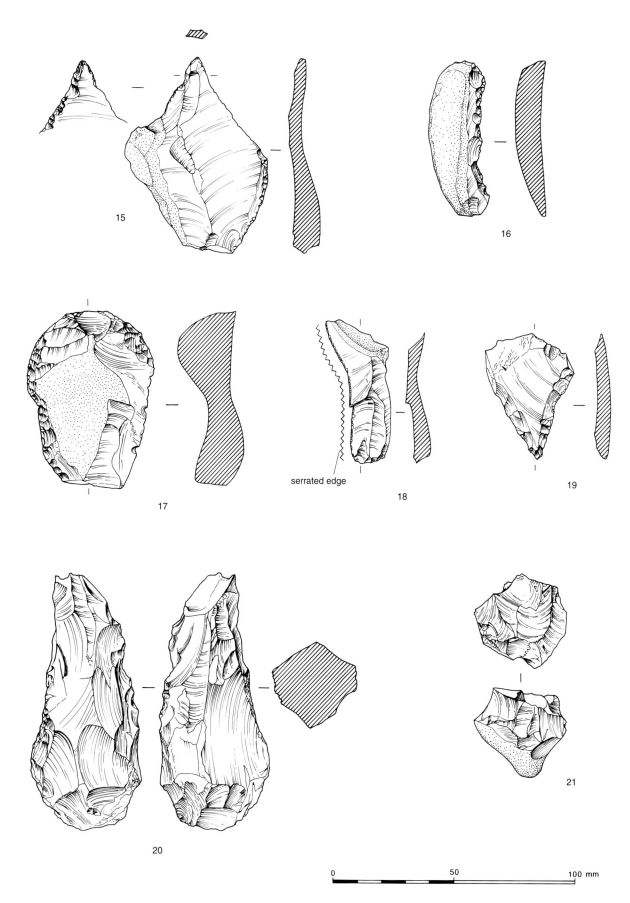

Figure 4.3   Flints: 15–20. Area 3017; 21. Area 3000B

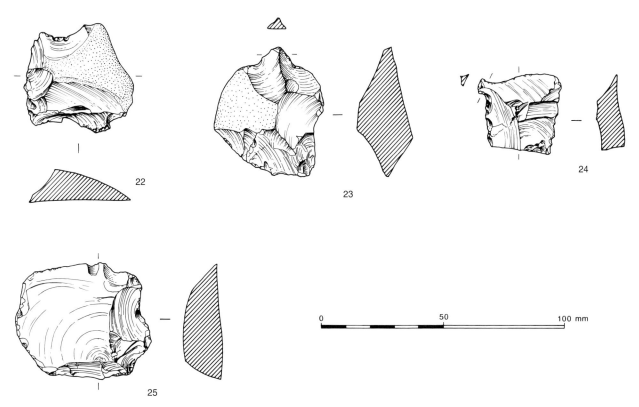

Figure 4.4   Flints: 22–5. Area 3000B

Earlier prehistoric pottery

by Alistair Barclay

Introduction

The excavation of Area 3017 produced a small quantity of earlier prehistoric pottery of mostly later Neolithic date. The only illustrated sherd is a decorated rim from a Woodlands style Grooved Ware vessel.

Methodology

The assemblage is quantified by weight and sherd number (see Table 4.9). Refitting fresh breaks are excluded from the sherd count. The pottery is characterised by fabric, form, surface treatment, decoration and colour, and a record was made of burnt residues. Only the more diagnostic featured sherds are listed in the catalogue. The sherds were analysed using a binocular microscope (×20) and were divided into fabric groups by principal inclusion type.

OAU standard codes are used to denote inclusion types: A = sand (quartz and other mineral matter), F = flint, P = pellets (ferruginous), S = shell. The size range for inclusions is: 1 = <1 mm, fine; 2 = 1–3 mm, fine-medium, and 3 = >3 mm, medium-coarse: the frequency range for inclusions is; rare = <3%, sparse = <7%, moderate = 10%, common = 15%, and abundant = >20%.

Table 4.9   *Quantification by context of earlier prehistoric pottery (Area 3017)*

Context	Peterborough Ware	Grooved Ware	Indeterminate	Total	
				no.	g
5004 (ss.501 & 507)	2 sherds, 2 g			2	2
5011 (ss.508)		1 sherd, 1 g		1	1
5013			1 sherd, 7 g	1	7
5164			3 sherds, 1 g	3	1
5189			1 sherd, 5 g	1	5
Total	2 sherds, 2 g	1 sherd, 1 g	5 sherds, 13 g	8	16

Fabrics

Six fabrics were identified of which three are considered to be Neolithic (F1, F3 and SA2) and three are of indeterminate, possibly earlier prehistoric date (S2, PA2 and A1):

Flint-tempered

F1 – a hard fabric with abundant fine angular flint.
F3 – a soft laminated fabric with sparse coarse angular flint.

Shell-tempered

S2 – a vesicular fabric with common plate-like voids.
SA2 – a vesicular fabric with common plate-like voids and with sparse coarse quartz sand.

Sand-tempered

A1 – a hard fabric with common coarse quartz sand.
PA2 – a soft fabric with common (possibly naturally occurring) ferruginous pellets and sparse, coarse quartz sand.

Peterborough Ware

Two very small sherds of pottery in flint-tempered fabrics (F1 and F3) from context 5004 (fill of pit 5005) are likely to be from Peterborough Ware vessels of middle Neolithic date.

Grooved Ware

Context 5011 (fill of pit 5010) contained a single rim sherd from a Woodlands style vessel. The rim is bevelled and decorated with an impressed wavy strip and the exterior surface has a slightly wavy raised cordon, which is impressed. The rim is from a thin-walled vessel. The fabric is now very vesicular, but may originally have been tempered with crushed shell (SA2). The rim form is very typical of this style (Wainwright and Longworth 1971, 238) and can be almost exactly paralleled with one from Radley, Oxfordshire (Cleal 1999) and from other sites in the Upper Thames Valley (Case 1982, fig. 69.11–2, 124–5). The sherd is small and abraded indicating that it might be residual. Alternatively it could have reached this state between breakage and deposition, as a result of trampling or exposure in a midden deposit.

Indeterminate, possibly earlier prehistoric

Five plain body sherds (contexts 5013, 5164 and 5189) are of indeterminate character and although all of these appear to be handmade and low fired, it is not certain whether they are all earlier prehistoric date. One relatively thin-walled sherd in a shell-tempered fabric could be of late Neolithic date.

Discussion

The earliest pottery is the middle Neolithic Peterborough Ware recovered from a fill (5004) of pit 5005, a context that also produced a small piece of late Bronze Age pottery. None of these sherds weighs more than 1 g and all are abraded. Given their size and abraded condition the Neolithic sherds could represent residual surface material that has been redeposited into the feature. The six remaining sherds were all recovered from three pits. Pit 5010 contained two sherds that included a Grooved Ware rim (Fig. 4.5, context 5011) and a body sherd of possible earlier prehistoric date (5013).

Relatively little later Neolithic pottery has been found in the Reading area of the lower Kennet Valley. Finds of Peterborough Ware are not common and tend to consist of stray sherds or small groups of sherds (Cleal 1991–3, 19), and Grooved Ware is particularly scarce. As with the finds from this site, much of this material has been recovered from deposits in pits, the upper fills of tree-throw holes and as surface material on preserved land surfaces.

Catalogue of illustrated pottery

Area 3000B

Figure 4.5

1. Decorated rim sherd from a Neolithic Grooved Ware Woodlands style vessel, fabric SA2, colour, exterior and interior brown, core dark grey, condition worn, 5011, SS.508, pit 5010.

0   50 mm

Figure 4.5   1. Neolithic Grooved Ware Woodlands style, Area 3000B

Later prehistoric pottery

by Elaine Morris (with a contribution by David Williams)

Introduction

A total of 4346 sherds of later prehistoric pottery from Area 3000B, weighing 59,863 g, was examined in detail (Table 4.10). In addition, pieces of pottery recovered from sieved environmental samples were

Table 4.10   Quantification of middle to late Bronze Age pottery by fabric type

Fabric type	Fabric grade	No. of sherds	% by number	Weight of sherds (g)	% of total by weight
Middle Bronze Age					
F15	int	18	0.4%	158	0.3%
F16	coarse	329	7.6%	7062	11.8%
F17	coarse	1	>0.0%	78	0.1%
Middle/late Bronze Age					
F5	coarse	97	2.2%	1802	3.0%
Late Bronze Age					
F1	int/coarse	1086	25.0%	11006	18.4%
F2	int	19	0.4%	803	1.3%
F3	coarse	508	11.7%	7876	13.2%
F4	coarse	667	15.3%	8120	13.6%
F6	fine	80	1.8%	489	0.8%
F7	int	34	0.8%	729	1.2%
F8	fine/int	5	0.1%	63	0.1%
F9	fine	17	0.4%	199	0.3%
F10	int	31	0.7%	396	0.7%
F11	fine	25	0.6%	387	0.6%
F12	coarse	5	0.1%	210	0.4%
F13	fine/int	3	0.1%	35	0.1%
F99	–	518	11.9%	1289	2.2%
FG1	coarse	28	0.6%	857	1.4%
G1	fine	6	0.1%	21	0.0%
IF1	int	178	4.1%	3917	6.5%
IF2	int/coarse	400	9.2%	7350	12.3%
IF3	coarse	109	2.5%	2749	4.6%
IF4	int/coarse	34	0.8%	693	1.2%
IF5	coarse	143	3.3%	3543	5.9%
IG1	coarse	1	>0.0%	13	<0.1%
Q1	fine	4	0.1%	18	<0.1%
Totals		4346		59,863	

simply confirmed as later prehistoric types, counted and weighed by context (Table 4.19), while a small number of body sherds from a few Romano-British contexts in Area 3017 were simply confirmed as redeposited later prehistoric pottery. The assemblage is predominantly flint-tempered and consists of two middle Bronze Age urns associated with cremations, sherds from other middle Bronze Age urns found in settlement features, and late Bronze Age material.

Condition

The condition of the pottery is highly variable due to the nature of the deposits, the location of many features from which pottery was derived in an area of high permanent water table (Robinson 1992), and the flooding of the local clayey soils during the winter (Moore and Jennings 1992, 5). Much of the pottery has been altered by the infusion of iron staining ('ironisation') through the entire thickness of some sherds. This ironisation has resulted in the encrustation of selected sherds with iron oxide deposits, the disintegration of many sherds into flakes and has seriously affected the colour of sherds making difficult any real appreciation of firing conditions resulting from manufacture. This aspect was not discussed in the previous publication (Hall 1992).

Nevertheless, many sherds are large and numerous rims and bases were reconstructable to diameter measurement. Some deposits have both large sherds and disintegrated flakes from these sherds. Therefore, it was considered unwise to use mean sherd weight as part of the investigation of this assemblage. In addition, one complete, small vessel was recovered and the cremation urns are partial vessels. Some sherds displayed characteristics which indicated that they had been refired to an overfired state as sherds. These were recovered, usually singly, from all types of features and included a most distinctive sherd, found in the burnt mound deposit (Fig. 4.8.15), and another example was recovered from the watching brief (Fig. 4.18.79).

Methodology

Each sherd was examined macroscopically to determine the fabric type, and each fabric type was subsequently examined using a ×10 power binocular microscope and compared to the pottery fabric series from the earlier phase of excavations on this site (referred to as RBP1) (Hall 1992, 63–4). Fabric series samples in the archive were also examined to provide some clarification of the published descriptions. The 25 fabric types were each assigned to one of five fabric grades, fine, intermediate, coarse, fine/intermediate and intermediate/coarse, defined by a combination of temper size, range, density and sorting (Table 4.10). Some fabrics lie between the grades due to the handmade, non-specialist nature of the pottery production. The fabric grades are:

Fine - 5 fabrics
Well sorted temper or primary inclusion <2 mm with any density

Intermediate - 5 fabrics
Moderately sorted temper <3–4 mm with, <common amount

Coarse - 10 fabrics
Poorly sorted temper usually 5 mm or more at least a common amount

Fine to intermediate - 2 fabrics

Intermediate to coarse - 3 fabrics

All features of the pottery were recorded according to the guidelines for the analysis and publication of later prehistoric pottery (PCRG 1997), and the records were used to demonstrate the occurrences of specific aspects of the assemblage.

Fabrics

A total of 25 fabric types has been defined for this assemblage and these are described in detail below. These are primarily different types of flint-tempered fabrics, with sandy- and grog-tempered pottery fabric occurring infrequently. The amount of pottery identified for each fabric type is presented in Table 4.10, with all undefined flint-bearing sherds and flakes classified as F99. The range of fabric types is not surprising due to, as mentioned above, the handmade and non-specialist nature of most if not

all late Bronze Age pottery production, which could be interpreted as household production for household use (cf. Peacock 1982, 8: Morris 1994, 374–5). It may well be that each household/family group made their own pottery during several generations of settlers at this site, resulting in both slightly different recipes for temper and selection of different clay pockets within similar geological sources.

Macroscopic examination also revealed the possibility that there were at least two primary clay sources, or a significant variation within a single clay source, used for the manufacture of the majority of this pottery. These sources were separated into different groups of fabrics. The F series indicates infrequent, naturally occurring iron oxide fragments and the IF series indicates the frequent and obvious presence of numerous iron oxide fragments in the clay matrix. Different potters using specific sources may have used these two clay sources, the fabrics could correlate to different forms, and the fabric groups may have been used by different people or by the same people at different times.

Six of the fabric types (F1, F3, F15, IF1, IF2, IG1) were thin-sectioned and examined using petrological analysis to confirm the identification and to determine if there were any diagnostic characteristics indicating whether the pottery had been made from local resources. The vessels were predominantly oxidised and irregularly fired creating an orange-based range of colours but the ironisation effect, as described above, had altered the variation of these colours for the majority of sherds.

Flint-tempered fabrics

This group of fabrics is characterised by a clay matrix containing rare to sparse amounts of well rounded to rounded, naturally occurring iron oxide pieces and calcined and crushed flint temper which was very angular to angular in shape. When quartz grains are present they are always well rounded to rounded and naturally occurring. Comparison of these flint-tempered fabrics with those from the RBP1 assemblage, particularly through visual examination of the archived fabric series revealed that, as would be expected, several types were common to both excavations. The fabric types from RBP1 (Hall 1992), which correspond to the fabrics in this report, are indicated in brackets in the fabric descriptions which follow. The most frequently occurring fabric from the previous investigations (RBP1, fabric A, Hall 1992, 63–4) is also the most common from the present excavations (RBP2, fabric F1). The division of fabrics into middle and late Bronze Age is based on the presence of diagnostic form and decoration.

Middle Bronze Age

F15 – an intermediate fabric characterised by a micaceous and very fine sandy clay matrix containing a moderate amount (15% concentration) of moderately sorted flint, ≤ 4mm, a common amount (20%) of well sorted quartz, ≤ 0.2 mm, and a sparse (3–10%) amount of mica; the majority of the quartz grains are silt-grade in size (RBP1, fabric M).

F16 – a coarse fabric containing an abundant amount (40–50%) of moderately to well sorted flint, ≤ 3 mm across with rare pieces up to 7 mm, in a non-sandy clay matrix containing only rare amounts each of quartz, ≤ 0.5 mm, mica and iron oxides.

F17 – a (very) coarse fabric containing an abundant (40–50%) amount of poorly sorted flint, ≤ 7 mm with majority ≤ 5 mm, in an unsandy clay matrix containing a sparse amount of iron oxide fragments and rare flecks of mica (Fabric N); the abundance of flint temper in this fabric and the thickness of the only sherd made from it (17 mm) strongly suggest that it is of middle Bronze Age date.

Middle to late Bronze Age

F5 – a coarse fabric containing a common to very common amount (20–30%) of moderately sorted flint, ≤ 3mm across, in a sandy clay matrix containing a moderate amount (10%) of quartz, ≤ 0.8 mm, and a rare (1%) amount of iron oxides, ≤ 1 mm (this fabric can be distinguished from F1 by a greater density of burnt flint and from F3 by better sorting and smaller size range of burnt flint) (RBP1, fabric D).

Late Bronze Age

F1 – an intermediate to coarse fabric containing a moderate to common amount (15–20%) of poorly sorted flint, ≤ 5 mm across with the majority of pieces ≤ 2 mm, in a sandy clay matrix bearing a variable amount (5–15%) of quartz, ≤ 0.5 mm across, a rare amount (1%) of mica flecks and a rare to sparse amount (1–3%) of iron oxide fragments, ≤ 5 mm across (RBP1, fabric A).

F2 – an intermediate fabric containing a moderate amount (10%) of moderately sorted flint, ≤ 4 mm across with the majority ≤ 3 mm, in a sandy clay matrix containing a sparse to moderate amount (7–15%) of quartz, ≤ 1 mm across, a rare amount of fine mica flecks and a rare amount of iron oxide fragments, ≤ 1 mm across.

F3 – a coarse fabric containing a common to very common amount (20–30%) of poorly sorted flint, ≤ 9 mm across with the majority ≤ 6 mm, in a slightly sandy, micaceous clay matrix containing a rare to moderate amount (1–15%) of fine flecks of mica and a sparse amount (5–7%) of quartz, ≤ 5 mm, with rare iron oxide fragments observed occasionally (this fabric can be distinguished from F1 by a greater size range and density of burnt flint and from F5 by greater size range and poor sorting of burnt flint) (RBP1, fabric L).

F4 – a coarse fabric containing a moderate to common amount (10–20%) of poorly sorted flint, ≤ 12 mm with the majority of pieces ≤ 8 mm across, in a fabric which is characterised primarily by the loose structure of the matrix and the absence of an exterior surface to the ceramic pieces; this fabric has rare pieces of quartz grains, mica and iron oxide fragments (there is some evidence to

suggest that this material is actually pit lining: see discussion below).

F5 – not used.

F6 – a fine fabric containing a sparse to moderate (3–10%) amount of well sorted flint, ≤ 2 mm across with the majority ≤ 1 mm, in a sandy clay matrix containing a sparse to moderate amount (5–15%) of quartz, ≤ 0.5 mm, a rare to sparse (1–3%) amount of iron oxide fragments, ≤ 0.5 mm, and rare mica flecks (RBP1, fabric B).

F7 – an intermediate fabric containing a sparse to moderate amount (5–10%) of poorly sorted flint, ≤ 10 mm with the majority ≤ 8 mm, in a very sandy clay matrix containing a common amount (20–25%) of quartz, ≤ 0.5 mm, and rare amounts of iron oxides and mica (this fabric can be distinguished from F2 by the greater density of quartz and larger flint).

F8 – a fine to intermediate fabric containing a moderate amount (10%) of moderately sorted flint, ≤ 4mm with the majority ≤ 2 mm, in a very sandy clay matrix containing a common amount (20–25%) of quartz, ≤ 1 mm, and rare amounts of mica and iron oxides.

F9 – a fine fabric containing a common to very common amount (20–30%) of well sorted flint, ≤ 3 mm across with rare larger pieces, in a sandy clay matrix containing a moderate amount of quartz, ≤ 0.8 mm and rare mica (RBP1, fabric I).

F10 – an intermediate fabric containing a common to abundant amount (30–40%) of moderately sorted flint, ≤ 3 mm across distinguished by the 20–25% concentration of flint ≤ 1 mm across, and extremely rare larger pieces up to 5 mm, in a sandy clay matrix containing a sparse to moderate amount (3–10%) of quartz, ≤ 0.8 mm.

F11 – a fine fabric containing a common to very common amount (20–30%) of moderately to well sorted flint, ≤ 3 mm with the majority ≤ 1 mm (well sorted and very fine), in a sandy clay matrix containing a moderate amount (10–15%) of fine quartz, ≤ 0.3 mm across (this fabric is distinguished by the fineness of the flint fragments which appear almost like 'dust' macroscopically).

F12 – a coarse fabric containing a moderate to common amount (15–20%) of poorly sorted flint, ≤ 5 mm, and a sparse to moderate amount (3–15%) of poorly sorted linear vesicles which once contained organic matter, ≤ 5 mm across, in a clay matrix containing rare amounts of mica and iron oxide fragments.

F13 – a fine to intermediate fabric containing a moderate to common amount (15–20%) of moderately to well sorted flint, ≤ 2 mm, in a clay matrix containing a sparse amount (3–7%) of iron oxides, < 2 mm, and rare to sparse (1–3%) mica flecks (this fabric is distinguished by the absence of quartz visible at ×10 power).

F99 – this code was given to all those ironised flakes which have broken off larger sherds of pottery and which cannot be correctly classified due to their discoloration and size but which do bear flint temper.

Flint- and grog-tempered fabric

There is only one fabric which contains both flint and grog temper. This is in contrast to the frequency of grog temper reported for the RBP1 assemblage

(Hall 1992, 63–4). Macroscopic examination of the fabric series in the RBP1 archive suggests that some of this grog could be iron oxide fragments which may have been mistaken for grog, but confirmation of this observation would require petrological analysis. Flint- and grog-tempered fabrics are known to occur in late Bronze Age assemblages, such as at Potterne, Wiltshire (Morris 1991, fig. 8; Lawson 2000) and Shorncote Quarry, Gloucestershire (Morris 1994).

Late Bronze Age

FG1 – a coarse fabric containing about equal amounts (10%) of poorly sorted flint, $\leq$ 7 mm, and angular grog, $\leq$ 5 mm, in a sandy clay matrix containing a moderate amount (10–15%) of sub-rounded to well-rounded quartz, 1.2 mm or less across with the majority $\leq$ 0.8 mm, and rare iron oxides (this fabric is similar to RBP1, fabric Y but has much more burnt flint).

Grog-tempered fabric

There is only one fabric which contains just grog temper.

?Late Bronze Age

G1 – a fine fabric containing a common amount (20–25%) of moderately to well sorted grog temper, $\leq$ 2mm, a rare amount (1–2%) of flint, $\leq$ 1 mm, and a rare amount (1–2%) of quartz, $\leq$ 1 mm (this fabric appears to be too hard-fired to be classified as a late Neolithic-early Bronze Age/Beaker fabric).

Flint-tempered and iron oxide-bearing fabrics

This group of fabrics is characterised by a clay matrix which contains various quantities of well rounded to rounded, moderately to well sorted, naturally occurring iron oxide pieces and calcined, crushed flint temper.

Late Bronze Age

IF1 – an intermediate fabric containing a sparse to moderate amount (7–15%) of moderately sorted flint, $\leq$ 2 mm across, in an iron-rich clay matrix with a highly variable amount (7–30%) of iron oxide fragments, $\leq$ 3mm with the majority $\leq$ 2 mm, and a sparse amount (3–5%) of quartz, $\leq$ 0.5 mm.

IF2 – an intermediate/coarse fabric containing a moderate amount (10–15%) of iron oxide fragments, $\leq$ 2 mm across, a moderate to common amount (15–20%) of poorly sorted flint, $\leq$ 5 mm with the majority $\leq$ 3 mm, and rare to sparse amount (2–3%) of mica and rare quartz, $\leq$ 0.5 mm (this fabric is very similar to F1 above but the clay matrix has a visually dominant amount of iron oxide pieces and very little quartz; related to RBP1, fabrics G and H but not identical).

IF3 – a coarse fabric containing a common to abundant (25–40%) amount of poorly sorted flint, $\leq$ 8 mm with the majority $\leq$ 3 mm, in an iron oxide-rich clay matrix containing a moderate to common amount (10–20%) of fragments, $\leq$ 4 mm and rare amounts each (1%) of quartz and mica (this fabric is the iron oxide-rich equivalent of F3 and is similar to RBP1, fabric D, but more flint and iron oxide pieces).

IF4 – an intermediate/coarse fabric containing a moderate (10–15%) amount of poorly sorted flint, $\leq$ 7 mm across, in a clay matrix containing a sparse to moderate amount of iron oxide fragments, $\leq$ 2 mm across and a sparse to moderate amount of well sorted quartz grains, $\leq$ 0.8 mm (RBP1, fabric H).

IF5 – a coarse fabric which contains a moderate to common (15–20%) amount of poorly sorted flint, $\leq$ 12 mm across, in a laminated and iron-rich clay matrix containing a sparse to moderate (3–15%) amount of iron oxide fragments, $\leq$ 3 mm across, and rare amounts (1–2%) of mica and quartz (this fabric is related to IF4 and therefore similar to RBP1, fabric H; the distinguishing features are the very poorly sorted range of flint and the laminated structure of the fabric due to incomplete wedging of the clay which frequently, but not always, displays clay bedding planes of different colours).

Iron oxide-bearing and grog-tempered fabric

There is only one fabric which contains grog temper in an iron-rich clay matrix.

?Late Bronze Age

IG1 – a coarse, grog-tempered, iron-rich fabric containing a common amount (20–25%) of poorly sorted grog, $\leq$ 5 mm, a sparse to moderate amount (5–10%) of iron oxide fragments, $\leq$ 1 mm, and a rare amount (1–2%) of moderately sorted flint, $\leq$ 3 mm (RBP1, fabric Y).

Sandy fabric

There is only one fabric which is dominated by quartz grains.

Late Bronze Age

Q1 – a fine, sandy fabric containing a common amount (20–25%) of well sorted quartz grains, $\leq$ 0.8 mm across with the majority $\leq$ 0.5 mm, and an extremely infrequent amount (< 1%) of angular to sub-angular, crushed burnt flint, $\leq$ 1 mm, which was most likely to have been casually, rather than deliberately, added to the clay matrix by association due to the small size range and infrequency of the pieces (RBP1, fabric W).

Petrological report

by David Williams

Six sherds were submitted for a fabric analysis by thin sectioning and study under the petrological microscope. In addition, three samples of fired clay were recovered from stratified contexts at the site were also thin sectioned for comparative purposes. Before thin sectioning, each of the sherds was also examined in the hand-specimen using a binocular microscope (×20). This site lies on Valley Gravel, in an area which is made up of Alluvium, London Clay, Loam, Plateau Gravel, Lower Bagshot Beds, Bracklesham Beds and Upper Chalk (Geological Survey 1″ Map of England sheet No. 268).

Results of analysis

Samples from pottery fabrics

F1 – context 1016, PRN (Pottery Reference Number) 4022. A fairly hard, rough fabric, with moderately frequent angular pieces of white flint of variable size scattered throughout in a fairly sandy clay paste. In thin section the fabric is characterised by angular pieces of flint ranging in size from 0.30 mm to about 2 mm, with the majority below 1 mm. These inclusions are scattered in a darkish brown clay matrix. Also present are frequent angular to sub-angular quartz grains ranging in size up to 0.50 mm, with the majority falling below 0.20 mm, flecks of mica and a little iron oxide.

F3 – context 1237, PRN 4498. A fairly hard, rough fabric, with moderately frequent angular pieces of white flint of variable size scattered throughout. Superficially this sherd appears similar to F1 above, but closer inspection shows that the clay matrix is of a much finer texture, lacking the relatively high quartz content of the former sherd. This difference is borne out in thin section, where the quartz content is only moderate to sparse. In addition, there is a relatively high content of red iron oxide present.

IF2 – context 1016, PRN 4077. In thin section there are similarities between this sherd and F3 above, in that both share a similar fairly fine-texture iron-rich clay matrix. In the hand-specimen, this sherd can be seen to contain much more flint than F3.

IF1 – context 1016, PRN 4071. A fairly hard, rough fabric with a moderate amount of angular white flint scattered about, together with small pieces of red iron oxide. Thin sectioning shows moderate inclusions of flint generally below 1 mm in size. The clay matrix contains frequent angular to sub-angular quartz grains of silt size and slightly above, with some flecks of mica and red iron oxide.

FG1 – context 1027, PRN 4168. A fairly hard, rough fabric with moderately frequent inclusions of white angular flint set in a somewhat sandy fabric. There are similarities in the hand-specimen with F1 above, but this particular sherd also contains some small argillaceous inclusions which are lacking in F1. In thin section, the angularity of these argillaceous inclusions suggests that they are probably grog rather than clay pellets. The size of the flint reaches 2.5 mm in some cases but is normally below 1 mm. Also present are frequent angular to sub-angular quartz grains ranging in size up to 0.50 mm, with the majority falling below 0.20 mm, flecks of mica and a little iron oxide.

F15 – context 1130, PRN 4424. A fairly hard, rough fabric containing frequent inclusions of small sized white angular flint. Thin sectioning shows angular pieces of flint generally below 1 mm across, together with frequent sub-angular silt-sized grains of quartz and flecks of mica.

Samples from fired clay

1. **Context 1014** – in thin section, this sample can be seen to contain frequent angular to sub-angular grains of quartz, generally below 0.20 mm, but with a few grains ranging up to 0.50 mm across. Also present are flecks of mica and a little iron oxide.
2. **Context 1466**
3. **Context 1969** – in thin section, these two pieces can be seen to contain less quartz than the clay sample above, are slightly more micaceous and have more red iron oxide. Occasional pieces of flint are present.

Comments

by David Williams

In the hand-specimen all of the Bronze Age sherds can clearly be seen to contain inclusions of white flint protruding through the surfaces. Moreover, the general freshness and angularity of the flint suggest that much of it was probably deliberately crushed and added as a temper by the potter during preparation of the clay. There are, however, some noticeable differences amongst the sherds in the frequency and size-range of the flint present and also both in the texture of the clay matrix and its visible iron content.

The thin section results suggest that the Bronze Age sherds can be classified on the basis of fabric. Sherds 1 and 2 seem similar to clay sample 1, minus the addition of flint. While the relatively high red iron content of sherds 2–4 bear comparison with the clay samples 2 and 3. The variation in the quartz frequency between sherds 2 and 3, in which it is moderate to sparse, and 4, where it is frequent, might be explained by poorly wedged clay. It is noticeable in thin section, for example, that in both the sherds and fired clay samples, there occur lenses of clay which contain a greater or lesser quantity of quartz grains than the main body of paste within view. It is possible, in this case, that the body of clay chosen for pottery making contained significant lenses of material which were incorporated into the pottery. Sherd 6 contains a generally smaller size-range of quartz than the other sherds and additionally lacks the high iron content noted above.

The similarity of fired clay with the majority of the pottery strongly suggests that both were probably obtained locally. It is difficult to be certain, but it seems possible that many, perhaps all, of the above sherds may have been made from a loamy type of clay which could quite easily have been obtained at no great distance from the find-site, while flints abound in the local Valley Gravels and on the Upper Chalk (Blake 1903).

Discussion

by Elaine Morris

The petrological analysis has demonstrated that the primary late Bronze Age fabric groups, F and IF, are most likely to have been made from local resources and that the differences between the content of the clay matrices, particularly the frequency of quartz sand and iron oxides may be a result of variation within actual clay deposits rather than between different deposits. The variation in quartz and iron oxide observed amongst the fabric types could simply be due to differences in clay preparation techniques.

Thin sectioning confirmed that grog-temper (fabric FG1) was differentiated from iron oxides by microscopy and that this technique could also differentiate sand-sized grains of quartz (fabrics F1, F3, IF1, IF2) from silt-sized grains (F15) accurately.

Detailed examination of the full range of fired clay materials might possibly reveal a fabric which is similar to this middle Bronze Age ware, but this analysis has not been undertaken. There was very little use of predominantly sandy wares in both the RBP1 and the RBP2 late Bronze Age assemblages (fabric W, 0.2%; Q1, 0.1% respectively). Quartz-dominated wares are more common amongst other late Bronze Age assemblages in the area, and this aspect is discussed further below.

Forms and vessel sizes

The assemblage contains a minimum of 102 separate vessels. This is based on the number of different examples identified for each rim form, and also each lug/boss type and decorated sherd, not combined with rim forms (Table 4.11). Each rim and base has been assigned to one of the following

Table 4.11   Correlation of middle to late Bronze Age pottery forms to fabric types by number of recorded occurrences

Form type	F1	F2	F3	F5	F6	F7	F9	F10	F11	F12	F15	F16	FG1	IF1	IF2	IF3	IF4	IF5	Total
Rims																			
R1	–	–	–	–	–	–	–	1	–	–	–	–	–	1	1	–	–	–	3
R2	1	–	–	–	–	–	–	–	–	–	–	–	–	–	–	–	–	–	1
R3	1	–	–	–	–	–	–	–	–	–	–	–	–	–	–	–	–	–	1
R4	–	–	–	–	–	1	–	–	–	–	–	–	–	–	–	–	–	–	1
R5	–	–	–	–	–	–	–	–	–	–	–	–	–	–	–	–	1	–	1
R6	–	–	–	–	1	–	1	–	–	–	–	–	–	–	–	–	–	–	2
R11	17	1	4	–	2	2	–	1	–	1	–	–	–	2	9	1	2	–	42
R12	10	–	10	1	–	–	2	–	1	–	–	–	1	–	1	1	–	–	27
R13	2	–	1	–	–	–	–	–	–	–	–	–	–	1	–	–	–	–	4
R14	2	–	2	–	–	–	–	–	–	–	–	–	–	–	–	–	–	–	4
R15	–	–	–	–	1	–	–	–	–	–	–	–	–	–	–	–	–	–	1
R16	2	–	–	–	–	–	–	–	–	–	–	–	–	–	2	–	–	1	5
R17	–	–	–	–	–	–	–	–	–	–	–	–	–	–	1	–	–	–	1
R21	–	–	–	–	–	–	–	–	–	–	–	–	–	–	1	–	–	–	1
R22	–	–	–	–	–	–	–	–	–	–	–	–	–	1	–	–	–	–	1
R30	1	–	–	–	–	–	–	–	–	–	–	3	–	–	–	–	–	–	4
Bases																			
B1	19	1	4	2	–	–	1	1	1	–	–	–	–	2	1	1	–	–	33
B2	5	–	1	–	–	–	–	–	–	–	–	–	1	1	3	1	–	–	12
B3	2	–	1	–	–	–	–	–	–	–	–	–	–	–	–	1	–	–	4
B99	14	1	6	1	–	1	–	–	–	–	–	–	1	1	6	2	–	1	34
Shoulders																			
A1	3	–	–	–	2	–	–	–	–	–	–	–	–	1	1	–	–	–	7
A2	2	–	–	–	–	–	–	–	–	–	–	–	–	–	–	–	–	–	2
Lugs																			
L1	–	–	–	–	–	–	–	–	–	–	1	–	–	–	–	–	–	–	1
L2	–	–	–	–	–	–	–	–	–	–	–	1	–	–	–	–	–	–	1
L3	–	–	–	–	–	–	–	–	–	–	–	1	–	–	–	–	–	–	1
Decorated body																			
D1	–	–	–	1	–	–	–	–	–	–	–	3	–	–	–	–	–	–	4
Totals	81	3	29	5	6	4	4	3	2	1	1	9	3	10	25	7	3	2	198

forms and the measurable examples are indicated in Table 4.12 and Figure 4.6a.

Middle Bronze Age

Several examples of Deverel Rimbury style bucket urns have been identified; one was recovered with cremated human bone (fabric F16) while three others were found in other settlement features (one of fabric F5 and two of F16) (Fig. 4.7.1–4). These middle Bronze Age vessels, often associated with cremations, are well known nationally and in the Thames and Kennet Valley region as at Sulhampstead (Lobb 1992, fig. 25, 5 and 7) and Knight's Farm subsite 3 (Bradley *et al.* 1980, fig. 32) in Berkshire, and from four cemeteries in Middlesex (Barrett 1973). Charcoal associated with the cremation from context 1160 at RBP2 was radiocarbon dated to 1220–890 cal BC (92.0% confidence NZA 9422, Appendix Table A1.1). Similarly the bucket urn context at Knight's Farm was radiocarbon dated to 1750–1200 cal BC (95.4% confidence BM-1954: Bradley *et al.* 1980, 268) indicating that these vessels date in this area to the middle Bronze Age period of the later second millennium BC. Bucket urn material has been recovered from a middle Bronze Age settlement at Bray (Barnes and Cleal 1995, fig. 19, P11), and in river deposits at Brimpton (Lobb 1986–90, fig. 2, 4–5), both in Berkshire.

The four opposing, sprigged lug/boss attachments (L2, Fig. 4.7.1) were found on one of the bucket urns associated with a cremation and is a common middle Bronze Age assemblage characteristic (Barrett 1973, figs 1, 7–8, 10 and 14; 2, 19–20; 3, 2; 4, 6; 5, 6; Bradley *et al.* 1980, fig. 32, 39; Lobb 1986–90, fig. 2, 7; Barnes and Cleal 1995, fig. 21, P22). The RBP2 horizontal lug type (L1; Fig. 4.7.5, fabric F15) without associated rim or vessel, has been recognised as a component of some Deverel Rimbury urns (Dacre and Ellison 1981, figs 14, D1; 15, D/E5; 17, E15). The thumbed lug (L3): Fig. 4.7.2) found on the other urn is also quite common on bucket urns elsewhere.

There are two different sizes of R30 type vessels in the assemblage, very large bucket urns – the two urns associated with cremations and the one from a pit which measure between 300–360 mm in diameter – and a medium sized rim (180 mm) recovered from the primary fill of a ditch. Therefore, it is possible that large and medium sized bucket urns were used at the middle Bronze Age settlement, while large urns were also used, or reused, as burial containers.

Bucket urn

R30 – straight-sided or slightly convex profile, neckless urn with rounded rim; rounded rim often altered in profile with the application of fingertip impressions (Fig. 4.7.1–4).

Table 4.12   Frequency of usewear evidence by fabric type amongst the middle to late Bronze Age pottery (number of occurrences)

Form type	Diameter measurement (mm)															Totals
	Small			Medium							Large					
	80	100	120	140	160	180	200	220	240	260	280	300	320	340	360	
R1	–	–	1	–	–	1	1	–	–	–	–	–	–	–	–	3
R2	–	–	–	1	–	–	–	–	–	–	–	–	–	–	–	1
R4	–	–	–	–	–	–	–	–	1	–	–	–	–	–	–	1
R5	–	–	–	–	–	–	–	1	–	–	–	–	–	–	–	1
R6	–	–	1	–	1	–	–	–	–	–	–	–	–	–	–	2
R11	–	5	1	1	4	1	3	–	1	–	–	1	–	–	1	18
R12	–	2	–	4	3	2	1	–	–	1	–	–	1	1	–	15
R13	–	–	–	–	1	1	–	–	–	–	–	–	–	–	–	2
R14	–	–	–	1	–	–	–	1	–	–	–	–	–	–	–	2
R15	–	–	–	1	–	–	–	–	–	–	–	–	–	–	–	1
R16	–	–	1	–	2	–	–	–	–	–	–	–	–	–	1	4
R17	–	–	–	–	–	1	–	–	–	–	–	–	–	–	–	1
R30	–	–	–	–	–	1	–	–	–	–	–	1	1	–	1	4
B1	3	2	5	6	1	1	–	1	1	–	–	–	–	–	–	20
B2	1	1	1	1	2	2	1	1	–	–	–	–	–	–	–	10
B3	–	–	–	2	–	1	1	–	–	–	–	–	–	–	–	4
Totals	4	10	10	17	14	11	7	4	3	1	0	2	2	1	3	89

Lugs/bosses

L1 – oval, horizontal attachment (Fig. 4.7.5)
L2 – applied, pinched protuberance/boss or peaked and rounded attachment (Fig. 4.7.1).
L3 – applied and thumbed clay fragment (Fig. 4.7.2).

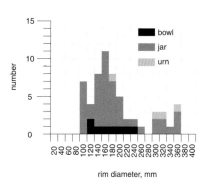

Figure 4.6a   Rim diameters of late Bronze Age bowls, jars and urns

Late Bronze Age

A total of six bowl types, seven jar types and two general vessel forms (Table 4.11) have been defined which date to the post-Deverel Rimbury, late Bronze Age period. Similar vessel forms were identified in the RBP1 assemblage, as would be expected, (Hall 1992, 64–8, figs 41–3) and these are indicated in brackets in the descriptions below. The assemblage is dominated by closed, ovoid jars of convex profile (R11, R12), straight-sided jars (R16), and sloping or slack-profile jars (R13, R15, R17) with a small number of shouldered or bipartite and tripartite bowls (R2, R3 and R6) and various hemispherical bowls (R1, R4, R5). Less diagnostic sherds possibly represent a bipartite jar (R14) and other vessels (R21/R22) but these unfortunately are too fragmented to determine the likely profile. Sherds from shouldered vessels, both angled (A1) and rounded (A2) were also recognised and recorded.

This range of forms is typical of the plain assemblage-style of late Bronze Age pottery defined by Barrett (1980) and exemplified in the immediate region by the assemblages from Aldermaston Wharf and Knight's Farm subsites 2 and 4 only (Bradley *et al.* 1980, figs 12–18 and 33). Widely separated radiocarbon dates were recovered from two pits at Aldermaston Wharf: 1900–1100 cal BC (1290±135 bc, BM-1592) for pit 6, with 1390–1110 cal BC (1050±40 bc, BM-1590) and 1010–830 cal BC (835±35 bc, BM-1591) from pit 68. The excavators are confident that the earliest date is possibly too early, particularly in the absence of any Deverel Rimbury activity on that site, but that the latter pair of dates 'bracket the range of occupation suggested by the pottery from the site' (ibid., 248). It is particularly noticeable how similar the three base types identified in the RBP2

assemblage are to those from Knight's Farm 2 and 4 (ibid., fig. 33. 52, 53, 57–9, 61–2, 70–1 and 83). At RBP2 an animal bone from pit 1518, context 1695, of the burnt mound complex was associated with two sherds of late Bronze Age pottery and was radio-carbon dated to 1220–890 cal BC (93.0% confidence NZA 9412, Appendix Table A1.1), similar to the dating from other sites as shown above.

The most striking aspect of this assemblage, however, is the lack of shouldered jars; the collection contains slack and rounded profiles but no true examples of shouldered jars, only rim sherds from a probable bipartite vessel (R14) and the angled sherds or suspected angled sherds from bipartite jars or bowls (A1 type). Shouldered jars are a very common vessel form at RBP1 (Hall 1992, types 10–13), Knight's Farm subsite 1 (Bradley *et al.* 1980, figs 34–6), and to a minor extent at Aldermaston Wharf in Berkshire, as well as further east at Carshalton (Adkins and Needham 1985, figs 3–11) and on the Thames at Runnymede Bridge (Longley 1980, 1991, type 12 jar) and Petters Sports Field (O'Connell 1986, 63), all in Surrey. Runnymede Bridge assemblages are dated to the 12th-7th centuries cal BC (Longley 1980, 71–4, fig. 47; Longley 1991, 169–70), while the deposition of pottery at Petters Sports Field is dated to the 8th-5th century cal BC (O'Connell 1986, 71, table 8).

Ovoid jars are one of the commonest forms in the earliest phases of the later prehistoric activity at

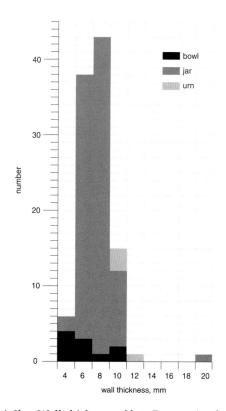

Figure 4.6b   Wall thickness of late Bronze Age bowls, jars and urns

Potterne in Wiltshire, where stratigraphical phases which have been radiocarbon dated to before the 11th-10th centuries cal BC (Morris 2000, 166). There is every reason to suggest that the late Bronze Age assemblage should date from prior to and during the occupation at Aldermaston Wharf, and definitely earlier than Runnymede and Petters Sports Field, that is, from the 11th-10th centuries BC and earlier.

One specific vessel form, the straight-sided jar R16 may well represent a transitional vessel type related to both bucket urns and ovoid jars. Frequent examples were found in the RBP1 assemblage (Hall 1992, type 15, 7% of classifiable vessels). This form has been identified as middle Bronze Age in the Knight's Farm 3 collection (Bradley *et al.* 1980, fig. 32.42 and 46) and as late Bronze Age in the Aldermaston Wharf assemblage (Bradley *et al.* 1980, type 4).

There are only eight examples of bowl rims which could be measured (Table 4.12), and these are recorded from 120–240 mm in diameter. The number of measurable jar rims is 43, and there appear to be three different size ranges amongst them, small (120 mm or less), medium (140–260 mm) and large (280–360), with peaks at 100 mm, 160 mm and 360 mm (Fig. 4.6a). The most frequent types of jars, the ovoid and the hooked rim ovoid (R11, R12), can be found in all three sizes, and this is also true for the less frequent straight-walled type (R16). This range of sizes was recognised by Barrett as a characteristic of the late Bronze Age ceramic tradition (1980, 302–3, fig. 2); the introduction of bowls and the frequency of small vessels are special to this period.

Table 4.11 presents the frequency of vessel form types to fabric types. Both major fabric groups, F and IF, were used to make the commonest vessel types, jars R11, R12 and R16. Similarly all three base types were made from the major fabric groups.

Bowls

R1 – hemispherical or conical bowl with rounded or flattened rim (RBP1, type 7).
R2 – round-shouldered, tripartite bowl with sharply everted, short rim (RBP1, type 5).
R3 – everted or flared rim, necked and shouldered bowl (RBP1, type 1).
R4 – rounded rim with steeply inturned profile which may be a lid or shallow bowl/dish (RBP1, type 25).
R5 – flanged rim bowl with deep profile.
R6 – bipartite bowl with upright and plain or simple rim (RBP1, type 4).

Jars

R11 – simple convex-profile, neckless, ovoid jar (RBP1, type 8).
R12 – hooked rim, ovoid jar (RBP1, type 8).
R13 – slightly everted to vertical rim on slack or sloping profile jar.

R14 – upright rim from a probable bipartite jar (RBP1, type 13).
R15 – out-turned or sharply everted rim from a sloping shoulder jar (RBP1, type 17).
R16 – straight-profile jar with simple rounded or flat-topped rim; the similarity of this rim form to the R30 urn is discussed below (RBP1, types 14 and 15).
R17 – slightly flared, vertical rim on necked, barrel-shaped profile jar.

Bowl/jars

R21 – everted rim merging directly onto a round-shouldered profile vessel (similar to RBP1, type 6a).
R22 – long-necked, slightly everted, rounded rim on probable bipartite vessel; single example overfired and slightly distorted in curvature.

Bases

B1 – simple, flat base.
B2 – flat base with exterior spur or lip effect; splayed or flared base.
B3 – extremely lipped or curled up base.
B99 – central part of base, no edge or angle visible.

Shoulders or Angled Sherds

A1 – gentle or very obtuse angle, shoulder sherd; can be from either bipartite bowls or jars (RBP1, type 2 or 10).
A2 – rounded-shoulder sherd; can be from either bowls or jars.

Decorations and surface treatments

Very few decorated vessels were identified in this assemblage, and the majority of these are middle Bronze Age in date.

Middle Bronze Age

Amongst the middle Bronze Age pottery, five out of seven identified vessels are decorated including both cremation urns, the bucket urn in pit 2271, a sherd from an urn made from fabric F5 and recovered from ditch 2201 (Fig. 4.7.6) and an unstratified sherd (Fig. 4.7.7). Middle Bronze Age decoration is confined to the application of a single, wide, applied strip or cordon around the vessel girth which is then impressed with a row of fingertip indentations or just the row of fingertip indentations at the girth, and a similar row of fingertip impressions around the inner edge of the rim.

Only one possible middle Bronze Age sherd was smoothed on the interior. This was made from fabric F17, is 17 mm thick and was recovered from post-hole 1851. Otherwise, the middle Bronze Age pottery has no surface treatment other than the excessive addition of fine, burnt and crushed flint chips on the underside of the base of the urn from pit 1753.

Late Bronze Age

Only five out of 95 identifiable late Bronze Age vessels (5%) are decorated, which contrasts to the frequency of decoration amongst the RBP1 assemblage where of 34 late Bronze Age vessels (out of between 220 (Hall 1992, 64) and 258 (Bradley and Hall 1992a, table 13)), about 13–15%, were decorated (ibid., figs 44–51).

The decoration in this assemblage is of two techniques: fingertip impressions on the interior edge of the rim of straight-sided and ovoid jars (Figs 4.13.45: 4.13.54: 4.14.59) or incised designs of either an irregular nature found on one thin-walled ovoid jar (Fig. 4.13.50) or a zig-zag effect on an everted vessel rim from the burnt mound (Fig. 4.8.15). The positioning of the fingertip impressions is very significant; these decorations are located only on the interior edge of the rim and not on the body of vessels. The noticeable absence of strongly shouldered jars in the assemblage (see above) and the positioning of this decoration on the interior of the rims are very derivative of the Deverel Rimbury middle Bronze Age tradition. This specific effect was noticed on one vessel from Aldermaston Wharf (Bradley *et al.* 1980, fig. 18.160) and on one from Green Lane, Farnham in Surrey (Oakley *et al.* 1939, fig. 78.22).

The presence of incised decoration on an ovoid jar (Fig. 4.13.50) is unique. The occurrence of a single example of an incised zig-zag motif below the everted rim and on the neck of a distorted vessel from within the burnt mound deposit (Fig. 4.8.15) is similar to a design recovered on a body sherd from Runnymede Bridge (Longley 1980, fig. 36.388).

Very few vessels display additional surface treatment effects suggestive of finewares, such as burnishing and smoothing. Table 4.13 provides the correlation of smoothing and burnishing to form types. Wiping, however, is a very common technique on the late Bronze Age pottery in this assemblage. Out of 1037 recorded occurrences 6 (0.6%) display burnishing, 8 (0.8%) smoothing, 3 (0.3%) possible slip application and 84 (8.1%) have been wiped with a cloth, brush or fingers.

Another surface treatment, the application of additional flint chips (Table 4.13), is a technique continued from the middle Bronze Age period but the flint fragments are larger and more ill-sorted in texture than those found on the single cremation urn. The use of extra flint is found on all three base types, and is a very common occurrence in this assemblage with 65% of all the bases having this treatment. Amongst the diagnostic forms, all four of the B3 bases, 92% of the B2 bases and 31% of the B1 bases have this surface treatment. Two bases, however, do not have flint chips but instead were placed on the grassed ground, turves or unpatterned matting since the impressions of dense quantities of organic matter can be seen on the undersides.

Ovoid jars (R11, R12) make up 80% of the jars in this assemblage and there are few bipartite or shouldered jars (R14, R22, 6%), so typical of the late Bronze Age. This is in contrast to the RBP1

Table 4.13   Frequency of surface treatment types by form type amongst late Bronze Age pottery (number of occurrences)

| Form type | Surface treatment | | | | | Totals |
	burnished	smoothed	?slipped	wiped	embedded flint	
R1	–	–	1	1	–	2
R6	–	1	–	–	–	1
R11	–	–	–	5	–	5
R12	–	1	–	2	–	3
R13	–	–	–	1	–	1
R14	–	1	–	–	–	1
R16	–	–	–	3	–	3
R17	–	–	–	1	–	1
B1	2	1	–	3	10	16
B2	–	–	–	–	11	11
B3	–	–	–	–	4	4
B99	–	–	–	–	29	29
A1	1	2	–	–	–	3
body sherds	3	2	2	68	–	75
Totals	6	8	3	84	54	155

assemblage with 46% ovoid types (types 8, 9, 14, 19) and 21% shouldered examples (types 10–13, 16–17) amongst its jars (Hall 1992, figs 42–3, 44–51).

It is very clear that this assemblage is quite different from the RBP1 excavated pottery assemblage with very few decorated sherds, little in the way of fine surface treatment and a very large number of roughened base vessels and a dominance of ovoid jars.

Classification of late Bronze Age vessels

In order to be able to compare the similarities and differences amongst late Bronze Age assemblages within the area, it seems sensible to try to classify the vessels according to the general scheme first devised by Barrett (1980, 302–3). This scheme relates to vessel function and higher productive investment based notionally on a combination of fabric, form, surface treatment and decoration. This classification scheme was also used by Bradley and Hall (1992a, tables 14–15) for the RBP1 assemblage, although the adaptation and application of the scheme is occasionally unclear. A bowl (RBP1, type 7) was identified as a jar form and the use of wall thickness for fabric type descriptions had some influence on classification.

The scheme was thus applied to this current assemblage, and a combination of five criteria was selected to determine the class of a vessel: fabric class (Tables 4.10 and 4.11), form type (Table 4.12), surface treatment (Table 4.13), wall thickness range (Fig. 4.6b) and type of decoration. It was hoped that differences amongst the convex-profile, ovoid jars (R11, R12) could be structured to conform to Barrett's Classes I (coarse) and II (fine) but this was not possible due to the variety of combinations of wall thickness and fabric textures as well as the absence of surface treatments and infrequency of decoration. A few ovoid jars were coarsely decorated with fingertip impressions, but one of the two incised examples in the assemblage is also an ovoid jar, and ovoid jars are thick- and thin-walled. Only 9% of the late Bronze Age assemblage is bowls so the differentiation between Barrett's Class III (coarse) and Class IV (fine) bowls would not be statistically significant.

Therefore, the simplest way to classify this assemblage is that it is dominated by Class I coarse jars, based purely on fabric class as described above with some possible jars of a finer nature (Class II), and a small quantity of bowls including both coarse (Class III) and fine (Class IV) varieties with some possible jars of a finer nature, and a small quantity of bowls including both fine and coarse varieties.

Evidence of use

One of the most interesting aspects of this assemblage is the lack of visible usewear evidence. Obvious usewear evidence includes sooting and burnt residues, while limescale can be visible on vessels which were used in areas with hard water. Interior pitting and various types of usewear abrasion were not recorded for this assemblage due to the nature of the fabrics and the condition of the material. Out of 1037 recorded occurrences of pottery, only 4.5% display evidence of use: 0.8% have burnt residues on their interior, 0.1% have sooting on the exterior and 4% display what may be limescale (Table 4.14). Coarse fabrics F1, F3 and IF2 were used to make both cooking vessels and possible water boiling pots.

The extremely low occurrence of evidence for cooking over a fire, and in particular the burning of food in ceramic containers, may provide useful information about the function of the burnt mound. If the shattered flint found to make up most of this structure had been used as 'pot boilers' to heat food, then sooting would not be expected to be found on vessels and the likelihood of carbonising food in pottery vessels would be low. This possibility would need to be tested using lipid residue analysis to determine which of the jars had been used to heat and cook foods and whether any pots without visible evidence belonged to this group. Only four ovoid jars display visible usewear evidence, two have burnt food and two probable limescale. Otherwise, the few examples of use were found primarily on body sherds with only four limescale examples on bases, two B1 and two B2.

Waterhole lining material or possible pottery?

Fabric 4 material is unusual. It is a fired clay matrix containing no obvious sand and which is coarsely tempered with crushed burnt flint. The pieces of F4 material have wiped interior surfaces but the exteriors are rough. There are no base or rim sherds in this fabric. Apparently identical material, some

Table 4.14 Frequency of usewear evidence by fabric type amongst the late Bronze Age pottery (number of occurrences)

Fabric type	Usewear evidence			
	burnt residue	soot	?limescale	Totals
F1	4	–	6	10
F2	–	–	3	3
F3	2	1	15	18
F4	–	–	4	4
F5	–	–	1	1
F7	1	–	–	1
F99	–	–	1	1
IF1	–	–	4	4
IF2	1	–	3	4
IF5	–	–	1	1
Totals	8	1	38	47

fragments with exteriors which 'could not be recognised at all' (Bradley *et al.* 1980, 244–5), were also recovered at Aldermaston Wharf, where the authors believed that similar ceramic material had been plastered into position and fired in situ. The question is whether this is pottery or fired clay. Due to the problems of the porous nature of the F4 fabric and the ironisation effect described above, it is extremely difficult to interpret the nature of this material based on form and fabric alone. It is unclear whether it is simply pottery without an exterior surface or pit lining bearing one interior surface. Some of the F4 pieces have a thin white residue on the interior surface which may be a whitewash.

Due to this problem of definition, the spatial distribution of the F4 material was examined. Three waterholes contained the majority of F4 sherds as follows: waterhole 2042 (349 pieces; 4346 g), waterhole 1144 (225; 2647 g) and waterhole 1118 (70; 774 g). This distribution accounts for 97% of the F4 material. However, waterhole 1015 had only two pieces (31 g) amongst 649 sherds (7267 g) of ceramic material and these F4 fragments were found in the tertiary infill. Therefore, there is every reason to support the original interpretation that this flint-tempered material, which has no exterior surface but is finished on the interior surface, has no rim or base sherds, and is frequently found in large quantities in waterholes but not in pits, tree-throw holes or ditches, is most likely to be some form of waterhole lining material at this site.

Middle Bronze Age features

The distribution of middle Bronze Age pottery is confined to ditches 1134 and 2201, pits 1390, 1753 and 2271, cremation 1161 and possibly posthole 1851 (single sherd of fabric F17) (Fig. 4.7, Table 4.15). Ditch 2201 and cremation 1161 are contiguous. Pit 1390 and ditches 1134 and 2201 contained only middle Bronze Age pottery including the single example of the horizontal lug and the undecorated R30 rim. Pit 2271 also contained sherds of late Bronze Age pottery in both pottery-bearing layers, and therefore the middle Bronze Age pottery is considered to have been redeposited. A further sherd was unstratified.

Late Bronze Age features

The burnt mound complex 1012 sealed a series of pits, postholes, ditches, waterholes and buried soils. The quantity of pottery recovered from features and the range of vessel forms identified are presented in Table 4.16.

Almost 100 sherds of late Bronze Age pottery were recovered from the nine features and buried soil stratified beneath the mound (97 sherds; 1553 g), but only six featured sherds were found and only one has a diagnostic vessel form. A hooked rim

Table 4.15 Frequency of middle Bronze Age pottery by feature (*joining sherds between contexts)

Feature	Total	Total	Form			Decorated
Context	no.	wt g	type			sherds – unattached
			R30	L1	L2	to vessels
Cremation 1161						
1160	45	2343	1*	–	1*	–
Pit 1753						
1754	264	3962	1	–	–	–
Ditch 1134						
1130	19	187	1	1	–	–
Ditch 2201						
2199	4	77	–	–	–	1
Pit 1390						
1317	1	254	–	–	–	1
1318	8	66	–	–	–	–
1334	4	114	–	–	–	–
Pit 2271						
2267	LBA	LBA	–	–	–	–
2268	3+LBA	98+LBA	–	–	–	–
Posthole 1851						
1852	1	78	–	–	–	–
Unstratified	1	101	–	–	–	1

ovoid jar and an angled or shoulder sherd from a bipartite vessel were recovered from ditch 1408, and the lower half of a possibly shouldered or bipartite jar was found in pit 1168 (Fig. 4.8.8–10). The latter is one of the two identifiable lower parts of vessels in the assemblage as a whole which can be called Class II (fine) jars due to the fabric type and thin vessel walls with burnished exterior and smoothed interior surfaces and the absence of embedded flint beneath the base; the other example is from waterhole 1015 (Fig. 4.9.16). Waterhole 1156 contained only one featured sherd, a B1 base, and pit 1172 had two B2 bases. The range of fabrics represented within this stratified collection includes fabrics from both the major groups, F and IF, but no examples of the rare fabric types with grog temper or predominantly quartz sand. The following fabrics were identified: F1, F3, F5–F7, F10, and IF1–IF4.

Partial excavation of the burnt mound complex revealed 259 sherds (1846 g). The mean sherd weight of this pottery is less than half that of the pottery recovered from beneath the mound (7 g vs 16 g respectively). Therefore, it is not surprising that only seven featured sherds, five rims and two bases, were identified. These include two ovoid jars, a slack-shouldered jar and a straight-sided jar, with

Table 4.16   Frequency of late Bronze Age pottery from the burnt mound complex by feature

Feature Context	Total no.	Total wt g	R1	R2	R3	R4	R5	R6	R11	R12	R13	R14	R15	R16	R17	R21	R22	A1	A2	B1	B2	B3
Alluvium																						
1013	12	119	–	–	–	–	–	–	–	–	–	–	–	–	–	–	–	–	–	–	1	–
Mound deposit																						
1012	8	111	–	–	–	–	–	–	–	–	–	–	–	–	–	–	–	–	–	–	–	–
1466	41	193	–	–	–	–	–	–	–	–	–	–	–	–	–	–	–	–	–	–	–	–
1014	180	1391	–	–	–	–	–	–	1	1	1	–	–	1	–	–	1	–	–	1	1	–
1448	30	151	–	–	–	–	–	–	–	–	–	–	–	–	–	–	–	–	–	–	–	–
Total	*259*	*1846*																				
Ditch 1408																						
1409	12	179	–	–	–	–	–	–	–	1	–	–	–	–	–	–	–	1	–	–	–	–
Ditch 1214																						
1215	14	88	–	–	–	–	–	–	–	–	–	–	–	–	–	–	–	–	–	–	–	–
1299	1	20	–	–	–	–	–	–	–	–	–	–	–	–	–	–	–	–	–	–	–	–
Total	*15*	*108*																				
Posthole 1624																						
1625	2	4	–	–	–	–	–	–	–	–	–	–	–	–	–	–	–	–	–	–	–	–
Pit 1300																						
1412	1	5	–	–	–	–	–	–	–	–	–	–	–	–	–	–	–	–	–	–	–	–
Waterhole 1156																						
1150	6	140	–	–	–	–	–	–	–	–	–	–	–	–	–	–	–	–	–	–	–	–
1616	13	90	–	–	–	–	–	–	–	–	–	–	–	–	–	–	–	–	–	–	–	–
1152	1	2	–	–	–	–	–	–	–	–	–	–	–	–	–	–	–	–	–	–	–	–
1153	27	521	–	–	–	–	–	–	–	–	–	–	–	–	–	–	–	–	–	1	–	–
Total	*47*	*753*																				
Pit 1168																						
1167	1	5	–	–	–	–	–	–	–	–	–	–	–	–	–	–	–	–	–	–	–	–
1201	2	274	–	–	–	–	–	–	–	–	–	–	–	–	–	–	–	1	–	1	–	–
Total	*3*	*279*																				
Pit 1170																						
1169	4	47	–	–	–	–	–	–	–	–	–	–	–	–	–	–	–	–	–	–	–	–
1422	2	58	–	–	–	–	–	–	–	–	–	–	–	–	–	–	–	–	–	–	–	–
1424	1	3	–	–	–	–	–	–	–	–	–	–	–	–	–	–	–	–	–	–	–	–
Total	*7*	*108*																				
Pit 1172																						
1171	3	35	–	–	–	–	–	–	–	–	–	–	–	–	–	–	–	–	–	–	1	–
1397	1	40	–	–	–	–	–	–	–	–	–	–	–	–	–	–	–	–	–	–	1	–
Total	*4*	*75*																				
Pit 1518																						
1516	1	8	–	–	–	–	–	–	–	–	–	–	–	–	–	–	–	–	–	–	–	–
1695	2	18	–	–	–	–	–	–	–	–	–	–	–	–	–	–	–	–	–	–	–	–
Total	*3*	*26*																				
Buried soil																						
1456	3	16	–	–	–	–	–	–	–	–	–	–	–	–	–	–	–	–	–	–	–	–
Overall totals	368	3518							1	2	1			1			1	2		3	4	–

the overfired and distorted everted rim sherd from a probable bipartite vessel decorated with incised zig-zag motif (Fig. 4.8.11–15). The closest parallel for this decorated vessel is a sherd from Runnymede, where the assemblage has been dated to the 12th-7th centuries cal BC (Longley 1980, 12: fig. 36, 388). The range of fabric types represented includes examples from both major groups, as well as examples of grog-tempered wares (IG1, G1). It is noticeable that there are fewer examples of the IF major fabric group in the burnt mound than from features located below the burnt mound and in particular F1, F3 and F5 are dominant. However, the nature of this feature and the processes behind its creation may well be biased towards heating and cooking activities, as discussed above. Therefore, the dominance of sherds made from well-tempered wares, known to have been associated with heating technology (Table 4.14) is not surprising.

It is possible that the IF fabric series may have gone out of use during the later occupation at this location, particularly in RBP1 areas, but this cannot be confirmed without a re-examination of the pottery focusing on this specific group of fabrics. The RBP1 fabrics which have been identified as part of the IF series, fabrics G and H, represent less than 4% of that pottery assemblage, while 20% of the RBP2 pottery is of the IF series. Careful fabric identification in conjunction with petrological analysis of new finds of middle and late Bronze Age pottery in this area are needed to investigate this hypothesis. Such work would need to examine the character of natural clay lenses within local resources and the degree of manufacturing effort observed in thin section as noted in the petrological report above.

Spatial distribution and contents of features

Several groups or types of feature produced significant quantities of pottery (Tables 4.17 and 4.19). These were examined individually and as clusters in order to identify any similarities in forms present or special depositional aspects. Due to the very restricted range of vessel forms in the collection, and the paucity of bowls, decorated sherds and well-finished vessels in contrast to the material discussed from RBP1 (Bradley and Hall 1992a, 71–82), this exercise was quite limited in its results.

Waterholes

All the waterholes contained large quantities of pottery, usually in secondary fills; at least one preserved part of a fineware vessel in the primary fill.

Waterhole 1015

Amongst the waterholes, 1015 is of considerable interest due to the types of infilling and the quantity and range of pottery present. The primary fill contained the lower half of a finely manufactured jar which was burnished on the exterior only and has no additional flint chips embedded in the underside (Fig. 4.10.37). This vessel, a Class II fine jar, could have been used to transport water from the feature to the domestic or working localities of the Area 3100/3000B complex because burnishing is a surface treatment which can aid the retention of liquids within vessels. There are no other sherds of this vessel within the feature. Instead, 13 coarse, ovoid, convex-profile jars, 3 of the 4 bipartite jars from the assemblage, a slack-shouldered jar, 3 bowls and the angled sherd from a shouldered vessel were found (Fig. 4.9.16–28). None of these joined between any contexts, which is in contrast to the infilling of waterhole 1127 described below. The range of fabric types includes sherds from both major groups but none of the other wares.

The pottery from waterhole 1015 displays several characteristics which suggest that it may have been contemporary with the occupation stratified beneath the burnt mound. The collection is dominated by ovoid jars but does have bipartite vessels and a Class II jar like the one from pit 1168 described above, with the vessels being made from F and IF fabrics only. There are no other fabric types and no decorated sherds in this large collection from a single feature.

Waterhole 1118

Waterhole 1118, located in the south-east part of Area 3000B, was another rich feature (Table 4.17) with numerous rim sherds from ovoid jars including an unusually thick-walled example, as well as two bowl sherds (Figs 4.16–4.17). The ratio of bowls to jars in this feature is similar to waterhole 1015. Amongst contexts 1053, 1054 and 1055 there are several joining sherds and sherds which appear to be from the same vessels but do not actually join and this is similar to waterhole 1127. Amongst contexts 1063, 1064 and 1065 there are no joins and only one rim sherd. It is possible to suggest that here there were at least two infilling episodes. Similar to waterholes 2024 and 1144, waterhole 1118 appears to have been lined with ceramic material (fabric F4).

Waterhole 1127

A large quantity of pottery was also recovered from waterhole 1127. Here nearly 500 sherds were recovered and a great range of featured sherds was recorded including two decorated rims (Fig. 4.13. 44–58).

The most striking aspect of this waterhole is with the nature of the deposition of the fills. Sherds from the same R16 vessel (Fig. 4.13.54) were distributed amongst contexts 1128, 1140 and 1141, while those from an ovoid jar were identified in 1140 and 1141 which strongly suggests that these layers were dumped into the waterhole feature as a single episode of purposeful backfill.

The R16 vessel is extremely distinctive as the only vessel in the site assemblage having been made from the poorly wedged, laminated fabric IF5 and it is generally roughly constructed. Both of the decorated rims were recovered from context 1128. Context 1128 has six rims from different vessels, 1141 has five rims from as many

Table 4.17   Frequency of late Bronze Age pottery from selected features (*joining sherds between contexts)

Feature Context	Total no.	Total wt	R1	R2	R3	R4	R5	R6	R11	R12	R13	R14	R15	R16	R17	R21	R22	A1	A2	B1	B2	B3
Waterholes																						
Waterhole 1015																						
1016	396	4237	–	1	1	–	–	–	8	3	2	–	–	–	–	–	–	1	–	8	1	–
1026	51	378	–	–	–	1	–	–	–	–	–	–	–	–	–	–	–	–	–	1	–	–
1027	115	1142	–	–	–	–	–	–	–	2	–	1	–	–	–	–	–	–	–	1	–	–
1031	33	199	–	–	–	–	–	–	–	–	–	–	–	–	–	–	–	–	–	1	–	–
1030	36	251	–	–	–	–	–	–	–	–	–	–	–	–	–	–	–	–	–	–	–	–
1032	2	35	–	–	–	–	–	–	–	–	–	–	–	–	–	–	–	–	–	–	–	–
1040	10	149	–	–	–	–	–	–	–	–	–	–	–	–	–	–	–	–	–	–	–	–
2143	1	220	–	–	–	–	–	–	–	–	–	–	–	–	–	–	–	–	–	–	–	–
1037	4	99	–	–	–	–	–	–	–	–	–	–	–	–	–	–	–	–	–	–	1	–
2329	1	557	–	–	–	–	–	–	–	–	–	–	–	–	–	–	–	–	–	1	–	–
Total	*649*	*7267*																				
Waterhole 1118																						
1053	69	947	–	–	–	–	–	–	1	–	–	–	–	–	–	–	–	–	–	2	1	–
1054	308	5615	1	–	–	–	1	–	6	2	–	–	1	–	–	–	–	–	–	2	3	–
1055	22	331	–	–	–	–	–	–	–	–	–	–	–	–	–	–	–	–	–	1	–	–
1063	11	88	–	–	–	–	–	–	–	–	–	–	–	–	–	–	–	–	–	–	–	–
1064	36	1365	–	–	–	–	–	–	–	1	–	–	–	–	–	–	–	–	–	2	–	1
1065	6	62	–	–	–	–	–	–	–	–	–	–	–	–	–	–	–	–	–	–	–	–
Total	*452*	*8408*																				
Waterhole 1127																						
1128	182	2733	–	–	–	–	–	–	4	2	–	–	–	2*	–	1	–	–	–	–	1	2
1139	13	72	–	–	–	–	–	–	–	1	–	–	–	–	–	–	–	–	–	–	–	–
1140	185	4776	–	–	–	–	–	–	2	1	–	–	–	1*	–	–	–	–	–	–	–	–
1141	118	1548	1	–	–	–	–	1	–	2	–	–	–	1*	–	–	–	–	–	–	–	–
Total	*498*	*9129*																				
Waterhole 1144																						
1060	20	101	–	–	–	–	–	–	—	–	–	–	–	—	–	–	–	–	–	–	–	–
1143	31	175	–	–	–	–	–	–	–	–	–	–	–	–	–	–	–	–	–	–	–	–
1146	138	2262	–	–	–	–	–	–	–	–	–	–	–	–	–	–	–	–	–	–	–	–
1147	72	659	–	–	–	–	–	–	–	–	–	–	–	–	–	–	–	–	–	–	–	–
1173	7	60	–	–	–	–	–	–	–	–	–	–	–	–	–	–	–	–	–	–	–	–
Total	*268*	*3257*																				
Waterhole 1156																						
1150	6	140	–	–	–	–	–	–	–	–	–	–	–	–	–	–	–	–	–	–	–	–
1152	1	2	–	–	–	–	–	–	–	–	–	–	–	–	–	–	–	1	–	1	–	–
1153	27	521	–	–	–	–	–	–	–	–	–	–	–	–	–	–	–	–	–	–	–	–
1616	13	90	–	–	–	–	–	–	–	–	–	–	–	–	–	–	–	–	–	–	–	–
Total	*47*	*753*																				
Waterhole 2042																						
2024	379	5436	–	–	–	–	–	–	3 (1*)	1	–	–	–	–	–	–	–	–	–	2	–	–
2038	78	966	–	–	–	–	–	–	1*	–	–	–	–	–	–	–	–	–	–	–	–	–
Total	*457*	*6402*																				
Waterhole 1264																						
1257	3	5	–	–	–	–	–	–	–	–	–	–	–	–	–	–	–	–	–	–	–	–
1262	2	177	–	–	–	–	–	–	1*	–	–	–	–	–	–	–	–	–	–	1*	–	–
Total	*5*	*182*																				

Table 4.17   (Continued)

Feature Context	Total no.	Total wt	R1	R2	R3	R4	R5	R6	R11	R12	R13	R14	R15	R16	R17	R21	R22	A1	A2	B1	B2	B3
Type 1 pits																						
Pit 1300																						
1412	1	5	–	–	–	–	–	–	–	–	–	–	–	–	–	–	–	–	–	–	–	–
Pit 1305																						
1302	17	108	–	–	–	–	–	–	–	–	–	–	–	–	–	–	–	–	–	–	–	–
Pit 1376																						
1377	2	21	–	–	–	–	–	–	–	–	–	–	–	–	–	–	–	1	–	–	–	–
Pit 1710																						
1714	2	41	–	–	–	–	–	–	–	–	–	–	–	–	–	–	–	–	–	1	–	–
Pit 1862 (part of roundhouse RH2)																						
1863	77	779	1	–	—	–	–	–	–	–	–	–	–	–	–	–	–	–	–	–	–	–
Pit 2011																						
2010	38	279	–	–	–	–	–	–	–	–	–	–	–	–	–	–	–	–	–	–	–	–
Type 2 pits																						
Pit 1114																						
1113	116	1398	–	–	–	–	–	–	2	1	–	–	–	–	–	–	–	–	–	1	–	–
1164	11	86	–	–	–	–	–	–	1	1	1	–	–	1	–	–	–	–	–	–	–	–
Total	*127*	*1484*																				
Pit 1168																						
1201	2	274	–	–	–	–	–	–	–	–	–	–	–	–	–	–	–	–	–	1	–	–
1167	1	5	–	–	–	–	–	–	—	–	–	–	–	–	–	–	–	–	–	–	–	–
Total	*3*	*279*																				
Pit 1172																						
1397	1	40	–	–	–	–	–	–	–	–	–	–	–	–	–	–	–	–	–	–	–	–
1171	3	35	–	–	–	–	–	–	–	–	–	–	–	–	–	–	–	–	–	–	–	–
Total	*4*	*75*																				
Pit 1269																						
1223	6	100	–	–	–	–	–	–	1	–	–	–	–	–	–	–	–	–	–	–	–	–
Pit 1387																						
1385	9	205	–	–	–	–	–	–	–	–	–	–	–	–	–	–	–	–	–	–	–	–
Pit 1403																						
1404	16	82	–	–	–	–	–	–	–	–	–	–	–	–	–	–	–	–	–	–	–	–
Pit 1723																						
1725	15	208	–	–	–	–	–	–	–	–	–	–	–	–	–	–	–	–	–	–	–	–
Pit 1752																						
1750	3	11	–	–	–	–	–	–	–	–	–	–	–	–	–	–	–	–	–	–	1	–
Pit 1770																						
1776	11	80	–	–	–	–	–	–	–	–	–	–	–	–	–	–	–	–	–	–	–	–
1777	5	97	–	–	–	–	–	–	–	1	–	–	–	–	–	–	–	–	–	–	–	
Totals	*16*	*177*																				
Pit 1967																						
1969	11	141	–	–	–	–	–	–	–	–	1	1	–	–	–	–	–	–	–	–	–	–

Table 4.17   (Continued)

Feature Context	Total no.	Total wt	R1	R2	R3	R4	R5	R6	R11	R12	R13	R14	R15	R16	R17	R21	R22	A1	A2	B1	B2	B3
Type 3 pit																						
Pit 1845 (part of roundhouse RH2)																						
1846	73	820	1	–	–	–	–	–	3	1	–	–	–	–	–	–	–	–	–	–	–	–
Type 4 pits																						
Pit 1480																						
1481	29	313	–	–	–	–	–	–	–	–	–	–	–	–	–	–	–	–	–	1	–	
1483	1	64	–	–	–	–	–	–	–	–	–	–	–	–	–	–	–	–	–	1	–	
Total	30	377																				
Pit 1550																						
1554	39	212	–	–	–	–	–	–	–	–	–	–	–	–	–	–	–	–	–	–	–	1
1545	14	66	–	–	–	–	–	–	–	–	–	–	–	–	–	–	–	–	–	–	–	1
Total	53	278																				
Pit 1551																						
1552	26	104	–	–	–	–	–	–	–	–	–	–	–	–	–	–	–	–	–	–	–	–
1697	26	122	–	–	–	–	–	–	–	–	–	–	–	–	–	–	–	–	–	–	–	–
Total	52	226																				
Pit 1559																						
1597	8	6	–		–		–		–		–		–		–		–		–		–	
Pit 1704																						
1705	2	8	–	–	–	–	–	–	–	–	–	–	–	–	–	–	–	–	–	–	–	–
1706	23	128	–	–	–	–	–	–	–	–	–	–	–	–	–	–	–	–	–	–	–	–
1707	17	117	–	–	–	–	–	–	–	–	–	–	–	–	–	–	–	–	–	–	–	–
Total	42	253																				
Pit 1927																						
1924	18	53	–	–	–	–	–	–	–	–	–	–	–	–	–	–	–	–	–	–	–	–
Irregular pit																						
Pit 1691																						
1692	56	915	–	–	–	–	–	–	1	1	–	–	–	2	–	–	–	–	–	–	–	–
Late Bronze Age ditches																						
Ditch 1905																						
1898	5	61	–	–	–	–	–	–	–	–	–	–	–	–	–	–	–	–	–	–	–	–
Ditch 1850																						
1848	2	5	–	–	–	–	–	–	–	–	–	–	–	–	–	–	–	–	1	–	–	–
Ditch 2147																						
2144	7	61	–	–	–	–	–	–	–	–	–	–	–	–	–	–	–	–	–	1	–	–
2145	7	31	–	–	–	–	–	–	–	–	–	–	–	–	–	–	–	–	–	–	–	–
Total	14	92																				
Ditch 2151																						
2148	3	18	–		–		–		–		–		–		–		–		–		–	
Tree–throw holes																						
Tree–throw hole 1023																						
1025	20	350	–	–	–	–	–	–	–	–	–	–	–	–	–	1	–	–	–	1	–	–
2280	7	177	–	–	–	–	–	–	–	–	–	–	–	–	–	–	–	–	–	–	–	–
2283	11	47	–	–	–	–	–	–	–	–	–	–	–	–	–	–	–	–	–	–	–	–
Total	38	574																				

Table 4.18 Frequency of late Bronze Age pottery from circular and other structures (*joining sherds between contexts: ** middle Bronze Age pottery)

Structure Posthole	Total no.	Total wt g	R1	R6	R11	R12	A1	B1	B2
Roundhouse RH1									
1881	1	3	–	–	–	–	–	–	–
1871	3	21	–	–	–	–	–	–	–
Total	*4*	*24*							
Roundhouse RH2									
1442	18	68	–	–	–	1	–	–	1
1889	2	7	–	–	–	–	–	–	–
Total	*20*	*75*							
Inside RH2									
1845	78	866	1	–	32	–	–	–	–
1862	77	779	–	–	–	–	–	–	–
Total	*155*	*1645*							
Roundhouse RH3									
1227	2	7	–	–	–	–	–	–	–
1229	2	71	–	–	–	–	–	–	–
1233	6	52	–	–	1	–	–	–	–
1235	2	14	–	–	–	–	–	–	–
1652	7	53	–	–	–	–	–	–	–
*1342	8	77	–	–	–	–	–	–	–
*1344	7	48	–	–	1	–	–	–	–
Total	*34*	*322*							
Inside RH3		–							
1283	16	74	–	1	1	–	–	–	–
1346	4	9	–	–	–	–	–	–	–
**1727	2	55	–	–	–	1	–	–	–
Total	*22*	*138*							
Roundhouse RH4									
1277	1	3	–	–	–	–	–	–	–
1403	16	82	–	–	–	–	–	–	–
1452	1	12	–	–	–	–	–	–	–
1668	2	103	–	–	–	–	1	–	–
1670	7	74	–	–	–	–	–	–	–
1730	8	11	–	–	–	–	–	–	–
1735	21	231	–	–	1	1	–	–	–
2342	4	43	–	–	–	–	–	–	–
Total	*60*	*559*							
Inside RH4									
1401	1	38	–	–	–	–	–	–	–
1405	3	49	–	–	–	–	–	–	–
Total	*4*	*87*							
Roundhouse RH5									
1183	1	3	–	–	–	–	–	–	–
1191	4	17	–	–	–	–	–	–	–
Total	*5*	*20*							
6-post structure SP6									
1235	2	14	–	–	–	–	–	–	–
1276	1	3	–	–	–	–	–	–	–
Total	*3*	*17*							
4-post structure FP12									
1840	8	3	–	–	–	–	–	–	–
4-post structure FP13									
1801	11	38	–	–	–	–	–	–	–
1805	10	36	–	–	–	–	–	–	–
1807	2	77	–	–	–	–	–	–	–
Total	*23*	*151*							

Table 4.18 (Continued)

Structure Posthole	Total no.	Total wt g	R1	R6	R11	R12	A1	B1	B2
4-post structure FP16									
1504	1	8	–	–	–	–	–	–	–
4-post structure FP17									
1585	1	3	–	–	–	–	–	–	–
1600	1	5	–	–	–	–	–	–	–
Total	*2*	*8*							
4-post structure FP19									
2337	13	268	–	–	–	–	–	2	–
2338	1	3	–	–	–	–	–	–	–
2339	71	702	–	–	–	1	–	–	–
Total	*85*	*973*							
2-post structure TP22									
1364	3	80	–	–	–	–	–	–	–
2-post structure TP24									
1180	6	28	–	–	–	–	–	–	–
1183	1	3	–	–	–	–	–	–	–
Total	*7*	*31*							
2-post structure TP25									
1049	4	53							

Table 4.19 Quantification of sieved pottery by number and weight in grams

Feature	Context	Sherds no.	Sherds wt g	Sample nos
Burnt mound group	1012	41	24	352 & 353
Alluvium	1013	10	6	1 & 2
Burnt mound	1014	11	4	61, 62, 85, 97
		5	4	360
		5	2	374
Waterholes				
1118	1064	11	10	–
	1065	5	7	–
1127	1128	113	78	70 & 71
	1139	43	26	123 & 124
	1140	62	34	122
1144	1143	30	20	96
	1147	12	12	316 & 317
1156	1152	1	1	197
Cremation				
1159	1159	9	3	127 & 128
Postholes				
1504	1503	4	2	251
1530	1529	1	1	162
1842	1841	1	1	209
Type 4 pits				
1704	1705	6	6	273 – 276
	1706	25	23	277 – 280
1927	1924	1	1	218, 220, 221
Land surface	2348	2	2	429 & 433
Gully 5075	5074	1	1	557 – 561

vessels, and 1140 has four rims from two different vessels. The best example of a B3 base with embedded flint chips was found in this pit. The fabrics are predominantly from the coarseware range but there is also a fine biconical bowl in the assemblage. This feature, therefore, has all of the hallmarks of a pre-burnt mound assemblage but is richer in both the quantity of pottery and the range of material present and therefore similar to waterhole 1015. However, waterhole 1015 had more examples of bowls, slack-profile jars and a bipartite jar.

Waterhole 1144

One waterhole, 1144, is much smaller in diameter than nearby pits 1690/1691 and waterhole 1127 but, while it has a large amount of ceramic material (268; 31,257 g), there are no featured sherds in the assemblage, not even bases. This may be because the commonest fabric type is the suspected pit lining material F4 (225 pieces), a few of which have the possible whitewash adhering to them.

Waterhole 2042

A rich feature, waterhole 2042 (Table 4.17) was located 4 m west of roundhouse RH4. Four vessels could be identified to form and all are convex-profile, ovoid jars (Fig. 4.15.60–63). There are numerous pieces of F4? ceramic lining, a few of which display the possible whitewash deposit on the interior surface. The range of fabrics is interestingly dominated by IF fabric sherds with F group sherds making up the remainder of material not classified as possible pit liner. This pit may have been infilled at a time similar to the pre-burnt mound features, waterholes 1015 and 1127 and pit 1690/1691. The waterhole 2042 was located to the west and behind roundhouses RH3 and RH4. The presence in the waterhole of similar vessel forms and fabrics (archive data) to those in these buildings (which had numerous sherds in their postholes) suggests that it may have been associated but unfortunately no joining sherds were found to connect them directly. Further investigation might assist with this association.

Features west of waterhole 1015

Several pits were excavated between waterhole 1015 and the edge of Area 3000B to the west. Four were located in a line 4 m to the west of the waterhole, pits 1387, 1389, 1704 and 1710, with 1–1.5 m between them. Two pits, 1723 and 1752, were found 5 m further west. Surprisingly, 87 sherds (817 g) of pottery were recovered from these, but no rim or angled shoulder sherds and only two base sherds, with a mean sherd weight of 10 g. The six pits were not used for the disposal or deposition of significant quantities of pottery remains.

Features south-east of waterhole 1015

This pattern was repeated amongst the pits, 4-post cluster and tree-throw hole with pottery located to the south-east of waterhole 1015. Waterhole 1264 and pit 1927 contained only 23 sherds between them (235 g). However, the only total profile vessel in the assemblage, a small jar, was found in 1264 (Fig. 4.10.38).

The 4-post structure FP13 made from postholes 1801, 1803, 1805, and 1807 had 23 sherds (151 g) amongst them but none are featured sherds (Table 4.18). Pits 1305 and 1480 had 47 sherds (485 g) between them but only two base sherds were recovered.

The tree-throw hole 1023, however, was slightly different. Amongst the 38 sherds (574 g) was found the only example of an R17 rim. This vessel was made from a very coarse fabric (IF3) and had an extremely well wiped exterior surface (Fig. 4.11.39). However, this vessel was not associated with sherds from any other specific vessel type.

Features north of waterhole 1015

Just north of waterhole 1015, one pit and three postholes were excavated which contained pottery. A total of 56 sherds (915 g) was recovered from pit 1691 and four rims were identified to form, two ovoids and two straight-sided jars (Fig. 4.12.40–3). The fabrics included numerous examples of both F and IF groups but no other types. Three of the sherds may have derived from pit lining; while the fabric was more similar to F2 than F4, the wall thickness of the pieces was in excess of 20 mm. Although there are no examples of bipartite forms or bowls in this feature, other characteristics of this pit assemblage would not be out of place as pre-burnt mound material.

Four features located to the south of the burnt mound, pits 1170 and 2271 and ditches 1850 and 1905, contained very few sherds amongst them. Pit 1170, discussed above as stratified beneath the burnt mound, and the ditches contained no featured sherds but pit 2271 contained sherds from a middle Bronze Age urn (Fig. 4.7.3) and also late Bronze Age body sherds (Table 4.15).

Structures

There are five identifiable circular roundhouse structures located between the burnt mound complex and waterhole 1015; pottery was present in a number of the postholes (Table 4.18). In addition, at least one 6-post structure and several 4-post structures also contained sherds of late Bronze Age pottery.

In roundhouse RH3 a total of 34 sherds were found including one large and decorated hooked rim, ovoid jar (Fig. 4.14.59) and sherds from two other ovoid jars.

Roundhouse RH4 contained sherds of ovoid jars in posthole 1735, and also a B2 base in posthole 1670 and a very abraded shoulder sherd from a bowl. Posthole 2339 located within the south-west interior of RH4 and identified as part of 4-post structure FP19 was relatively rich for this type of feature; it had an R12 ovoid jar amongst many sherds.

To the south of all these buildings and just west of waterhole 1015, the postholes of roundhouse RH1 were excavated. Very little pottery (4 sherds) was recovered from this building despite the proximity of the richly infilled waterhole.

Only posthole 1442 in roundhouse RH2 contained featured sherds, the rim from a medium size ovoid jar

(140 mm) and a B2 base, and also sherds from the F group of fabrics as well as fabric type G1 (5 sherds; 17 g). The only other G1 fabric pottery (1 sherd; 4 g) comes from within the burnt mound. However, the pits from within this structure, 1845 and 1862 contained a large number of sherds (155 sherds; 1645 g) including a bowl and several ovoid jars.

Therefore, there is a contrast between the frequency of pottery recovered from the postholes which make RH3 and RH4 and those which make all of the other structures, although the limited range of forms and the consistency of fabric groups (archive data) suggest that there is no reason to consider them to be anything but broadly contemporary.

Summary of the stratigraphic and spatial evidence

Examination of the types of pottery and the presence of ceramic lining material within waterholes has shown that wherever there are features which contain numerous sherds it is possible to indicate that these are similar in several respects to the material stratified beneath the burnt mound.

There is nothing which would suggest that any of the richer features located south of the burnt mound in Area 3000B were not broadly contemporary. In particular, roundhouses RH3 and RH4 and waterhole 2042 are rich in pottery within their class of features at this site and their location suggests that there was some connection amongst them. The other structures consistently contain less material (with the exception of 4-post structure FP19 within roundhouse RH4), and therefore may have been occupied for a shorter period of time or functioned in a different capacity to roundhouses RH3 and RH4. Waterholes 1015, 1127 and 1144 and several pits to the north of 1015 were also likely to have been infilled with material of a similar date to that of RH3 and RH4, and waterholes 1127 and 2042 are similar in their richness and variety of vessels.

All of these features could be contemporary with the pre-burnt mound features. The distorted and decorated rim sherd, which is unique in form amongst the RBP2 material, from the burnt mound suggests that there may have been a significant chronological difference possible between the mound and pre-mound features.

General discussion

Middle Bronze Age to late Bronze Age continuity

This assemblage of pottery is particularly useful for exploring the continuity of pottery production traditions between the middle and late Bronze Age. Five main characteristics show that, while continuity can be demonstrated between these ceramic phases, there is also ample evidence that a distinctive potting tradition developed during the late Bronze Age. Where appropriate, material from both RBP1 and RBP2 excavations at Reading Business Park will be used to support the interpretation.

Amongst the RBP2 assemblage, there are seven diagnostic vessels, and one other possible body sherd, which can be dated to the middle Bronze Age (Fig. 4.7.1–7). Four of these were classified as bucket urns including one decorated cremation urn, two decorated urns from pits, and an undecorated urn from a ditch. In addition, two decorated body sherds display all the characteristics of Deverel Rimbury style middle Bronze Age urns, one from a ditch and the other unstratified. The seventh vessel, recovered from a ditch, is represented by a horizontal lug. Therefore, middle Bronze Age pottery from both cemetery and settlement contexts were present on the site and these were made from flint-tempered fabrics F5, F15 and F16. Another possible sherd is unique; it is the only one made from fabric F17, is unusually well smoothed on the interior surface although the vessel was thick-walled, and was the only pottery found in posthole 1851.

All of the middle Bronze Age pottery is flint-tempered and made using non-iron oxide-rich clay resources. The majority of the vessels were made from moderate to well sorted, but coarse, flint-tempered fabrics (F5, F16), while two others were produced from a fine, silty and micaceous clay matrix with moderately sorted, intermediately sized flint temper (F15) and an extremely coarse flint temper (F17) respectively. These fabrics may be seen as the precursors to the late Bronze Age potting tradition which also employs flint temper to create fine, intermediate and coarse fabrics; in fact the fabric F5 was used to make both middle Bronze Age pottery (Fig. 4.7.4 and 6) and late Bronze Age pottery in the form of an R12 rim (Table 4.11). The late Bronze Age pottery, however, generally was made using less well selected temper and often less density of temper, a characteristic also noted by Raymond in her assessment of the middle and late Bronze Age pottery from fieldwork on Salisbury Plain (1994). The late Bronze Age tradition at RBP2 was also enhanced by the utilisation of a new source for clay, the iron-rich resource, and the addition on rare occasions of grog temper to the flint temper to create a mixed recipe, the use of grog temper alone, and the exploration of quartz sand as a suitable medium for the production of selected vessels. There is only one sandy fabric in the assemblage from RBP1 (Hall 1992, fabric W). However, the ability to make and use quartz sand fabric pottery is well known elsewhere during the full late Bronze Age. It appears that this technological and cultural change is truly a hallmark of the late Bronze Age.

In addition, the bucket urns are similar in profile to the commonest vessel type of late Bronze Age date, the two ovoid jar forms (R11, R12). Ovoid jars are very common in both the RBP1 (types 8 and 9; 27%) and RBP2 (73%) assemblages of classifiable vessels. It is also significant that one vessel type in particular is made in a straight-sided profile form (R16 – 5%; Hall 1992, type 14 – 3% of vessels) which is again similar to bucket urns. The late Bronze Age assemblage, however, is significant for the manufacture and use of a brand new vessel form, the bowl (Barrett 1980, 302–3), which may be indicative of transformations in ceramic function and use or symbolic meaning and effect (Raymond 1994, 75). This is no exception within the RBP2 assemblage where out of 95 identifiably different late Bronze Age vessels (Table 4.11), nine are bowls, representing 9% of the late Bronze Age assemblage. At RBP1 the development of vessel forms continued with the appearance of various distinctively shouldered jars (Hall 1992, types 10–13; 9% of classifiable vessels) which, as stated previously, are present (R14; some A1 examples) but infrequent in Area 3000B of RBP2.

While the vessel forms of urns and both ovoid and straight-sided jars are not dissimilar in profile, the sizes of these vessels are also repetitious. The straight-sided jars and the bucket urns are few in number but both have medium sized vessels (140–260 mm) as well as large vessels (300–360 mm). The ovoid jars also have a range of medium sized and large sized vessels but they, like the straight-sided vessels are distinctive for the additional manufacture of small vessels (less than 140 mm), a late Bronze Age development.

A fourth characteristic which both links and separates the middle and late Bronze Age pottery from this site is decoration. The use of fingertip impressions on the interior edge of rims is a related characteristic; the bucket urns, the ovoid jars, and the straight-sided jars use this decorative technique. The straight-sided jar is an obvious candidate to be recognised as a transitional form based on fabric, vessel shape, location and type of decoration, and size range.

However, the decorative tradition of the late Bronze Age itself develops further with the use of fingertip impressions on the point of shouldered jars and the exterior edge of the rims of jars, as commonly indicated amongst the RBP1 pottery (Bradley and Hall 1992a, figs 45, 66–9; 46, 71; 47, 104; 48, 144, 150; 50, 184, 186, 190–1, 193–4, 196) but not in RBP2 Area 3000B. A new decorative technique, the incising of simple and complex designs on both jars and bowls (Bradley and Hall 1992a, figs 47, 127; 50, 185) was also introduced. This incising technique can be seen on only two vessels from RBP2 Area 3000B, one thin-walled ovoid jar (Fig. 4.13.48) and one burnt and distorted, everted rim vessel from the stratigraphically late burnt mound (Fig. 4.8.15).

And finally, the fifth characteristic is the use of embedded flint chips on the underside of bases. This middle Bronze Age technique continued into the late Bronze Age but was altered, with the chips being ill sorted and larger in size. One specific characteristic which does not continue into the late Bronze Age repertoire, however, is the use of lugs.

Chronologically, therefore, the RBP2 assemblage from Area 3000B is distinctive due to the strong links which have been demonstrated between the middle Bronze Age Deverel Rimbury material and the late Bronze Age material in fabric, form, rim decoration and vessel size. There is every reason to suspect that the late Bronze Age occupation followed on immediately from the middle Bronze Age landscape delineation and settlement occupation with its distinctive burial activity.

Only one other site in the region is recorded as having a direct link between middle and late Bronze Age occupation. Excavations at Pingewood, located less than 2 km west of Reading Business Park, revealed a series of large and moderate sized Bronze Age pits, postholes and stakeholes containing pottery, animal bones, clay weights, querns and rubbers (Johnston 1983–5). The occupation debris was dated to the middle and late Bronze Age based on the presence of Deverel Rimbury bucket urn sherds, straight-sided jars and diagnostic late Bronze Age hooked rim and simple rim, ovoid jars made from the same fabrics and within the same features (Bradley 1983–5, figs 7–9). This pottery was also ironised, unabraded and in generally good condition as discussed for the RBP2 assemblage.

At Pingewood at least 62 vessels were identified amongst the 10 kg of flint-tempered pottery. Identical late Bronze Age form and decorative details include fingertip decoration on the interior edge of ovoid, hooked and straight-sided jar rims, a pinched protrusion or boss, and both splayed and simple bases. The lack of concern about the appearance of these vessels is suggested by the exterior evidence for coil building apparent on one illustrated, straight-sided vessel (ibid., fig. 8.54), and the description that a few display rippling or smearing on the exterior. Possible biconical or shouldered vessels are suggested by the profiles of two necked jars (ibid., fig. 7.9–10), although these are described as bowls. Therefore, the recovery of both middle and late Bronze Age pottery made from similar fabrics and originating from very similar features at a site located within the immediate area suggests that the occupation at Reading Business Park is simply a continuum of that activity during the later Bronze Age.

The activities at Pingewood and RBP2 took place during a period which can now be recognised as transitional between the middle Bronze Age Deverel Rimbury tradition of bucket urns and the post-Deverel Rimbury late Bronze Age tradition of ovoid jars, bipartite jars and bowls. Bradley first recognised this as a distinctive phase of activity in the Thames Valley which was only rarely found and suggested a date of 'probably in the 11th century bc' (1983–5, 28), but it is only now that a second location of similar activity has come to light.

Nowhere else is there recorded such a strong link between vessels defined as middle Bronze Age and late Bronze Age pottery. On Salisbury Plain, in the 'Upper Study Area', the differences between the

Deverel Rimbury pottery and the plain assemblage late Bronze Age pottery were much more distinctive despite the recognition that several of the late Bronze Age sites began as middle Bronze Age foci (Raymond 1994, 72–4, fig. 51). The interpretation of the laying out of the land divisions in the Upper Study Area was assigned to the late Bronze Age phase rather than the middle Bronze Age which is quite different from RBP2 where the land division ditches are middle Bronze Age in date. On the Marlborough Downs, three sites were examined, Dean Bottom, Rockley Down and Burderop Down, which revealed both middle Bronze Age and non-Deverel Rimbury pottery (Gingell 1980). Detailed analysis of the pottery demonstrated that a variety of jars and round-shouldered bowls can be easily distinguished on form alone from the Deverel Rimbury component in these collections, but that there are no clear distinctions between the majority of fabrics (Cleal and Gingell 1992, 99–103). At these sites the pottery is tempered with flint, and only the very heavily tempered body sherds are typical of Deverel Rimbury pottery. The authors are firmly of the opinion that the post-Deverel Rimbury fabrics were 'sufficiently rooted in the preceding pottery traditions' (ibid., 103), and it is interesting to note that the vessel forms are not equally derivative.

Instead, the assemblage from Rams Hill is suggested as being a more typical transitional collection for comparison of material from the Upper and Middle Thames Valley region. Barrett first used this assemblage as an important collection for understanding and characterising the plain assemblage phase of the later Bronze Age (1980, 307–9). The earliest phase of pottery from this site, located 40 km north-west of Reading, is dominated by simple and hooked rim, ovoid jars and has several straight-sided jars (Bradley and Ellison 1975, fig. 3.5, 1–10, 15–18), in association with shouldered jars and rims from probable bipartite vessels but lacks any of the middle Bronze Age Deverel Rimbury bucket urns found at Reading Business Park. It is now possible to suggest a refined chronological ceramic development from the middle through the middle/late transition and into the late Bronze Age which needs to be tested with absolute dating from a variety of sites.

Late Bronze Age settlement shift

The late Bronze Age occupation at Reading Business Park as a whole continued throughout the plain-ware ceramic phase and the decorated ware phase. The frequency of decoration amongst the pottery from RBP1 excavations can be compared to that from elsewhere in order to determine when the occupation ceased. At Aldermaston Wharf which is dated to the late 2nd-early 1st millennium cal BC, 5% of the assemblage is decorated (Bradley *et al.* 1980, figs 12–18) and at Runnymede Bridge of the same date, 15% of the assemblage is decorated (Longley 1991, 167). At Petters Sports Field, dated from the early-middle 1st millennium cal BC, 25% is decorated (O`Connell 1986, 63). Amongst the Knight's Farm subsite 1 assemblage, dated to 1050–750 cal BC (740±80bc, HAR-1011) and 830–410 cal BC (600±80bc, HAR-1012), up to 50% may be decorated (Bradley *et al.* 1980, figs 34–6). This suggests, as discussed by Barrett, that assemblages generally become more decorated during the late Bronze Age in this area.

At RBP1, 37% of the assemblage was decorated (Bradley and Hall 1992a, table 13). It was suggested that certain features in Areas 5 and 3100 of this site were part of the decorated ware ceramic phases of the late Bronze Age as defined by Barrett while other features in the same area contained plain assemblage late Bronze Age groups (Bradley and Hall 1992a, 80). Area 5 also had sherds of Deverel Rimbury pottery. Area 3100 did not have Deverel Rimbury pottery according to Bradley and Hall (1992a, table 13; *contra* Moore and Jennings 1992, 120). It was concluded that the occupation recovered during the RBP1 excavation represented limited middle Bronze Age activity and a continuous re-establishment of buildings in succession at the same location during both the plain and decorated ceramic phases of the late Bronze Age.

There appears to be significant middle Bronze Age occupation, in the form of land division with burial activity, in RBP2 Area 3000B. This activity was immediately followed by late Bronze Age occupation represented by the circular post-built structures and 4-post structures associated with the digging of pits, the digging and lining of waterhole facilities, and the use of pottery of which only 2% displayed little decoration. The occupation of RBP2 Area 3000B changed its nature before the full development of the significant indicators of late Bronze Age ceramic tradition characterised by common coarse and fine shouldered jars with surface treatment, and the use of fingertip decoration on the exterior of jars. The use of this area appears to have altered with a number of features removed from the landscape by the establishment of a major burnt flint dumping zone, which may represent an unidentified industrial activity. The possible industrial burnt mound deposit contains pottery which is generally similar to that from the rest of Area 3000B assemblage with the addition of a single decorated rim sherd which suggests that it continued in use during the shrinking and shifting of the settlement focus west into RBP1 Area 3100 prior to the appearance of the full late Bronze Age tradition. The distribution of pottery in RBP1 Area 5 (Bradley and Hall 1992a, table 13) indicates that that area, too, was occupied well after RBP2 Area 3000B was avoided as space for building structures but continued in use as a cooking or heating activity zone.

Flint transformed

The overwhelming dominance of flint-tempered later Bronze Age pottery at this site, and other sites in the Thames Valley from this period, is undoubtedly connected to the availability of flint within the Valley Gravels and in the Upper Chalk deposits. If and when flint is used as 'pot boilers', it becomes crazed and shattered, and thus even more readily available for use as temper in the next generation of pots.

Also occurring is the transformation of natural resources by heat into cultural materials. In the first instance there were flint gravels or nodules used as hot pot boilers, heated natural material to cook and transform food into edible cultural material and which were also then available for use as temper to transform clays into serviceable vessels through firing. It is possible to see a cycle of reinforcements whereby natural elements were transformed by heat into cultural phenomena with food and flint having been inextricably linked. It is also possible to understand a reinforcement which brings the past and the land, chips from old pot boilers/food cooking material, actually into the current food storage or presentation as the temper of vessels, jars and bowls. The fabrics of the vessels belong to the past and the earth but act in the present social arena in the consumption of food.

It is also important to realise that there is at this time a transformation of natural resources into cultural materials by heat. This may have been a very important focus during the middle and late Bronze Age when other transformations were taking place such as changes in burial practices or disposal of the dead with the ending of cremation cemeteries and alteration of the landscape with the demarcation of territory through linear boundaries. The end of this transformation may be seen in the culmination of the extraordinary mounds of cultural debris, or middens, which characterise the end of the late Bronze Age (Gingell and Lawson 1984, 1985; Lawson 2000; Brown *et al.* 1994; McOrmish 1996; Needham 1991).

Catalogue of illustrated pottery – Area 3000B

Middle Bronze Age

Figure 4.7

1. Bucket urn, F16, 98% of 300 mm diameter R30 rim, decorated with fingertip impressions on interior edge, four opposing L2 type lugs attached prior to horizontal row of fingertip impressions around girth, two pairs of repair hole perforations on either side of major vessel wall cracks, PRN (Pottery Record Number) 4452–4453, 1160 (pit 1159, cremation 1161).
2. Bucket urn, F16, 47% of 320 mm R30 rim, decorated with fingertip impressions on interior edge, at least one L3 type lug, possibly two, but unlocated position on vessel, *c* 40% of *c* 200 mm diameter B99 base with

added fine, burnt, crushed flint fragments on the underside of the base, very fragmented vessel with no base angle sherds, PRN 4691–4694, 1754 (pit 1753).
3. Bucket urn, F16, 5% of 360 mm R30 rim, decorated with fingertip impressions on interior edge, PRN 4840 and 5037, 2268 (pit 2271).
4. Bucket urn, F5, 10% of 180 mm R30 rim, PRN 4425, 1130 (ditch 1134).
5. Lug, type L1, F15, PRN 4424, 1130 (ditch 1134).
6. Decorated sherd, F5, applied strip with fingertip impressions at girth of urn, PRN 4815, 2199 (ditch 2201).
7. Decorated sherd, F16, applied strip with fingertip impressions, PRN 5009 (unstratified).

Late Bronze Age

Burnt mound complex

Figure 4.8

8. Ovoid jar, F3, <5% of R12 rim present, PRN 4552, 1409 (ditch 1408).
9. Shoulder sherd from probable bipartite jar, F6, A1, PRN 4547, 1409.
10. Lower half of jar, IF1, A1, B1, burnished exterior, smoothed interior, PRN 4455, 1201 (pit 1168).
11. Ovoid jar, IF1, 7% of 100 mm R11 rim, PRN 4982, SF122, 1014 (burnt mound complex 1012).
12. Ovoid jar, F1, 5% of 200 mm R12 rim, PRN 4914, SF30, 1014.
13. Slack-profile jar, F3, <5% of R13 rim, wiped exterior, PRN 4965, SF101, 1014.
14. Straight-sided jar, F1, 10 of 200 mm R16 rim, wiped exterior, PRN 4930, SF51, 1014.
15. Everted rim vessel, IF1 overfired, distorted shape, incised zig-zag motif on upper neck zone, PRN 4925, SF43, 1014.

Waterhole 1015

Figure 4.9

16. Ovoid jar, F1, 7% of 160 mm R11 rim, PRN 4006, 1016.
17. Slack-profile bowl, F1, 5% of 140 mm R2 rim, PRN 4007, 1016.
18. Bipartite, everted rim bowl, F1, <5% of R3 rim present, PRN 4008, 1016.
19. Ovoid jar, F1, <5% of R11 rim, possible limescale on interior, PRN 4009, 1016.
20. Ovoid jar, F1, <5% of R11 rim, PRN 4010, 1016.
21. Ovoid jar, F1, 5% of 140 mm R11 rim, PRN 4011, 1016.
22. Ovoid jar, F1, <5% of R11 rim, PRN 4012, 1016.
23. Ovoid jar, F1, <5% of R11 rim, PRN 4013, 1016.
24. Hooked rim, ovoid jar, F1, 5% of 140 mm, R12 rim, PRN 4014, 1016.
25. Hooked rim, ovoid jar, F1, 5% of 140 mm R12 rim, PRN 4015, 1016.
26. Slack-profile jar, F1, 6% of 160 mm R13 rim, PRN 4016, 1016.
27. Shoulder of bipartite vessel, F1, either from a jar or bowl, PRN 4017, 1016.

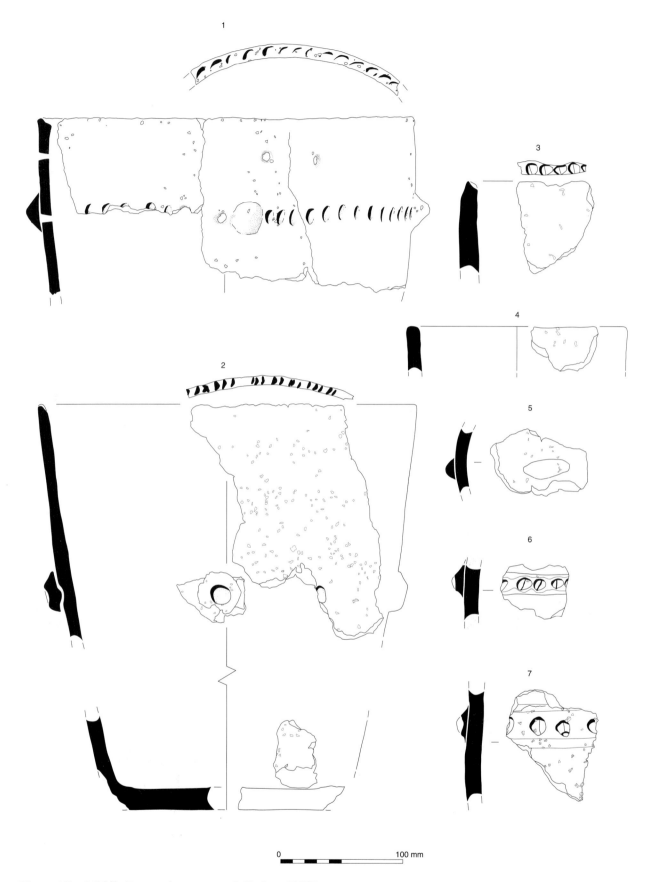

Figure 4.7   Middle Bronze Age pottery: 1–7. Area 3000B

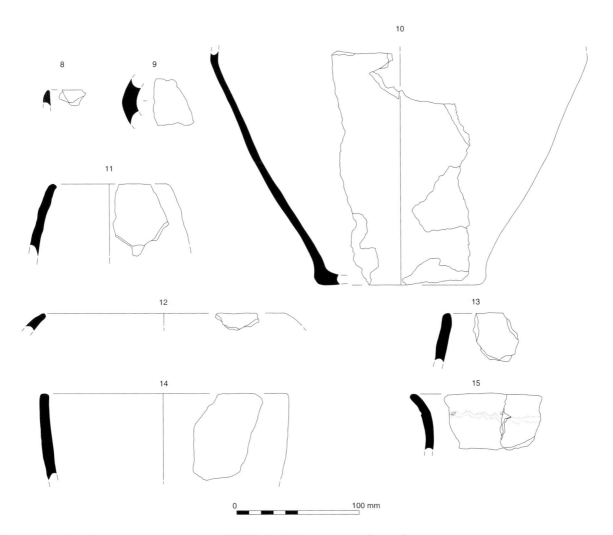

Figure 4.8   Late Bronze Age pottery, Area 3000B: 8–15. Burnt mound complex

28. Ovoid jar, F3, 5% of 200 mm, R11 rim, fingering marks on exterior, PRN 4033, 1016.

Figure 4.10

29. Bipartite jar, F3, 7% of 140 mm R14 rim, unusual fired effect on interior, PRN 4034, 1016.
30. Bipartite jar, F3, <5% of R14 rim, PRN 4035, 1016.
31. Hooked rim, ovoid jar, F9, 6% of 100 mm, R12 rim, PRN 4057, 1016.
32. Ovoid jar, IF1, <5% of R11 rim, limescale on interior, PRN 4066, 1016.
33. Inturned profile bowl (or lid), F7, 6% of 240 mm R4 rim, wiped on exterior, PRN 4092, 1026.
34. Ovoid jar, F1, <5% of R11 (? R12) rim, PRN 4101, 1027.
35. Bipartite jar, F1, 5% of 220 mm R14 rim, smoothed on exterior, PRN 4102, 1027.
36. Hooked rim, ovoid jar; F11, 7% of 160 mm R12 rim, smoothed on exterior but effect may be due to fineness of fabric, PRN 4106, 1027.
37. Jar, F2, 50% of 100 mm B1 base, burnished exterior, PRN 4129, 2329.

Waterhole 1264

Figure 4.10

38. Ovoid jar, F1, total profile, 15% of 100 mm R11 rim, 62% of 80 mm B1 base, embedded flint on base underside, PRN 4504, 1262.

Tree-throw hole 1023

Figure 4.11

39. Slightly flared or vertical rim, necked, slack-shoulder or barrel-profile jar, IF3, 6% of 180 mm R17 rim, 1025.

Pit 1691

Figure 4.12

40. Straight-sided jar, IF2, 5% of 160 mm R16 rim, wiped on exterior, PRN 4641, 1692.
41. Ovoid jar, F1, 5% of 300 mm R11 rim, PRN 4645, 1692.
42. Hooked rim, ovoid jar, F3, <5% of R12 rim, PRN 4646, 1692.
43. Straight-sided jar, F1, <5% of R16 rim, PRN 4547, 1692.

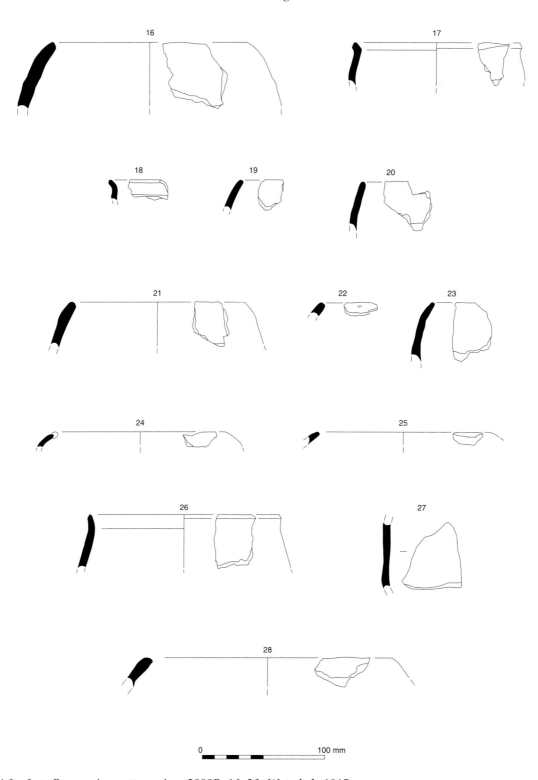

Figure 4.9   Late Bronze Age pottery, Area 3000B: 16–28. Waterhole 1015

Waterhole 1127

Figure 4.13

44. Curled base vessel, IF3, 25% of 180 mm B3 base, embedded flint on based underside, PRN 4289, 1128.

45. Straight-sided jar, IF2, <5% of R16 rim, decorated with fingertip impression on interior side of top edge, PRN 4290, 1128.

46. Everted rim, round-shoulder vessel, IF3, <5% of R21 rim, PRN 4291, 1128.

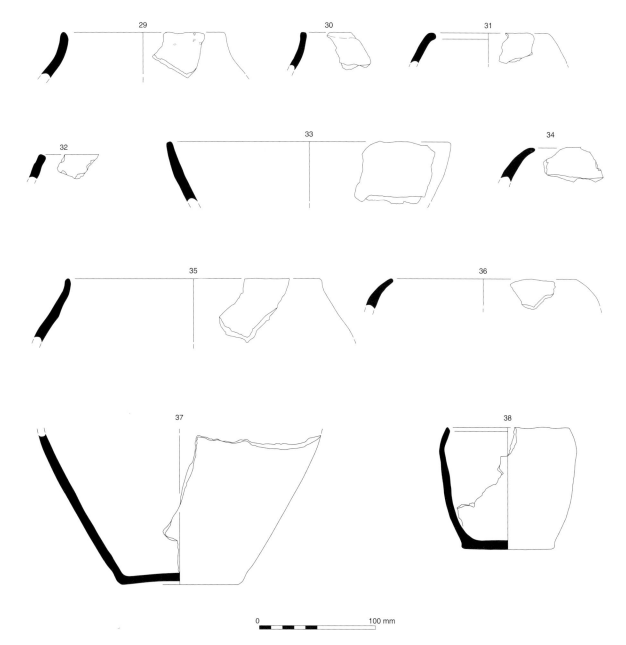

Figure 4.10   Late Bronze Age pottery, Area 3000B: 29–37. Waterhole 1015: 38 Waterhole 1264

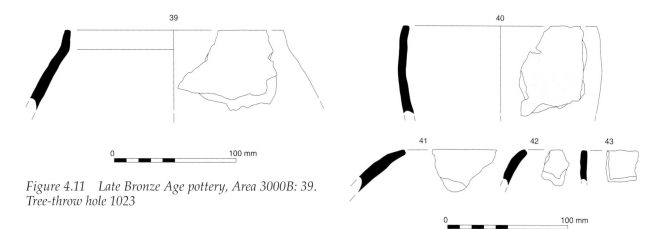

Figure 4.11   Late Bronze Age pottery, Area 3000B: 39. Tree-throw hole 1023

Figure 4.12   Late Bronze Age pottery, Area 3000B: 40-3. Pit 1691

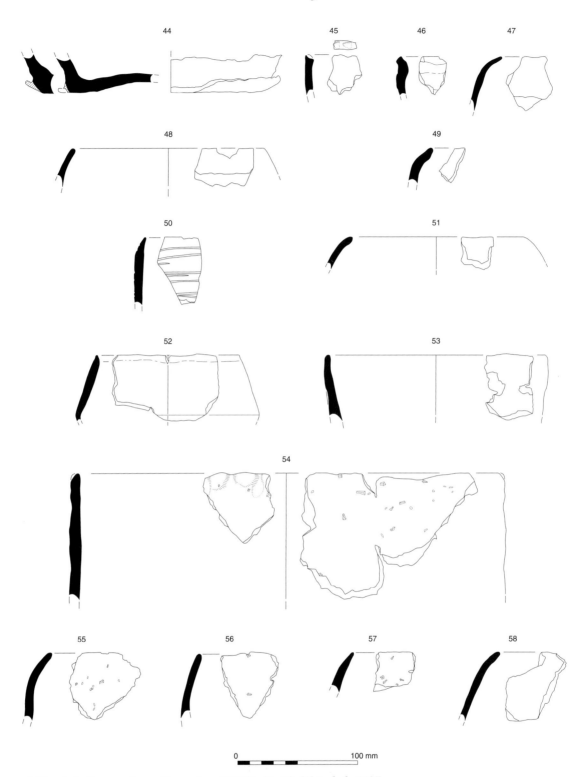

Figure 4.13   Late Bronze Age pottery, Area 3000B: 44–58. Waterhole 1127

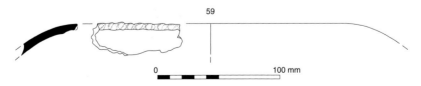

Figure 4.14 Late Bronze Age pottery, Area 3000B: 59. Roundhouse RH3

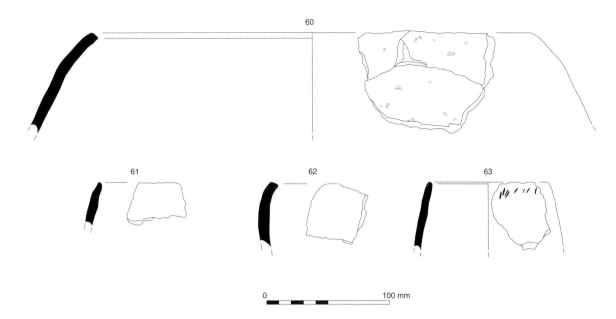

Figure 4.15   Late Bronze Age pottery, Area 3000B: 60–3. Waterhole 2042

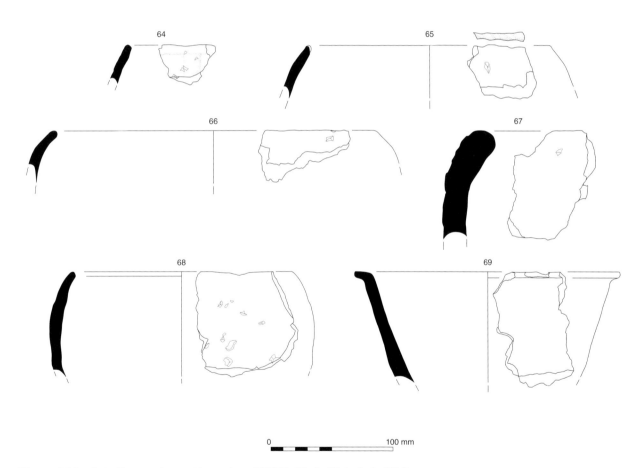

Figure 4.16   Late Bronze Age pottery, Area 3000B: 64–9. Waterhole 1118

47. Hooked rim, ovoid jar, IF2, 5% of 100 mm R12 rim, brittle effect to firing condition, PRN 4292, 1128.
48. Ovoid jar, F6, 8% of 160 mm R11 rim, PRN 4293, 1128.
49. Hooked rim, ovoid jar, F3, <5% of R12 rim, PRN 4294, 1128.

50. Ovoid jar, F6, <5% of R11 present, decorated with apparently random but generally horizontal, incised lines, PRN 4295, 1128.
51. Hooked rim, ovoid jar, F3, 7% of 140 mm R12 rim, PRN 4319, 1139.

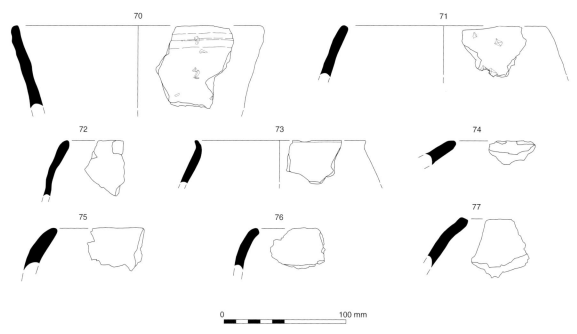

Figure 4.17   Late Bronze Age pottery, Area 3000B: 70–7. Waterhole 1118

52. Bipartite bowl, F9, 25% of 120 mm R6 rim; smoothed on exterior; PRN 4320, 1141.
53. Hemispherical bowl with slight shoulder, F10, 7% of 180 mm R1 rim, wiped on exterior; PRN 4346, 1141.
54. Straight-sided jar, IF5, 21% of 360 mm R16 rim, wiped on exterior; PRNs 4347/4375/4379, 1128/1141/1140.
55. Hooked rim, ovoid jar, F3, <5% of R12 rim, PRN 4358, 1141.
56. Ovoid jar, F3, 6% of 190 mm R11 rim, PRN 4367, 1140.
57. Ovoid jar, IF3, <5% of R11 rim, PRN 4370, 1140.
58. Hooked rim, ovoid jar, IF3, <5% of R12 rim, wiped on exterior, PRN 4371, 1140.

Roundhouse RH3

Figure 4.14

59. Hooked rim, ovoid jar, F3, 6% of 320 mm R12 rim, decorated with fingertip impressions on inner edge of rim, brittle effect to firing conditions, PRN 4670, 1728 (posthole 1727).

Waterhole 2042

Figure 4.15

60. Ovoid jar, IF2, 25% of 360 mm R11 rim, wiped on exterior, PRNs 4774/4782, 2038/2024.
61. Ovoid jar, F1, 10% of 100 mm R11 rim, wiped on exterior, PRN 4786, 2024.
62. Hooked rim, F1, <5% of R12 rim, PRN 4789, 2024.
63. Ovoid jar, IF2, 10% of 100 mm R11 (or R16) rim, finger nail decoration below rim, PRN 4790, 2024.

Waterhole 1118

Figure 4.16

64. Ovoid jar, F7, <5% of R11 (or R12) rim, PRN 4138, 1053.
65. Ovoid jar, F7, 5% of 200 mm R11 rim, slight impressions on rim, PRN 4159, 1053.
66. Hooked rim, ovoid jar, FG1, *c* 12% of *c* 260 mm R12 rim, PRN 4167, 1054.
67. Ovoid jar, F12, <5% of R11 rim, PRN 4169, 1054.
68. Ovoid jar, IF4, 10% of 180 mm R11 rim, PRN 4171, 1054.
69. Flanged rim bowl, IF4, 7% of 220 mm R5 rim, PRN 4173, 1054.

Figure 4.17

70. Conical or hemispherical bowl, IF2, 5% of 200 mm R1 rim, PRN 4185, 1054.
71. Ovoid jar, F7, 10% of 160 mm R11 rim, PRN 4188, 1054.
72. Ovoid jar, F1, <5% of R11 rim, PRN 4193, 1054.
73. Everted rim, sloping shoulder jar, F6, 8% of 140 mm R15 rim, PRN 4198, 1054.
74. Ovoid jar, F11, <5% of R11 rim, PRN 4199, 1054.
75. Ovoid jar, F2, <5% of R11 rim, PRN 4201, 1054.
76. Ovoid jar, F3, <5% of R11 rim, PRN 4202, 1054.
77. Hooked rim, ovoid jar, F5, <5% of R12 rim, PRN 4229, 1064.

Watching brief pottery

Introduction

A total of 147 sherds (807 g) of middle and late Bronze Age pottery was recovered. The range of fabrics represented amongst this assemblage is the same as that identified during the detailed excavation of RBP2. The range of forms is also the same, with the addition of two new rim forms. The pottery was derived from a variety of feature types including postholes, a ditch, a pit or tree-throw hole and the burnt mound. The condition of this material is generally very good, and therefore in contrast to much of the main assemblage with only two sherds in a flaked condition and very few which are ironised. The burnt mound produced body sherds, apparently from the same vessel which had been extremely overheated, creating a bloated and distorted appearance.

Fabrics

Among the late Bronze Age pottery, the commonest fabric types are F1 (36%), F11 (28%) and IF2 (15%) which is similar to the frequency of these fabrics from the main excavations. Minor fabric types include F2 (17%), F7 (4%) and IF1 (3%), with all others represented by 2% or less with the assemblage. There are three body sherds (2%) of middle Bronze Age pottery made from fabric F16. The provenance of the pottery by fabric is presented in Table 4.20, and the form types are shown in Table 4.21.

Forms and context

Only seven rims, two bases and a single angled shoulder sherds were identified. Four of the rims were from ovoid jars, two simple ovoids (R11) and two hooked rim types (R12). A single example from a bowl (R3: Fig. 4.18.78) was recovered from the top of an unexcavated posthole. A probable shouldered jar (R18: Fig. 4.18.79) which had been extremely overheated and twisted out of shape was also identified. This vessel appears to have been a bipartite or shouldered jar with a strongly everted rim which suggests it may have been similar to vessel types 10 and 11 of RBP1 (Bradley and Hall 1992a, figs 442–3) and is not dissimilar to R22 from RBP2 (Fig. 4.8.15). In addition, a simple, slightly everted rim with a rounded appearance from a necked vessel of uncertain profile (R23: Fig. 4.18.80) was found in the secondary fill (91) of a pit or tree-throw hole (89).

The largest group of sherds with identifiable form was recovered from the burnt mound and includes two ovoid jars, the distorted, bipartite or shouldered jar with everted rim, a simple flat base and the angled shoulder sherd from another bipartite vessel. The original collection from the mound included

Table 4.20   Quantification of pottery from watching brief by context and fabric type

Feature Test pit	Context	F1 no.	F1 wt g	F2 no.	F2 wt g	F3 no.	F3 wt g	F5 no.	F5 wt g	F7 no.	F7 wt g	F11 no.	F11 wt g	F16 no.	F16 wt g	IF1 no.	IF1 wt g	IF2 no.	IF2 wt g	IF3 no.	IF3 wt g
Test pits																					
TP28–32	5	1	11	–	–	–	–	–	–	–	–	–	–	3	30	–	–	–	–	–	–
TP28, feature 7	6	1	5	8	8	2	42	–	–	–	–	20	36	–	–	–	–	4	33	–	–
?TP29	29	–	–	–	–	–	–	1	11	–	–	–	–	–	–	–	–	–	–	–	–
4-Post structure 132																					
Posthole 82	31	2	47	–	–	–	–	–	–	–	–	–	–	–	–	–	–	–	–	1	50
Posthole 83	32	5	36	–	–	1	16	–	–	–	–	1	5	–	–	–	–	–	–	–	–
Postholes																					
Posthole 59	35	23	118	–	–	–	–	–	–	–	–	19	43	–	–	–	–	–	–	–	–
Posthole 60	34	1	10	2	18	–	–	–	–	–	–	–	–	–	–	–	–	–	–	–	–
unexcav posthole	30	–	–	–	–	–	–	1	24	–	–	–	–	–	–	–	–	–	–	–	–
unexcav posthole	33	–	–	–	–	–	–	–	–	–	–	–	–	–	–	–	–	17	95	–	–
Ditch																					
Ditch 56	55	1	5	–	–	–	–	–	–	–	–	–	–	–	–	–	–	–	–	–	–
Burnt mound complex																					
Burnt mound	67	9	41	–	–	–	–	–	–	6	62	–	–	–	–	–	–	1	4	–	–
Pit/Treehole																					
Feature 89	90	9	17	–	–	–	–	1	7	–	–	1	2	–	–	4	18	–	–	–	–
	91	1	9	–	–	–	–	–	–	–	–	–	–	–	–	1	4	–	–	–	–
Total		53	299	10	26	3	58	3	42	6	62	41	86	3	30	5	22	22	132	1	50
%		36.1		6.8		2.0		2.0		4.1		27.9		2.0		3.4		15.0		0.7	

Table 4.21 Quantification of pottery from watching brief by context and form

| Feature | Context | Form Types | | | | | | |
Test pit		R3	R11	R12	R18	R23	B1	A1
Test pits								
TP28-32	5	–	–	–	–	–	1	–
TP28, feature 7	6	–	1	–	–	–	–	–
4-Post structure 132								
Posthole 83	32	–	–	1	–	–	–	–
Postholes								
unexcav posthole	33	1	–	–	–	–	–	–
Burnt mound complex								
Burnt mound	67	–	1	1	1	–	1	1
Pit/treehole								
Feature 89	91	–	–	–	–	1	–	–
Total		1	2	2	1	1	2	1

three ovoid jars, the shoulder from a bipartite jar, a straight-sided jar, a slack-profile jar (Fig. 4.8.8–14) and the zig-zag decorated everted rim vessel (Fig. 4.8.15) which had also been overheated and distorted in form. The distorted rim from the watching brief is most likely to have been contemporary with the bipartite jars (R14, A1 jar examples) based on form. The infrequency of this type with the rest of the RBP2 material must be chronologically significant; only eight other examples of bipartite jars were recovered. The watching brief examples reinforce the interpretation that the mound is the latest prehistoric feature in the RBP2 Area 3000B since straight-sided (R16) and ovoid jars (R11 and R12) are clearly derived from the middle Bronze Age vessel repertoire of the Thames Valley. While bipartite vessels, both jars and bowls, are a diagnostic late Bronze Age pottery style which continues to be used in the early Iron Age.

Overheated sherds

The group of six overheated sherds from the burnt mound are bloated, twisted and distorted quite severely due to the apparent melting of the fabric: they appear to be from the same bipartite or shouldered jar. Both surfaces and the broken edges of these sherds are pitted due to the incineration or evaporation of unidentified inclusions. The fabric is porous and extremely light in weight and the typical density of the flint-tempered ware has gone.

The condition of this vessel and the decorated rim sherds from the detailed RBP2 excavations (Fig. 4.8.15), is similar to that of many sherds recovered from the postholes of an early Iron Age double ring post-built roundhouse at Brighton Hill (South Site X/Y) which had been burned down (Morris 1992, 13–16, table 3, fig. 6). This pottery was examined by Andrew Middleton (British Museum) using scanning electron microscopy which revealed that the pottery had been heated to about 100°C for up to 1 hr. The distorted sherds from the excavation and watching brief phase RBP2 must have been subjected to a similar temperature. It is not clear whether this was due to the activity which created the burnt mound and incorporated these sherds in the creation of the mound. Alternatively, the extreme temperature could have occurred elsewhere and the sherds may represent redeposited material within the burnt mound structure. The infrequency of distorted sherds within the mound suggests that the burning activity had occurred elsewhere, with the mound itself being an above ground pile of waste. Only eight other distorted and bloated sherds from different vessels, based on fabric variation, were recovered as isolated occurrences elsewhere within the RBP2 excavations.

Catalogue of illustrated pottery

Figure 4.18

78. Bowl, IF2, <5% of R3 rim, wiped on exterior, PRN 6019, 33 (unexcavated posthole).

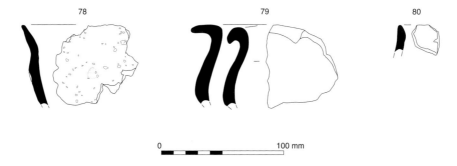

Figure 4.18 Late Bronze Age pottery: 78–80. Watching brief area

79. Probably bipartite/shouldered jar, uncertain fabric type, <5% of R18 rim, overheated, bloated, twisted and distorted condition with pitted surfaces due to loss of fabric inclusions, PRN 6030, 67 (burnt mound).
80. Necked vessel, ?IF1, <5% of R23 rim, PRN 6037, 91 (pit/tree-throw hole 89).

Medieval pottery

by Paul Blinkhorn

The medieval pottery assemblage comprised 35 sherds with a total weight of 1089 g. The minimum number of vessels was 0.69. The occurrence per context by number and weight of sherds per fabric type is shown in Table 4.22.

Fabrics

The medieval fabric types can be paralleled with material from other sites in Reading, particularly those on the waterfront (Underwood-Keevil 1997, 144).

F1 – 21 sherds, 781 g, MNV = 0.35. Flint and limestone tempered fabric which is similar to Underwood-Keevil's fabric FLS (ibid.) and also Mellor's East Wiltshire Ware, classified in the Oxford type-series as fabric OXAQ (ibid., 100–6). This fabric is datable to the early 12th century in Hampshire (ibid., 106), but also occurred in small quantities in pre-Conquest deposits at Eynsham Abbey, Oxfordshire (Blinkhorn in press). There are rim sherds from two jars and a full profile of a wide, shallow bowl which shows evidence of having been heated (Fig. 4.19.1).
F2 – Sandy coarseware I. 10 sherds, 192 g, MNV = 0.14. Moderate to dense sub-rounded white, grey and clear quartz up to 0.5 mm. Equivalent to Underwood-Keevil's fabric SM (ibid., 144). Two rim sherds, both from jars.
F3 – Sandy coarseware II. 4 sherds, 116 g, MNV = 0.2. Sparse to moderate clear, sub-rounded quartz up to 0.5 mm. Rare angular white flint and red ironstone up to 1 mm, rare fine silver mica. Equivalent to Underwood-Keevil's fabric SIw (ibid., 144). Rim and spout from a spouted bowl (Fig. 4.19.2).

Chronology

All the wares are typical of pottery of the 11th-12th centuries. The sandy coarsewares are unremarkable, and are very similar to a range of types found in the Thames Valley and its hinterland (cf. McCarthy and Brooks 1988; Mellor 1994), but fabric F1, the East Wiltshire Ware, although in general use from the 12th century, could be pre-Conquest. The total absence of glazed wares in the assemblage suggests that this material belongs to the early part of the currency of these types, as such material occurs on sites in Reading from about the mid-12th century onwards at the latest (Underwood-Keevil 1997, 152). The socketed bowl and wide shallow pancheon are also typical of early medieval vessel forms, although such pots were used throughout the period. It seems most likely therefore that all these groups of pottery date to the 11th or early 12th century.

Discussion

The average sherd weight (31.1 g) is quite large and there is little rim fragmentation (mean = 10% complete) of the assemblage. Also the sherds are not abraded which suggests that the assemblage has remained quite undisturbed since its initial deposition. The partially complete state of the bowl in particular suggests that there was early medieval occupation in the vicinity of these excavations.

Catalogue of illustrated pottery

Figure 4.19

1. Shallow bowl, F1 (OXAQ 1), grey-brown fabric with exterior scorched red, and thick patches of soot on outer body, 5195 (tree-throw hole).
2. Spouted bowl, F3 (SC1), dark grey fabric with inner buff surface and variegated brown and orange exterior, 5083 (ditch).

Table 4.22   Medieval pottery: occurrence per context by number and weight of sherds per fabric type

Fabric context	F1		F2		F3		Assemblage possible date
	no.	wt g	no.	wt g	no.	wt g	
A3017	5	68	–	–	–	–	11th/12th century
5083	10	89	7	121	1	65	11th/12th century
5090	5	93	–	–	2	25	11th/12th century
5195	1	531	–	–	–	–	11th/12th century
5203	–	–	3	71	1	26	11th/12th century
Total	21	781	10	192	4	116	

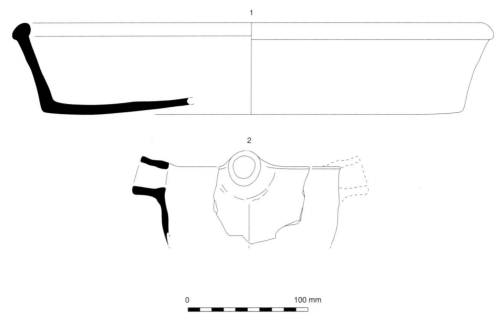

Figure 4.19   Medieval pottery: 1–2. Area 3000B

Fired clay

by Alistair Barclay

Introduction

The fired clay assemblage was mostly recovered from the excavation area, although a significant deposit (75 fragments, 3620 g) of possible hearth clay came from the watching brief. The total assemblage includes 426 fragments (5410 g) of fired clay. The only identifiable objects are fragmentary cylindrical loomweights and part of an oven plate, with the remainder of the assemblage made up of amorphous fragments. The occurrence of possible clay pit lining and the problems of its identification are discussed as part of the prehistoric pottery report (see Morris, this Chapter).

Methodology

The material is quantified by number of fragments and weight (Table 4.23). The fired clay was examined for evidence of wattle or other impressions, possible objects and structural pieces, and the fabrics were recorded.

Fabrics

Six fabrics have been identified (A–F) on the basis of texture and inclusion types. Five of the fabrics (A–D, F) would appear to represent unmodified clay, while fabric E is similar to fabric A, with the addition of crushed calcined flint. This fabric is equivalent to pottery fabric F4 (Morris, this Chapter). Fabric A (context 1014, part of a cylindrical loomweight) was thin sectioned by Williams along with two other fragments of fired clay (Williams, this Chapter).

Loomweights were manufactured from fabric A and rarely fabrics D–E. Part of an oven plate was manufactured from fabric E and amorphous fired clay occurred in all six fabrics.

Fabric types

A – medium-coarse sandy clay matrix with sparse reddish-brown ferruginous pellets, sometimes contains rare flint.
B – as above but with sparse ill sorted flint gravel (3–5 mm).
C – sandy clay with no other inclusions.
D – silty clay with no other inclusions.
E – sandy clay matrix with sparse ferruginous pellets and moderate-common medium (1–3 mm) calcined flint.
F – coarse sandy fabric with sparse, well-rounded clay pellets.

Loomweights

Ten contexts (1012, 1014, 1027, 1030, 1054, 1076, 1697, 1777, 1863 and 2144) contained fragments from cylindrical weights. Typologically these are generally seen as being of mid-late Bronze Age date and are also indicators for the production of textiles on the site. These weights were manufactured from fabric A with the exception of a single weight fragment from context 1027 that was manufactured from fabric E, and a possible weight fragment manufactured in fabric D from 2144. In every case the loomweights were fragmentary and none was more than 25% complete. Three weights (contexts 1014, 1027, 1697: for example see Fig. 4.20) had approximate diameters of 100 mm and a fourth had a diameter of 120 mm (context 1054). One fragment from context 1030 would appear to come from a

Table 4.23 Quantification of fired clay by context, with number of fragments and weight

Context	?Oven plates		Hearth clay		Loomweights		Miscellaneous		Comments
	no.	wt g	no.	wt g	no.	wt g	no.	wt g	
WB 93			75	3620					
Burnt mound									
1012					1	11	1	1	Includes ss.353
1014					8	53	27	66	Includes sf.40, 58, 79, 80, 83–5, 98
1448							35	22	
1466							11	17	
Waterhole									
1016 (1015)					12	116	5	23	Mostly amorphous, some surfaces and ?pottery fragments
Alluvium									
1021							4	8	
1027					3	106			Loomweight fragments
1030					44	283			Fired clay with surviving surfaces as well as amorphous fragments
1054	8	53			1	172	1	3	?Loomweight fragment, ?pottery and amorphous fragments
Postholes (no.)									
1080 (1081)							1	5	
1084 (1085)							1	4	
1176 (1175)							4	8	
1306 (1307)							1	3	
1343 (1344)							1	1	
1404 (1403)							10	30	
1406 (1405)							20	20	
1503 (1504)							1	3	
1505 (1506)							1	1	
1533 (1534)							10	9	
1590 (1600)	1	85					1	3	Part of clay disc or oven plate
1778 (1768)							1	2	Amorphous
1874 (1875)							6	23	
Type 1 pits (no.)									
1714 (1710)							2	2	
1863 (1862)					11	48			Loomweight fragments
Type 2 pits (no.)									
1223 (1269)							30	16	
1777 (1770)					1	52			
1969 (1967)							10	23	
Type 3 pits (no.)									
2116 (pit 2115)							1	1	
Type 4 pits (no.)									
1552 (1551)							6	28	Amorphous
1697 (1551)					1	168	49	213	Includes cylindrical loomweight fragments
1697 (1551)					1	168	49	213	Includes cylindrical loomweight fragments
1707 (1704)							1	1	
Buried soil									
1157							2	17	Amorphous
1456							3	1	
MBA ditch (no.)									
2144 (2147)					1	38			Loomweight fragment, edge piece
Large pits (no.)									
2267 (2271)							3	7	
2268 (2271)							6	6	Amorphous
Total	9	138	75	3620	84	1215	301	780	422 Pieces, 5753 g

massive weight with an estimated diameter in the region of 200 mm. Cylindrical weights were also found at Knight's Farm, while at Aldermaston Wharf most of the weights were of pyramidal form and only two were cylindrical (Bradley *et al.* 1980, 243, 275). It is noticeable from the illustrated weights that the size range (diameter) from these two sites, between 100–150 mm, is comparable to that from Reading. At RBP1 both cylindrical and pyramidal forms were present, although only the former are associated with stratified late Bronze Age pottery. At Pingewood both cylindrical and annular forms occur (Johnston 1983–5, 33).

Fragment of possible oven plate

At least one rim-like fragment in flint-tempered fabric E would appear to be from the edge of an oven plate (1590). These objects have been found on numerous sites in the Middle and Lower Thames Valley and are often assumed to have functioned as part of an oven (Champion 1980, 238). Sometimes these plates can be perforated with six or more holes (Adkins and Needham 1985, 38) and, like the contemporary pottery, are often tempered with flint-grits. Often such plates are found with more substantial deposits of fired clay that are of an amorphous character. Such deposits could be interpreted as the redeposited remains of collapsed oven structures. Of relevance here is a perforated fragment with moulded edge from RBP1. This fragment was originally described as coming from an annular loomweight, but could in fact be part of an oven plate (Bradley and Hall 1992b, 87, fig. 52.1). Interestingly this object was found in a feature that also produced clay slabs and what is interpreted as pit lining. The fabric of this material is generally found to be very similar to that of some of the pottery and it is sometimes difficult to differentiate the two. For this reason the pit lining is discussed within the pottery report (Morris, this Chapter).

Possible hearth clay

The watching brief context produced a large quantity of burnt clay (75 pieces, 3620 g). This deposit would appear to represent the burnt clay base of a hearth or fire that had been dumped in a pit. Alternatively it could represent no more than the firing of the natural clayey subsoil.

Miscellaneous fired clay

The vast majority of the fired clay is of amorphous character (see Table 4.23), although most of this material is fired reddish-brown. The majority probably derives from either hearths, ovens or from the accidental burning of natural clay, for example, through the clearance of vegetation.

Discussion

Fired clay is a good indicator of domestic settlement and is a common find on certain types of prehistoric settlement. Although the assemblage is relatively small, it does provide indirect evidence for textile production in the form of fragmentary loomweights. In this respect it is rather similar to the assemblage found during the previous phase of excavation (Bradley and Hall 1992b, 87). Apart from the loomweights, most of the remaining component of the assemblage includes amorphous fragments. No fired clay evidence for bronze working was identified. Such evidence is generally rare, although mould fragments were found during the previous phase of the excavation (Northover 1992, 87–9). The only other find was part of a probable oven plate fragment that was found in a feature that also produced so-called clay lining (Morris, this Chapter). Oven plates are a common find on later Bronze Age sites in the Lower and Middle Thames Valley (Adkins and Needham 1985, 37), but are less so in the Kennet and Upper Thames Valley.

The fired clay was recovered from a variety of feature types (see Table 4.23). The burnt mound produced a significant quantity of amorphous fired clay (contexts 1448, 1466) as well as a few fragments from cylindrical loomweights (contexts 1012 and 1014). A few fragments of amorphous fired clay also came from the buried soil beneath the mound (contexts 1157, 1456). The cylindrical loomweight fragments were recovered from either pits (1697, 1777, 1863), waterhole 1015 (contexts 1016, 1027, 1030) and from the middle Bronze Age ditch 2147 (fill 2144). In contrast all of the fired clay recovered from postholes is of amorphous character. Possible oven clay was recovered from one of the fills (1054) of the waterhole (1118) that also produced the loomweights, while a fragment of oven plate came from the fill (1590) of posthole 1600, part of structure FP17.

Catalogue of illustrated fired clay

Figure 4.20

1. Fragment from a cylindrical loomweight, *c* 100 mm diameter, fabric A, SF224, 1697 (pit 1551).

Worked stone

by Fiona Roe

Introduction and quantification

A total of 19 pieces of worked stone came from nine contexts in Area 3000B, with one worn pebble from Area 3017. Some stone found in both areas was unworked (Tables 4.24 and 4.25). The assemblage consisted predominantly of probable quern or rubber fragments, including two-thirds of a saddle quern. A further seven pieces appeared to have worked

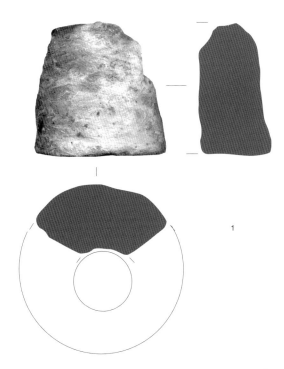

Figure 4.20   Fired clay, Area 3000B: 1. Loomweight, c 100 mm diameter

surfaces. A dolerite polished stone axe and flint hammerstone were also present. A fragment of shale bracelet is discussed separately (Boyle, this Chapter).

Methodology

The stone is quantified by finds type and material. The stone axe was thin sectioned and examined at Imperial College, London. The other finds were examined using a ×8 hand lens.

Materials and sources

Five different varieties of stone were used for artefacts, three of which, sarsen, Tertiary sandstone and flint, came from local sources, while two others came from outside the immediate area. Imported greensand was used for a saddle quern, and dolerite for a Neolithic stone axe.

Local stone

Sarsen was the most frequently used local material, accounting for pieces from seven contexts. Five of these pieces were associated with late Bronze Age pottery, two joining fragments coming from the burnt mound (1014), and the rest from pits (1026, 1173, 1454 and 1695), while two other pieces were undated. This serviceable sandstone was used mainly for querns and rubbers. Tertiary iron-oxide cemented sandstone only occurred in two contexts. It is dark red/purple due to its high iron content,

and was probably too friable for intensive use. The fill (1552) of the late Bronze Age pit (1551) produced six small fragments, one with a worn surface, suggesting possible use as a rubber. The final fill of the pit included three further fragments of the same sandstone. The third material to be utilised was flint, and a hammerstone, now burnt, came from the fill (1173) of a small pit, which also contained late Bronze Age pottery.

All the materials discussed above could have been obtained in the immediate locality, either from primary sources such as the chalklands and the local Tertiary sandstone, or else from secondary sources comprising the Pleistocene gravels of the area. The Plateau Gravel between the rivers Thames and Kennet contains blocks of sarsen, as well as pieces of flint and sandstone (Blake 1903, 68–9). Small blocks of sarsen are common, for instance, in the gravel on Tilehurst Common, located 5.8 km from the site. These gravels would have been a source of material for much of the worked stone on the site, though it may have been necessary to search further afield for sarsen slabs large enough to use as the lower stones of saddle querns (Blake 1903, 83).

Imported stone

A saddle quern (Fig. 4.21.1) made from a distinctive variety of the Lower Greensand was recovered from the upper fill of a late Bronze Age pit (1892). The quern was approximately two-thirds complete and would have measured about 300 × 155 mm. The greensand, which contains small, highly polished quartz pebbles, was available from around Culham, Oxfordshire approximately 35 km from the site.

A stone axe (Fig. 4.21.2) was recovered from buried soil sealed by the burnt mound. Thin sectioning has shown that it is made from a decomposed dolerite, in which all the feldspar and much of the pyroxene has been reduced to a clouded mass. This variety of rock cannot be attributed to any specific source. Both the butt and the blade of the axe have been damaged, but the weathering across the implement suggests that the damage took place after abandonment. The axe may not be of Bronze Age date, but may represent a residual find relating to earlier prehistoric activity, as may the flint hammerstone.

Burnt material

Burnt stone is often found on prehistoric sites as here (Tables 4.24 and 4.25). The large quantity of burnt flint has been described above (Bradley, this Chapter), and the amounts of non-flint material are small. All of the burnt stone could have been collected from the local gravels. Quartzite accounts for the majority of the burnt fragment (630 g), but burnt sarsen also occurs (95 g), with a smaller amount of sandstone (25 g).

Table 4.24 Worked, burnt and unworked stone from Area 3000B

Context	SF	Description	Type of stone	Context type
Worked stone				
–	235	Quern or rubber fragment, worked surface, burnt; now 90 × 65.5 × 50 mm	Sarsen	Unstratified
1014	233	Quern or rubber fragment, worn on two surfaces, partly burnt, fits SF 234	Sarsen	Layer, part of burnt mound feature, LBA pottery
1014	234	Quern or rubber fragment, worn on two surfaces, partly burnt, fits SF 233; together now 158 × 82.5 × 53 mm	Sarsen	Layer, part of burnt mound feature, LBA pottery
1026	–	Fragment with worn surface, burnt; now 61.5 × 39.5 × 23.5 mm	Sarsen	Fill of large pit, cut 1015; LBA pottery
1157	129	Stone axe, nearly complete; 96.5 × 65 × 29 mm max; thin section R 300: Fig. 4.21.2	Decomposed dolerite	Layer, buried soil beneath burnt mound
1173	127	Part of burnt pebble with possible wear, could be a rubber; now 67 × 57.5 × 43 mm	Sarsen	Fill of small pit; LBA pottery
1173	128	Hammerstone, burnt; now 65 × 62.5 × 60 mm	Flint	Fill of small pit; LBA pottery
1454	223	Quern or rubber fragment, weathered, one worked surface; now 140 × 94 × 49 mm	Sarsen	Fill of pit 1453; LBA pottery
1552	–	6 small fragments, one with possible worked surface; part of rubber?	Tertiary iron sandstone	Upper fill of pit 1551; LBA pottery
1695	222	Part of quern or rubber, flat worked surface, burnt; now 102 × 86.5 × 64 mm	Sarsen	Fill of pit 1518; LBA pottery
1697 (2 bags)	–	3 small fragments, unworked, but a possible rubber material	Tertiary iron sandstone	Final fill of pit 1551; overlies 1552 which contained LBA pottery
1876	229	Part of saddle quern, about two-thirds complete, well worn, slightly concave grinding surface, rough on underside; now 205 × 155 × 40 mm: Fig. 4.21.1	Lower Greensand from around Culham, Oxfordshire	Upper fill of pit 1892
Burnt stone				
1040	–	Fragment of pebble; 25 g	Sandstone	Fill of pit, cut 1015; LBA pottery
1054	–	Fragment of pebble; 10 g	Quartzite	Upper fill of pit, cut 1118; LBA pottery
Unworked stone				
1406	–	4 small fragments	Light in weight; might be consolidated ash from burnt wood?	Fill of posthole 1405; LBA pottery

Table 4.25   Worked, burnt and unworked stone (Area 3017)

Context	Description	Type of stone	Context type
Worked stone			
5004	Pebble, burnt, with possible wear on one flat side; 100 × 72 × 52.5 mm	Sarsen	Fill of tree-throw hole 5505
Burnt stone			
5004	2 fragments pebble; 155 g	Quartzite	Fill of tree-throw hole 5505
5004	Fragment; 5 g	Flint?	Fill of tree-throw hole 5505
5019	2 fragments pebble; 25 g	Sarsen	Fill of tree-throw hole 5018
5060	9 fragments pebble; 460 g	Quartzite	Fill of pit 5059
5118	Fragment pebble; 50 g	Sarsen	Upper fill of large pit 5119
5138	Fragment pebble; 5 g	Quartzite	Secondary fill of pit 5136
5206	Fragment; 5 g	Flint	
5317	Fragment; 20 g	Sarsen	
Unworked stone			
5004	Fragment	Malmstone/weathered chert	Fill of tree-throw hole 5505
5004	Small fragment	Quartzite	Fill of tree-throw hole 5505

Discussion

The local lithic materials in use at Reading Business Park may have been utilised in the area since at least the Neolithic period, and the choice of materials in RBP2 may reflect earlier established traditions. Sarsen saddle querns are fairly common on Neolithic sites, such as Wayland's Smithy, Wiltshire (Whittle 1991, 87) and Staines, Middlesex (Robertson-Mackay 1987, 118). The use of sarsen must have been common in areas where it was available. Much broken sarsen was found at Rams Hill, Berkshire (Bradley and Ellison 1975; Reading Museum 1976.71), although querns were not recorded from Bronze Age levels (Bradley 1986, 46). At Pingewood, Berkshire, sarsen quern or rubber fragments had been reused as post packing (Johnston 1983–5, 22; Reading Museum 1979.2). Both sarsen and Tertiary sandstone were in use during the middle Bronze Age at Weirbank Stud Farm, Bray, Berkshire (Montague 1995, 24–5). By the late Bronze Age, sarsen was one of the materials used for saddle querns at Carshalton, Surrey (Adkins and Needham 1985, 38), and it was also one of the main grinding materials in use at Runnymede Bridge (Needham 1991, 136), where the worked stone again also included Tertiary iron sandstone, and also flint pebbles were used as hammerstones (Needham 1991, 136; Needham and Spence 1996, 165). The first phase of excavations RBP1 produced artefacts made from locally obtained stone, similar to those described above, with the addition of tools utilising quartzite pebbles (Moore and Jennings 1992, 93). Such quartzite artefacts are very common in areas where the pebbles can be collected from Pleistocene river gravels. They have been noted in Bronze Age contexts at Wallingford, Oxfordshire (Barclay and

Roe forthcoming) and also at Yarnton Floodplain, Oxfordshire (Roe in prep.).

The smaller and more mundane stone artefacts such as hammerstones and rubbers were not always recorded from early excavations in the Reading area. However, at Runnymede Bridge a wide range of stone tool types was recovered, and an attempt was made to identify their possible uses (Needham 1991, 137). In addition to the basic grinding of corn and the use of hammerstones, many activities were suggested including the sharpening of bronze tools, the sanding of wood, bone or antler, the production of temper for pottery and subsequent burnishing of the pots.

With plentiful supplies of sarsen near to the site, imported quern stone at Reading Business Park was not a necessity. Lower Greensand from Culham may have been considered a superior grinding material, or it may have had prestige value. This greensand, could easily have been brought down the Thames by boat alongside other commodities (Bradley *et al.* 1980, 256). A second saddle quern made from the Culham greensand came from the RBP1 excavations (Moore and Jennings 1992, 93). Further finds of Bronze Age date which utilised this particular greensand are known from Yarnton Floodplain, Oxfordshire (Roe in prep.). Saddle querns of Iron Age date made from Culham greensand have a wide distribution in the Upper Thames Valley, reaching as far north as Steeple Aston (Roe in prep.), and eastwards to Blewburton Hill (Collins 1947, 21; 1953, 49). However, on current evidence the two saddle querns from RBP2 represent the eastern edge of this distribution.

Two other nearby late Bronze Age sites in the Kennet Valley have saddle querns of rock that appears to have been imported over considerable

Figure 4.21   Worked stone, Area 3000B: 1. Saddle quern, 2. Stone axe

distances. At Knight's Farm, Burghfield, a quern of altered gabbro was found (Bradley *et al.* 1980, 275), while at Aldermaston Wharf there was one of granite or diorite (ibid., 245). Boulders of igneous rock of any size are a rare occurrence in the local gravels, and in the immediate area only rhyolite has been recorded at Tilehurst Common (Monckton 1893, 309), and thus these two querns of igneous rock had probably been brought to the sites. At Runnymede Bridge, Lodsworth greensand was brought in from a source in Sussex some 50 km away (Needham 1991, 381; Needham and Spence 1996, 165).

There has been some emphasis on the external contacts of high status sites such as Runnymede Bridge and Petters Sports Field (Longley 1980; Needham and Burgess 1980), where the goods acquired included amber and shale. Knight's Farm and Aldermaston Wharf were considered to be relatively wealthy sites (Bradley *et al.* 1980, 289). For metalworking obtaining copper, tin and lead required far-reaching contacts, and this resulted in the acquisition of unusual varieties of stone being used for querns, moulds and even for bracelets. The Reading Business Park site may therefore have been a somewhat lower status agricultural settlement,

but there was an interest in trade along the Thames, and also the ability to acquire goods from some distance away, such as shale for bracelets. This settlement, along with the neighbouring communities, was not an isolated group.

Catalogue of illustrated worked stone

Area 3000B

Figure 4.21

1. Saddle quern, part of quern of Lower Greensand, about two-thirds complete, well worn, slightly concave grinding surface, rough on underside, now 205 × 155 × 40 mm, SF229 (pit 1892).
2. Stone axe, almost complete, of decomposed dolerite, 96.5 × 65 × 29 mm maximum, SF129, 1157 (soil beneath burnt mound).

Shale bracelet

by Angela Boyle

A fragment of a D-shaped bracelet was recovered from the burnt mound (1014). Shale bracelets are quite common on sites which date to the late rather than the middle Bronze Age and are often of high status. Examples are known from the late Bronze Age enclosure at Eynsham, Oxfordshire (Boyle 2001) and the late Bronze Age riverside settlement at Runnymede Bridge (Needham and Longley 1980, fig. 3.6). Two incomplete shale armlets were recovered from a late Bronze Age settlement at W34 Fargo Wood II, Wiltshire (Richards 1990, 207, fig. 147). The Kimmeridge area of Dorset is the likely source for the shale (Calkin 1953), suggesting that this material was brought some distance to the site.

Catalogue of illustrated shale

Area 3000B

Figure 4.22

1. Shale bracelet, fragment of shale bracelet with D-shaped section: max surviving length 52 mm, thickness 10 mm, SF44, 1014 (burnt mound).

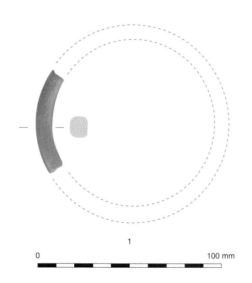

Figure 4.22   Shale, Area 3000B: 1. Fragment of shale bracelet

Worked bone assemblage

by Angela Boyle

Two bone points were recovered from fills (1128 and 5038) of two pits (1127, Area 3000B and 5136, Area 3017). Fill 5038 also contained two sherds of late Bronze Age pottery. Fill 1128 did not contain any pottery, but a substantial quantity of late Bronze Age pottery was derived from the earlier fills of pit 1127, which was located adjacent to a 4-post structure. A third worked piece derived from the burnt mound (1014).

A bone point was recovered from a posthole in association with late Bronze Age pottery during the

RBP1 excavations (Moore and Jennings 1992, 93, fig. 54.643). Similar objects of earlier prehistoric date have also been recovered from Durrington Walls (Wainwright and Longworth 1971, 181, fig 79) and Runnymede Bridge (Foxon 1991, fig. 65.B1).

A single fragment of worked human bone was recovered from context 1037 (SF230). It has been identified as a portion of adult human skull vault (probable parietal) which appears originally to have formed a disc or roundel. The rounded edge has been cut and smoothed and there are cut marks on both the ectocranial (outer surfaces) and endocranial (inner surfaces). In addition, part of a drilled perforation can be seen. The edges have been worn very smooth, perhaps suggesting that the disc was originally suspended. Examples are known from a number of settlement sites of comparable date (Brück 1995, 269–72).

Human cranial fragments were recovered during excavations at Wallingford in 1951, from dark occupation soil described as a midden deposit. The layer contained abundant pottery of late Bronze Age date, animal bone, flint flakes and burnt pebbles as well as bronze metalwork. A date in the 8th century BC was suggested for the site. The presence of human cranial fragments suggested the disposal or perhaps display of human remains at or near the site (Thomas *et al.* 1986) and similar events may have taken place at the Reading Business Park site in the late Bronze Age.

Catalogue of illustrated worked bone

Area 3000B

Figure 4.23

1. Bone point, from animal long bone shaft fragment, tip broken off, surface smoothed and slightly polished, length 77 mm, width 21 mm, thickness 7 mm, SF42, 1128 (waterhole 1127).
2. Worked bone, possible bone point derived from animal long bone shaft fragment, with slight polishing on one edge, length 50 mm, width 18 mm, thickness 4 mm, SF124, 1014 (burnt mound).

Area 3017

3. Bone point, from animal long bone shaft fragment, surface smoothed and polished, particularly towards tip, length 65 mm, width 12.5 mm, thickness 7 mm, SF500, 5138 (pit 5136).

Area 3000B

4. Worked human skull, fragment of adult skull vault, probable parietal, incomplete disc of bone with a partially surviving perforation, smoothed rounded edge and surfaces, cut marks present on both surfaces, maximum surviving diameter 73 mm, thickness 4 mm, SF230, 1037 (waterhole 1015).

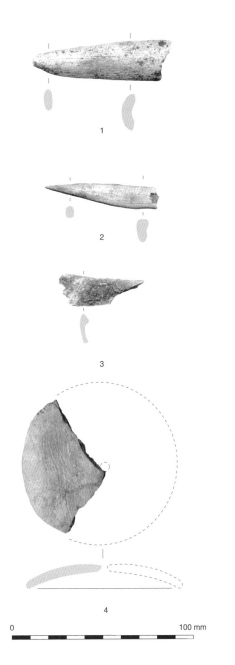

Figure 4.23   Worked bone, Area 3000B: 1. Bone point, 2. Worked bone Area 3017: 3. Bone point. Area 3000B: 4. Worked fragment of human skull

Worked wood

by Maisie Taylor

Introduction

The assemblage of wood from RBP2 represents a reasonable range of woodworking debris, and is particularly interesting because it comes from a series of pits and waterholes. Unfortunately there is not enough material for extensive statistical analyses, and much of the material was broken during excavation. The length of many pieces is listed and where there is a likelihood that the length has been truncated by sampling, the measurement has been placed in parentheses. All the wood is catalogued in Table 4.26.

Species

A relatively limited range of species has been identified. Oak (*Quercus* sp.) is the most common and accounted for more than half of the material. All the other species were much less frequent. It can be difficult to distinguish hazel from alder and as some of the wood from the pit 1551 was very decayed, a precise identification could not be made. Alder (*Alnus glutinosa*), hazel (*Corylus avellana*), and the wood which could not be precisely identified, all occurred in equal quantities, as did field maple (*Acer campestre*). There was also a single sample which was either willow (*Salix* sp.) or poplar (*Populus* sp.). The samples from 1551 showed oak to be the most common species, followed by field maple, which did not occur elsewhere on the site.

Roundwood

None of the roundwood from the site is particularly large and mostly seems to be derived from branch-wood or from coppiced stems. The wood from the pit 1201 is largely branchwood with side shoots, none of which appeared to have been trimmed. The roundwood from 1153 is also branchwood, but of a slightly larger diameter, and some of it is trimmed. There is, however, only a limited amount that can be deduced from branchwood and it could simply represent debris from trimming up a few trunks.

Some of the roundwood from the pit 1551 shows distinct signs of coppicing, with parts of heels and some stems with the distinctive curve associated with the growth of coppiced wood.

The range of species identified from the round-wood is all from shrubs and trees which would have been commonly available in the area.

Stakes

Two stakes were retrieved from the palaeochannel, both were oak. One was roundwood (236) and one was half split (237). The stakes have points shaped from all sides, and although the working was clear, the points were too well finished for the precise shape of the axe to be evident.

Timber and woodchips

The half split timber with a well-made slot from waterhole 1015 is the only finished piece. The remaining pieces, which have been classified as timber, are all debris from timber working or trimming of a felled tree rather than actual timbers. Woodchips were absent from all the samples.

Felled tree

Although there are no actual felled trunks surviving, two fragments of timber debris were almost certainly derived from a felled trunk or trunks. The shape of the end of a felled tree is very distinctive. This end is often trimmed off before wood is split.

Artefact

A wooden disc (SF231, 2328) 16 mm thick and carefully made from split oak was found in water-hole 1015. The disc is almost circular, measuring 130 × 126 mm, with a central hole 33 × 26 mm. The edge of the disc is possibly worn and the edge of the hole is chamfered.

Discussion

Much of the worked wood from the site is oak. Worked oak is common on sites of all periods, as it is a strong and versatile wood, and was often selected for general work, and for fuel. Alder can be common on sites which are low-lying and wet, and willow and poplar are both wet-loving trees. Hazel prefers drier conditions and does not often grow alongside alder and willow. All three are very common species with wood which displays similar properties. They might, for example, be used for small items and, because of their flexibility, for weaving baskets and wattle. The field maple from 1551 was only in a very limited range of diameters, slightly above 20 mm.

The diameter of the roundwood from the site varies from over 50 mm down to less than 20 mm, and a high proportion of the roundwood was found in pit 1551. The sample of roundwood from this context showed that 85% fell within the diameter range 20–40 mm, with some of the remaining pieces being a little larger. This percentage is well over double that of all roundwood at Flag Fen (Taylor 2001), where only 40.49% fall within this size range. All were within the range of diameters used in wattle fencing and building.

Two fragments from felled trees (2040) were found in the fill of waterhole 2042. A large number of felled trunks have been retrieved from Flag Fen and some experimental work has been carried out with replica axes (ibid.). Felled tree ends are very distinctive in shape and often display toolmarks, especially when the felled end is cut off and discarded. Under these circumstances, rough marks where the axe has bitten in are more likely to survive. On a finished artefact, care would be taken to remove these marks, but it is these which are most likely to produce complete profiles. The axe that felled the tree at RBP2 left clear marks 40 mm across and not deeply curved.

A timber from 1015 was half split oak with a slot cut through it. Slots are simply elongated mortices and are cut in a similar way. Cuts are made with an axe, first across the grain, and then along the grain, gouging out the wood between the two cross cuts. This leaves a distinctly 'waisted' shape, which is evident in this fragment. Two timbers worked in a similar way have been identified from the excavations at Flag Fen (Taylor 1992, 491, fig. 14). In all three cases the timber is a half split oak trunk of between 170 and 250 mm diameter. The slotted timber here, however, has a shorter slot than the timbers from Flag Fen, but it is otherwise closely similar. The timber may have been placed in the bottom of the well for someone using the well to stand on, but if this is the case then it was undoubtedly reused.

The wooden disc is very similar in size and fabrication to one from the Iron Age site at Haddenham, with a slightly bevelled edge. The disc is slightly oval (130 × 126 mm) which might suggest that it is the base of a two piece, carved vessel. It is a simple matter to construct a circular stave-built vessel, but much more difficult to find a perfectly circular log or trunk from which to carve a one-piece body. Both this disc and the one from Haddenham are quite small (the Haddenham example is 110 × 100 mm) which would favour a carved body, rather than staves. One piece carved vessels also occur (Taylor 1992), but where the whole vessel is carved from one log, there would be a tendency for the base to split radially as wood shrinks as it seasons. If the base was made from a separate piece, there would still be shrinkage in the body but this could be partly controlled by strapping. Two piece carved vessels occur from the middle of the 1st millennium BC onwards (Earwood 1993, 162). Some vessels have bases that are sewn or pegged into place but the pieces from Reading Business Park and from Haddenham do not have holes to attach them, so they were sprung into place, facilitated by the slightly tapered edge. The hole in the base (33 × 26 mm) is larger than that in the piece from Haddenham (15 × 13 mm), but the edges are not as sharply cut and more chamfered, suggesting that the shape and size of the hole was exaggerated by wear. It is difficult to identify specific functions for parts of artefacts, but the most obvious use for a wooden vessel with a carefully made hole in the base would be as part of a press, such as used in making cheese.

The assemblage does not include any wood chips which might suggest that, although there is debris from working wood, both roundwood and small timber, that there was no woodworking in the immediate vicinity. Some of the roundwood in the large sample was trimmed, but there is not the volume of material or debris to suggest that this was the material from coppicing, as seen at Yarnton. Possibly this roundwood represents off-cuts of coppiced wood, brought in only roughly trimmed and then finished for use on site.

Table 4.26 Worked wood (Area 3000B). All measurements are in mm: measurements in brackets indicate that the length has probably been truncated by sampling

Samples no.	Context and description	No. of samples R=roundwood W=weathered fragments TD=timber debris	R=roundwood TD=timber debris T=timber length × diameter or width × thickness	Description
1	1153, fill of waterhole 1156 R (140) × 50	4 R, 6W Quercus sp. (oak)	R (120) × 55 R (120) × 27 R (72) × 12/14	Quercus sp. (oak) branchwood, possible trimmed 1 end /1 direction Quercus sp. (oak) branchwood, trimmed 1 end /1 direction Corylus avellana / Alnus glutinosa (hazel or alder) very immature stems
2	1201, primary fill of pit 1168	5 R, 1 TD	R (115) × 35/46 R (180) × 33/42 R (100) × 34/45 R (100) × 34/45 R (40) × 22 R (50) × 24 TD (70) × 70 × 20	Quercus sp. (oak) branchwood, badly buckled Alnus glutinosa (alder) branchwood with side shoots, badly buckled Alnus glutinosa (alder) branchwood, buckled Alnus glutinosa (alder) branchwood, buckled Alnus glutinosa (alder) branchwood Alnus glutinosa (alder) Quercus sp. (oak) tangentially split (or hewn) fragment, damaged by roots
3	1776, fill of LBA pit 1770	2 R	small fragments	Quercus sp. (oak)
4	2040, secondary fill of waterhole 2042	2 TD	TD (180) × 155 × 50 T (126) × 155 × 50 fragment	Quercus sp. (oak), very slow grown – possibly debris from trimming up felled tree. Many toolmarks on possible felling face Quercus sp. (oak), very slow grown – possibly other end of above, very deteriorated.
5	2360, SF 236, from the palaeochannel 1879/2361	1 Stake	R 310 × 70	Quercus sp. (oak) trimmed 1 end/all directions, very small axe marks
6	2358, SF 237 from the palaeochannel 1879/2361	1 Stake	R ½ split, 230 × 50 × 42	Quercus sp. (oak), very slow grown – trimmed 1 end/all directions – wood slightly mineralised
7	1015, waterhole	1 T	T ½ split, 1000 × 250 × 85 with slot 400 × 70	Quercus sp. (oak) – broken and badly crushed one end
8	2328, SF 231, waterhole 1015	1 Artefact, Fig. 4.24.1	Disc 130 × 126 × 16 thick, hole 33 × 26	Quercus sp. (oak)
9	1551, pit 3 bags of samples taken	1 T, 1 R, 1 sample bag	T 520 × 72 × 52 thick R approx 24 mm D Sample bag – 40 R frags	Quercus sp. (oak) – tangential split, trimmed across the grain Roundwood – totally dried out in storage 4 pieces were trimmed, 2 trimmed from 2 directions, 2 trimmed in one direction. 2 stems were slightly curved at one end, as from coppicing, and one had part of a possible stool still attached. Diameters ranged from 15–50. 50% sample taken for identification. 20 samples detailed below
			D 16–34 D 22–24 D 30–40 D 32–36 D 33 D 22	Quercus sp. (oak) – 7 samples Acer campestre (field maple) – 4 samples Corylus avellana (hazel) – 4 samples C. avellana / A. glutinosa (hazel or alder) – 3 samples, very decayed Alnus glutinosa (alder) – 1 sample Salix sp./Populus sp. (willow or poplar) – 1 sample

Catalogue of illustrated worked wood

Area 3000B

Figure 4.24

1. Disc of split oak (*Quercus* sp.) 130 x 126 x 16 mm thick, with central hole chamfered hole, 33 x 26 mm, SF231, 2328 (waterhole 1015).

1

0   100 mm

Figure 4.24   Worked wood, Area 3000B: 1. Disc of split oak with central hole

Chapter 5:   Environmental Evidence

Animal bone

by Bob Wilson

Introduction

Over 2000 animal bones from the RBP2 excavations in Areas 3017 and 3000B were examined and recorded. Of these 1862 bones and antler fragments were assignable to chronological periods and 297 could be identified to species level. In the normal hand-picked samples 18% were identified while in the small fragments of the sieved samples only 8% could be identified. The bones were fragmented by sieving and by both old and new breakages, making them difficult to identify and interpret.

Table 5.1 shows the fragment frequencies and percentages of bones according to the abundance of animal species, and of the unidentifiable and burnt debris. Also shown is the number of bones from hand-picked and sieved deposits within each period. The medieval bone assemblage was too small to assess reliably. Table 5.2 provides information on the skeletal parts of the commonest species of animals.

Neolithic assemblage

Pit 5010 contained two unidentifiable bones of Neolithic date associated with Grooved Ware pottery. Some bones from apparently later deposits were separated out before the bones of 17 feature contexts could be discerned as Neolithic, partly due to the distinctive species represented and partly to dating by other archaeological evidence.

Many bones were fragmented and others were further destroyed by burning and were unidentifiable. This included 97% of the unsieved Neolithic bone from pit 5136 (fill 5138) and 14% of the sieved bone dated to the Neolithic from pit 5005 (fill 5004).

Most of the identified bones (68%) came from two pits, 5005 and 5059. Bones were sparsely spread throughout the other 16 features, but present a relatively homogeneous assemblage dominated by pig bones and to a lesser extent by bones of cattle and red deer. Occasional bones of aurochs and beaver were noteworthy as was the virtual absence of sheep and horse bones, as shown on Table 5.1. The sample is small but quite important since some species were not present in the small sample

---

Table 5.1   Fragment frequencies and percentages of animal bones

	Handpicked bone groups					Sieved bone groups	
	Neolithic		Late Bronze Age		Medieval	Neolithic	Late Bronze Age
No. of contexts	18		70		5	6	13
	Frequency	%	Frequency	%	Frequency	Frequency	Frequency
Cattle	21	21	81	66	5	–	6
Aurochs	1	1	–	–	–	–	–
Sheep	1	1	31	25	1	–	2
Pig	63	63	8	7	4	17	–
Horse	–	–	2	2	2	–	–
Dog	–	–	–	–	–	1	–
Red deer	11+31A	11	1	1	–	–	–
Roe deer	–	–	A	+	–	–	–
Beaver	3	3	–	–	–	3	–
Identified	100+31A		124+A		12	21	8
Unidentified	560		626		22	264	93
Total	660+31A		750+A		34	285	101
Burnt bones	228		5		6	41	7

A + Antler fragment

Table 5.2 Fragment frequencies and percentages of the main groups of skeletal elements for the most numerous animal species

Period	Neolithic		Late Bronze Age	
	Cattle	Pig	Cattle	Sheep
No. of bones	21	63	82	31
	%	%	%	%
Head	19	67	51	39
Foot	29	16	7	13
Body	52	17	42	48
% of loose teeth	5	37	28	32
Degradation index				67%

examined from the adjacent site (Levitan1992, table 21). This new assemblage gives a better indication of species presence and abundance.

Bones from all parts of animal carcasses are represented (Table 5.2). About half of the high percentage of pig head elements was due to the abundance of loose teeth recorded. This was due to bone degradation and did not have any special cultural significance such as butchery or ritual activity.

Information on animal mortality patterns was very limited. Three pig jaws showed estimated mandible wear stages (Grant 1982) of 8, 13–16 and 40–42 months, indicating that the animals were dying at different age stages. There were two fused epiphyses of cattle, and one pelvis from a cow.

The evidence suggests the bones were primarily dietary remains and additionally may be indicative of the environment of the Neolithic site. Both woodland and wetland environments are indicated by the presence of wild species, by the abundance of pig and cattle and by the virtual absence of sheep among the domesticated species. It is very difficult, however, to estimate the proximity and extent of these environments as cattle and pig are able to forage successfully in a variety of habitats. The status and role of pigs at Runnymede, for example, has recently been discussed by Serjeantson (1996, 219–23). Another complicating factor is consideration of the density of humans in the area. A low density might allow wild animals like deer to exploit grassland with less need for the shelter of scrub or woodland. A higher density of herders and hunters, and presumably their domesticated animals, might tend to exclude wild species unless significant shelter was available.

Nevertheless, it can be concluded that woodland and wetland were much more evident locally during the Neolithic occupation than during the Bronze Age. Indeed the RBP2 Neolithic assemblage showed some resemblance to that from the Mesolithic site of Thatcham (King 1962; Robinson and Wilson 1987, table 1).

Late Bronze Age assemblage

Bones were sparsely but homogeneously spread throughout the 70 feature contexts of this period with no context yielding many identifiable bones. Few burnt bones occurred in this group compared to the Neolithic group. General preservation of bones was not specially good and a bone degradation index calculated from the late Bronze Age sheep bones and teeth (Wilson 1985; see Table 5.2) gave a figure of 67%, which is fairly typical of prehistoric bone collections from the Thames river gravel sites. Better and much worse preservation has been seen on sites elsewhere such as Watkins Farm and Mingies Ditch, Oxfordshire (Wilson 1990, table T12; Wilson 1993, table T41).

Cattle bones predominated in the RBP2 assemblage with more sheep bones and far fewer pig, deer and other wild species bones than in the Neolithic assemblage (Table 5.1). The carcass part-representation of the cattle and sheep is not unusual although loose teeth comprise half of the head debris of cattle and most of the head debris of sheep (Table 5.2).

The higher percentage of bones from larger species and the lack of burnt bones could suggest that the animal bones had originated on the periphery of the settlement (Wilson 1996), but this was not the case as houses were apparent in the RBP2 excavations of Area 3000B. The percentages of cattle, sheep and pig in the RBP1 assemblage (Levitan 1992) were similar to the RBP2 excavations and it may be that the species differences observed were determined less by taphonomic factors and more by culture and environment. In this RBP2 assemblage, and also that of RBP1 (ibid.), the mandible wear stages of the cattle suggest that most were killed before they reached maturity. The mandible wear stage of one sheep suggested a moderately mature animal at death.

The species presence and abundance results indicate woodland environments were more remote than during the Neolithic, as the Bronze Age percentages of pig and deer bones were very low. The sizeable increase in the percentage of late Bronze Age sheep bones indicates more grass pasture was available for grazing. The surrounding meadowland was largely treeless, and its dampness would have favoured cattle, and tended to exclude deer and perhaps beaver.

Human skeletal assemblage

by Angela Boyle

Middle Bronze Age cremations

Segmented ring ditch, Area 3017

A single deposit of cremated human bone (5151) was recovered from the fill (5095) of a section (5094) through the segmented ring ditch in Area 3017 (Fig. 2.2). The section was located approximately 2.70 m

Table 5.3 Cremation details (Areas 3017 and 3000B)

Context	Wt g	Age	Sex	Identifiable bones	Minimum no. of individuals	Comments
Segmented ring ditch						
5151	542	Adult	Prob Female	Skull vault, dentition, mandible, ribs, vertebrae (including odontoid), ulna, radius, femur, tibia, patella, fibula, metapodials	1	A single fragment of slightly charred animal bone was identified; no charcoal was present: possible date MBA
MBA ditches						
1158	182	Adult	?	Skull vault, mandible, dentition, rib shaft, long bone shaft fragments	2	–
		Sub-adult	–	Skull vault		
1160	1215	Adult	?		2	–
		Sub-adult	–	Skull vault, dentition, odontoid process Skull vault, orbit, maxilla, mandible, dentition, rib shaft, vertebrae, long bone fragments		
Possible late Bronze Age features						
1163	9	–	–	Long bone fragments	1	–
1308	11	Adult	Male?	Skull vault, long bone shaft	1	Pit truncated by field drain
1343	<1	–	–	–	1	–
1857	141	–	–	Skull vault, long bone	1	–

from the western terminus of the southern segment. The cremated material was uncontained and there were no associated artefacts. The deposit weighed 542 g and comprised the partial remains of a possible adult female. Flint and animal bone were recovered from the fill of this segment. The cremated bone was uniformly white and well calcined with the exception of two fragments. The detailed analysis of the cremated material appears on Table 5.3. An associated pig humerus gave a single radiocarbon date of 1700–1440 cal BC (93.1% confidence NZA 9508, see Table A1.1).

Pit 1159, Area 3000B

A single deposit of cremated human bone was contained within a complete middle Bronze Age pottery vessel 1160 which had been placed in a small pit 1159. A second pit 1753 contained a similar vessel but there was no associated cremated bone. Both pits were located within the area of the middle to late Bronze Age ditches which formed part of a field system (see Fig. 3.1).

Pit 1159 was circular in plan, 0.60 m in diameter and 0.15 m deep, with slightly sloping sides, a flat bottom and two fills. The primary fill 1158 was dark grey sandy loam mixed with cremated bone and located immediately around the urn, and the secondary fill 1174 was loose grey silty sand with frequent gravel inclusions. A middle Bronze Age

Deverel Rimbury urn (Fig. 4.7.1) had been inverted in the pit and its base was truncated by later ploughing. The urn was lifted and excavated in spits as described below, and all the spits were dry and wet sieved. No structured deposition of the bone was identified.

Spit 1 – the upper fill of the vessel was ploughsoil which had slumped into the inverted pot when the base was damaged. This fill was dark brown silty clay 0.01 m thick with a coarse sand component and 35% gravel. Pieces of burnt flint and pottery were present, and less than 2 g of burnt bone was recovered.

Spit 2 – a shallow uneven layer measuring up to 0.02 m thick. This was dark brown silty clay with 20% gravel, and a small quantity of burnt flint and pottery. About 5 g of burnt bone was recovered.

Spit 3 – this was dark black clay which contained pottery. A total of 117 g of burnt bone was recovered during hand excavation and a further 34 g after dry and wet sieving.

Spit 4 – this was the most substantial layer and most of the burnt bone was contained within it. It was very black silty clay containing quite substantial pieces of charcoal.

Spit 5 – this was a dense concentration of burnt bone confined to a single quadrant of the vessel.

In pit 1159 the cremated bone from the pot weighed 1215 g and comprised the mixed partial remains of at least two individuals, an adult and a sub-adult (Table 5.3). Cremated bone from pit fill 1158 weighed 182 g and also represented the

Table 5.4   Charred plant remains

Taxa		501–7 5004 Neolithic pit	557–61 5074 Neo. ring ditch	609 5160 Neo. pit	611 5164 Neo. pit	– 1158 BA cremation	– 1160 BA cremation	47–8 1065 LBA waterhole 1118	100–3 1153 LBA waterhole 1156
Cerastium sp.	mouse-ear chickweed	–	–	–	–	–	–	1	–
Montia fontana L.	blinks	–	–	–	–	–	1	–	–
Chenopodium cf *album* L.	fat hen	–	–	–	–	–	1	–	–
Chenopodiaceae indet.	–	–	–	–	–	–	1	–	–
Medicago type	medick, clover etc	–	–	–	–	–	–	–	3
Vicia / Lathyrus sp.	vetch/ tare	–	–	–	–	–	–	1	–
Leguminosae (small) indet.	small legume	–	–	–	–	1	–	–	–
Rubus fruticosus agg.	blackberry	–	–	–	–	–	–	1	–
Prunus spinosa L.	sloe	–	1	–	–	–	–	–	1
Polygonum sp.	bistort, knotgrass	–	1	–	–	–	–	–	–
Corylus avellana L. (nut frag)	hazel	288f (3)	–	259f (4)	682f (4)	–	–	–	–
Sambucus nigra L.	elder	–	1	–	–	–	–	–	–
Poa annua type	annual meadowgrass	–	–	–	–	–	–	1	–
Bromus sp.	brome	–	–	–	–	–	–	1	1
Arrhenatherum elatius ssp. *bulbosum* (Wild.) Schübler & Martens (tuber)	onion couch	–	2	–	–	–	–	–	–
Gramineae (large) indet.	grass	–	–	–	–	–	–	–	1
Gramineae (small) indet.	grass	–	–	–	–	–	–	–	2
cf Gramineae indet.	grass	1	–	–	–	–	–	–	–
Triticum dicoccum (Schrank) Schübl. (glume base)	emmer wheat	–	–	–	–	–	–	11	–
T. dicoccum type (grain)	emmer wheat	–	–	–	–	–	1	–	–
T. cf *dicoccum* (spikelet fork)	emmer wheat	–	–	–	–	–	–	1	–

T. cf dicoccum (rachis internode)	emmer wheat	–	–	–	–	–	3	–
T. cf dicoccum (glume base)	emmer wheat	–	–	–	–	–	2	1
T. monococcum / dicoccum (glume base)	einkorn or emmer wheat	–	–	–	–	–	–	1
T. spelta L. (glume base)	spelt wheat	–	–	–	–	–	1	1
T. dicoccum / spelta (grain)	emmer or spelt wheat	–	–	–	–	–	1	–
T. dicoccum / spelta (glume base)	emmer or spelt wheat	–	–	–	–	–	4	1
Triticum, cf free-threshing type (grain)		4	–	–	–	–	–	–
Triticum sp. (grain)	wheat	–	–	–	–	–	2	1
Triticum sp. (glume base)	wheat	–	–	–	–	–	2	1
Triticum sp. (spikelet fork)	wheat	–	–	–	–	–	–	–
cf *Triticum* sp. (grain)	wheat	–	–	1	–	–	–	–
Hordeum vulgare ssp. *vulgare* L. (rachis)	six-row barley	–	–	–	–	–	–	1
Hordeum sp. (hulled twisted grain)	hulled barley	–	–	–	–	–	1	–
Hordeum sp. (grain)	barley	–	–	–	–	–	1	–
Hordeum sp. (rachis)	barley	–	–	–	–	–	1	1
Secale / Hordeum sp. (rachis)	rye or barley	–	–	–	–	–	2	2
Cereales indet. (grain)		–	1	–	–	–	1	–
Cereales indet. (rachis frags)		–	–	–	–	–	–	3
tuber indet.		–	1	–	–	+	–	–
moss stalk		–	–	–	–	–	–	1
Ignota		–	2	–	–	–	1	1
Total no. of items identified		293	8	260	682	8	40	23
Litres of soil sieved		113	75	60	8	18	16	40
Items per litre		2.59	0.11	4.3	85.25	0.44	2.5	0.58

remains of at least two individuals, an adult of unknown sex and a sub-adult. On excavation it was thought that the bone around the urn was not the result of accidental spillage of the contents of the urn. However, as adult and sub-adult bones were present in both contexts, both within and outside the urn, it seems very likely that the cremations had been combined by later disturbance. The adult remains predominated in fill 1158 around the urn while the sub-adult remains were mainly in the urn 1160 (Fig. 3.4). Two odontoid processes were present in deposit 1160 and both have been tentatively identified as adult. Given the fact that no further duplicate adult bones could be identified the possibility that the second odontoid represents an accidental, rather than a deliberate inclusion, must be considered.

A single radiocarbon date of 1220–890 cal BC (92% confidence NZA 9422; Table A1.1) was obtained from charcoal associated with the cremation deposit 1160 found within the Deverel Rimbury urn in pit 1159. The dating of the pottery in this context is discussed in Chapters 4 and 6.

Discussion

The largest cremation deposit 1160 came from the near complete Deverel Rimbury bucket urn, where it would have been protected as the urn was inverted in a pit. Charcoal associated with the cremation gave a date in the late 2nd to early 1st millennium BC. Bronze Age pottery of this type is well known and often associated with cremations both in the Thames and Kennet Valley region and elsewhere (Morris, Chapter 4). Cremations of this period have also been found to be associated with contemporaneous field systems at other similar sites elsewhere, such as Weir Bank Stud Farm, Bray (Barnes and Cleal 1995, 18).

Possible late Bronze Age cremations

Two deposits of cremated bone, 1163 and 1343, were associated with late Bronze Age pottery. Cremation deposit 1163 was found in pit 1114 which had a distinctive fill of black sandy loam with charcoal and burnt sand. Cremation 1343 was found in posthole 1344 of RH3. Two further cremations, 1308 from badly truncated pit 1309 and 1857 from pit 1859, were undated but possibly late Bronze Age. Three of the cremations could not be aged or sexed; 1163 of 9 g, 1343 of 1 g and 1857 of 141 g. Cremation deposit 1308 weighed 11 g and was identified as adult and possibly male.

Deposit 1308 from pit 1309 was located 0.10 m south-east of pit 1159 which contained the complete middle Bronze Age bucket urn. Pit 1309 was circular in plan, 0.50 m in diameter and 0.08 m deep, with sloping sides and a flat bottom. However, a field drain cut through the centre of the pit and this deposit remains undated.

Three late Bronze Age cremations were also recovered during RBP1 excavations (Boyle 1992, 98). These ranged in weight from 60 g to 700 g and all comprised the partial remains of unsexed adult individuals.

Charred plant remains

by Gill Campbell

Introduction

A series of samples were taken from contexts of Neolithic and Bronze Age date for the recovery of environmental remains. Samples were taken from the burnt mound and from most of the late Bronze Age pits and waterholes including those which were waterlogged. Samples were floated onto a 0.5 mm mesh with the residue being retained on a 0.5 mm mesh. The preservation in waterlogged features was rather poor and no analytical work was undertaken on these samples as nothing could be added to the information obtained from waterlogged features analysed during the previous excavation phase (Campbell 1992). However two Bronze Age waterholes did produce well preserved charred plant remains, and assemblages from these two contexts were analysed.

Elsewhere on the site the preservation of charred plant material was similar to that found in the previous excavation phase (ibid.) with the exception of Area 3017 where well preserved material was recovered from Neolithic features. Samples from the burnt mound were also rather disappointing, as they contained no charred plant remains other than charcoal. This would appear to be consistent with results from the sampling of other burnt mounds in the country (P Murphy, pers. comm.)

In addition to the two samples from late Bronze Age waterholes, samples from three Neolithic pits and one from the segmented ring ditch were analysed along with samples from the two Bronze Age cremations. The results are given in Table 5.4. Nomenclature follows Clapham *et al.* (1989), excepting Miller (1987) for wheat, and Zohary and Hopf (1994) for barley.

Results

The Neolithic samples with the exception of those taken from the segmented ring ditch, all produced large numbers of hazelnut shell fragments, although the number of whole hazelnuts that these fragments represented was very few. Several wheat grains, which were short and fat resembling *Triticum compactum* Host. were found in pit fill 5005 while a single seed of *Sambucus nigra* L (elder) was recovered from gully 5075 (fill 5074).

The assemblages from the two cremations included a seed of *Montia fontana* (blinks) and indeterminate tuber fragment. The assemblages from the two waterholes were much more substantial and included chaff from both emmer and spelt wheat and remains of six-row hulled barley.

Discussion

The assemblages from the Neolithic contexts are typical of this period and have been interpreted as evidence for the continued use of woodland resources alongside the cultivation of cereals (Moffett *et al.* 1989). This aspect of the Neolithic economy has recently been the subject of much debate (Thomas 1991, 20–1, 80; Legge *et al.* 1998; Robinson 2000). However while the frequencies of hazelnut shell vs cereal grain cannot be taken as an indication of their relative importance in the economy, they can be regarded as the result of particular activities which are largely absent in later prehistory. It is possible that hazelnut shells were used as a fuel or for particular ritual activities. These could also be used for the drying of cereal grain prior to grinding.

The results from the Bronze Age cremations are also typical of this type of deposit. Most remains in cremations of this date, with the exception of cereal grain, probably derive from local vegetation or turf burnt during the cremation process rather than food offerings.

The two late Bronze Age waterholes produced the largest assemblages and form a useful comparison with the charred plant remains recovered from the RBP1 excavations (Campbell 1992). These assemblages from the waterholes produced mainly chaff, including emmer wheat rachis internodes and barley rachis fragments. This would appear to represent waste from threshing or winnowing (Hillman's stage 5–7, Hillman 1981, 132–5) and therefore indicates that the inhabitants were growing their own crops. This is unlike the impression given by the RBP1 excavation where the absence of rachis fragments and culm nodes was taken to suggest that cereals were being transported to the site in their hulls and were grown elsewhere. In addition, the Bronze Age waterholes produced evidence for spelt wheat which was absent in the samples from the previous excavation.

Overall the charred plant evidence from the site still contrasts with the evidence from other locations in the Thames Valley (Clapham 1995; Greig 1991). Other sites have produced rye and possibly oats. In addition, spelt wheat is generally more common in the Thames Valley.

Pollen analysis of a Bronze Age waterhole

by Robert Scaife

Introduction

Pollen analysis of this late Bronze Age waterhole feature (1015) (column <257>) was undertaken in conjunction with plant macrofossil analysis (Campbell this Chapter) in order to provide information on the character of the local vegetation and environment. Well preserved pollen was obtained from the lower waterlogged silts of the profile thus providing data on the local habitat. The upper section was, however, drier with much poorer pollen preservation and skewing of the assemblages in favour of those with strong exines pollen walls (exine). Taphonomy of pollen in such contexts may be complex but useful information can be gained on local prehistoric land use.

Methodology

Samples for pollen analysis were taken from the excavated sections using box monolith profile tins. The chosen monolith was sub-sampled and described in the laboratory. Standard techniques were used for the extraction of the sub-fossil pollen and spores (Moore and Webb 1978; Moore *et al.* 1991). Micromesh sieving at 10 μm was used to assist with the removal of clay. Samples of 2 ml volume were used and absolute pollen frequencies were measured using exotic markers/spikes (Stockmarr 1971: *Lycopodium* spores) to the known sample volume. A pollen sum of 300 total dry land pollen was counted (where preservation allowed) for each level plus extant pollen of marsh/wetland taxa and spores of ferns and miscellaneous elements. Taxonomy follows that of Moore and Webb (1978), modified to Stace (1991), according to Bennett *et al.* (1994).

Percentages are calculated as follows:

Pollen sum = % sum of total dry land pollen (t.d.l.p.)
Marsh taxa (Cyperaceae) = % sum of t.d.l.p.+ marsh
Spores = % sum t.d.l.p. + spores
Misc. = % sum t.d.l.p. + misc.

These procedures were carried out in the Department of Geography, University of Southampton. Pollen was identified and counted using an Olympus biological research microscope at magnifications of ×400 and ×1000.

Stratigraphy

The stratigraphy observed in the monolith section during pollen sampling comprised:

Depth cm	
0–7	Sand and gravel
7–22	Grey silty clay
22–35	Grey sand with silty levels, gravel
35–46	Grey clayey silt
46–55	Organic, dark silt with pebbles
55–61	Basal gravel in clay matrix

The pollen data

The pollen assemblages obtained from the 61 cm of this profile can be divided into two broad sections.

The lower (52–34 cm) may be regarded as a local pollen assemblage zone in which pollen preservation was moderate to good with relatively high APF (arboreal pollen frequency) values (to 53,000 grains/ml at 44 cm). The upper half of the profile is markedly different due to the effects of poor pollen preservation, small absolute pollen frequencies (with absence or as low as 1800 grains/ml at 24 cm) and skewing of the data towards those few taxa which have a robust exine (specifically spores of *Pteridium aquilinum* (bracken) and Lactucae (dandelion types) which are present in much greater numbers than in the lower waterlogged sediment. Interpretation must be cautious as this upper zone does not reflect the true vegetation at the time of sediment deposition.

Local pollen zone: 1 (52 cm–34 cm)

This basal unit comprises a diverse range of herbs with few trees and shrubs. For the latter, there are small but consistent values (<5%) of *Quercus* and *Corylus avellana* type. Herbs are dominated by Poaceae (to 65%) with Cereal type (to 8%). Lactucae increase upwards (to 50% at 34 cm). There is a diverse range of herbs compared with the subsequent zone. These include a range of weeds which include *Chenopodium* type, *Polygonum aviculare* type, *Persicaria maculosa* type, *Fallopia convolvulus*, *Rumex* spp., *Plantago lanceolata* and Asteraceae types. *Linum bienne/Linum usitatissimum*, albeit a single grain, is recorded in the basal level. Some wetland types are present and include Cyperaceae, *Typha angustifolia/Sparganium* type. Spores of *Pteridium aquilinum* and *Equisetum* are present.

Local pollen zone: 2 (34 cm–8 cm)

The upper half of the profile has low APF values and pollen is absent in some levels. Pollen counts were small because of the paucity of pollen. Taxonomic diversity is small compared with Zone 1. Lactucae (to 65%) is the predominant taxa with Poaceae, and substantial increase in *Pteridium aquilinum* (to 55% tp [tree pollen] + spores). Other taxa include *Plantago lanceolata* and *Chenopodium* type.

Discussion

Taphonomic factors are especially important in any interpretation of this profile given that the catchment for airborne pollen would have been small and secondary inputs from crop processing and domestic waste might be also present. In addition, post-depositional degradation of pollen has occurred in the upper levels (from 35 cm) of this sediment possibly through drying out and oxidation making this data unreliable. Pollen in the basal levels of Zone 1 was well preserved and is not skewed through such excessive degradation of those grains with thin exines but, however, may be skewed towards local and/or introduced pollen statistically suppressing the ratios of numbers of arboreal elements.

Bearing in mind the above factors, it is clear that Zone 1 provides a more realistic indication of the local vegetation present during the period of deposition. Towards the top of the zone, however, pollen preserving conditions start to deteriorate as evidenced by the expansion of Lactucae. This perhaps marks the top of the groundwater table level (and fluctuations) above which pollen has been degraded. Consequently, the upper Zone 2 is not discussed further.

The inferred vegetation

There is a notable absence of trees and dominance of herbs. Whilst local over-representation of the herbs may have suppressed the numbers of more regional trees and shrubs, it nevertheless appears that woodland was not present in the near/local landscape. Elements which might have been expected in greater quantity such as *Quercus* (oak), *Corylus avellana* (hazel) and especially *Tilia* (lime/lindens) had apparently been cleared by the late Bronze Age, which is the suggested date of the feature. Lime is thought to have been dominant over a larger part of southern and eastern England during the middle and late Holocene prior to widespread late prehistoric deforestation for agriculture (largely during the late Bronze Age but asynchronously from the Neolithic to post-Roman/historic period).

In contrast, there is a strong representation of herbs of agriculture. Cereal pollen and possible associated weeds of cultivation are present including *Polygonum aviculare* (knotweed), *Persicaria maculosa* type (various types including redshank), *Fallopia convolvulus* (black bindweed), *Spergula* type (corn spurrey, Chenopodiaceae (goosefoots and oraches), *Artemisia* (mugwort) and possibly *Sinapis* (charlocks) *Plantago major* (greater plantain or hoary plantain) and *Urtica* (nettle or pellitory). This is clear indication of arable cultivation taking place. However, it should also be considered that these taxa might derive from secondary sources such as crop processing with pollen trapped in the inflorescences (Robinson and Hubbard 1977) being liberated during winnowing and threshing activities. Alternatively, pollen may derive from domestic waste, floor coverings and human and animal faecal material which may have been disposed of in this feature. Pastoral agriculture is less easily distinguished in pollen spectra since grassland taxa may easily derive from 'natural' marsh and floodplain communities. Here, Poaceae (grasses) are dominant and undoubtedly derived from grassland. This however as noted may have derived from the damp floodplain vegetation surrounding the site or from dry grassland pasture. *Linum usitatissimum* (*Linum bienne* type: cultivated and wild flax) is the only other possible cultigen. Flax is extremely poorly represented in pollen spectra producing very small numbers of pollen grains. A Bronze Age pit at West Row Fen, Mildenhall, Suffolk contained *Linum* capsules possibly indicating its use for retting but was certainly evidence of local cultivation (Murphy 1983) contained only a very small number of pollen grains. Although only a single occurrence at Reading, this may be of some significance indicating local flax cropping and/or processing. It should also be considered that the grain might come from *L. bienne* (pale flax).

The sediment fills of waterhole 1015 therefore produced well preserved pollen from the lower waterlogged levels. The upper levels, however, display extreme pollen degradation. Pollen assemblages in such small features are likely to have a small pollen catchment representing on, or very near, site plant communities. There is a notable absence of tree and shrub pollen contrasting strongly with a dominant and diverse range of herbs. This implies that the local region had been deforested for agriculture. This is shown by predominance of pastoral taxa (largely Poaceae; grasses), but also with evidence of cereal cultivation, or crop processing. There is also tentative evidence of flax cultivation.

Wood charcoal

by Rowena Gale

Introduction

Charred seeds and plant macrofossils were relatively rare compared to the charcoal deposits. Charcoal was present in a Neolithic segmented ring ditch, pits and postholes, a Bronze Age burnt mound and cremation and possible medieval contexts. Neolithic features were truncated in the medieval period so the deposits from some ditch fills and a ring gully may be of Neolithic or medieval date. Several other pits (including the fills of tree-throw holes) also contained charcoal and although these were thought to be prehistoric, there were no associated artefacts.

Charcoal samples from these features were assessed for their potential to provide environmental evidence of woodland and on-site use of woodland resources during these periods, with particular reference to the burnt mound. Forty samples were examined, including those from the undated features.

Materials and methods

Charcoal was processed from bulk soil samples by flotation and separated from the seed and other plant remains by Gill Campbell. Fragments measuring >2 mm

in radial cross-section were considered for assessment. The charcoal from the gravel terrace tended to be better preserved than the material from the floodplain. Sediments had permeated through the tissues of all charcoal fragments leaving thin layers deposited on the surfaces of the cell walls, which made the charcoal very difficult to examine. This was probably the result of fluctuations in the water table. Some samples selected for assessment (such as 589 and 587 and three from the cremation 1160) proved to contain insufficient material for identification.

Charcoal fragments for each sample submitted were initially scanned under low magnification, sorted to type based on the anatomical features seen on the transverse surfaces and counted. Representative fragments were selected and prepared for examination by fracturing to expose fresh transverse, tangential and radial surfaces. These were supported in sand. The anatomical structure was viewed using a Nikon Labophot incident-light microscope at up to ×400 magnification. The samples were matched to reference material.

Results

The taxa identified are listed with details of contexts in Table 5.5. The taxa groups included *Acer* sp. (maple), *Alnus* sp. (alder), *Betula* sp. (birch), *Corylus* sp. (hazel), *Fraxinus* sp. (ash), Pomoideae, *Prunus* spp. (blackthorn, cherry and bird cherry), *Quercus* sp. (oak), *Rhamnus cathartica* (purging buckthorn) and Salicaceae. Pomoideae is a sub-family of the Rosaceae, which includes *Crataegus* spp. (hawthorn), *Malus* sp. (apple), and *Sorbus* spp. (whitebeam, wild service and rowan). These genera are anatomically similar. The species of *Prunus* spp. are often difficult or impossible to distinguish from their anatomical structure, however, in this instance the charcoal was more characteristic of blackthorn (*P. spinosa*). Salicaceae includes *Salix* sp. (willow) and *Populus* sp. (poplar) and it is not possible to separate these genera with any certainty using anatomical features.

Neolithic

Pits

Charcoal sample 501–7 from the fill (5004) of pit 5005 and sample 508–10 from the fills (5011, 5012, 5013) of pit 5010 were associated with flint and other remains. Although the charcoal was not particularly well preserved it was relatively abundant. The taxa identified from the samples were more or less similar (see Table 5.5) and included oak (*Quercus*), ash (*Fraxinus*), hazel (*Corylus*), alder (*Alnus*), and members of the Pomoideae (hawthorn, apple, whitebeam, wild service, rowan). The oak was mostly sapwood, except in fill 5013 of pit 5010 which also included heartwood.

Ring ditch 5093

The Neolithic ring ditch was truncated by a medieval field boundary ditch. Artefactual evidence

Table 5.5   Charcoal identifications by context

Context	Sample	Acer	Alnus	Bet.	Corylus	Frax.	Pomoid.	Prun.	Quercus	Rham.	Salic.
5004	501–7	–	–	–	25	3	3	–	20	–	–
5011	508	–	5	–	–	6	–	–	26	–	–
5012	509	–	–	–	–	4	2	–	39	–	–
5013	510	–	–	–	4	14	5	–	12	–	–
1012	352	1	?2	–	?2	–	2	8	13	–	–
	353	–	–	–	–	–	2	4	13	1	–
1014	62	1	–	–	–	–	9	–	33	–	1
	69	–	–	–	–	–	1	–	1	–	1
	372	–	–	–	–	–	1	–	7	–	1
	374	–	–	–	?1	–	2	–	11	–	–
1160	F1	–	–	–	–	–	–	–	1	–	–
	F3	–	–	–	–	–	–	–	–	–	?1
	F4	–	?13	–	?13	–	–	?1	–	–	–
	S4	–	–	–	3	–	–	–	–	–	–
5083	548	–	16	–	–	17	–	–	5	–	–
5090	549	–	8	–	–	3	–	–	–	–	–
5092	590	–	10	–	3	8	–	–	10	–	–
5150	588	–	–	–	1	21	1	5	10	–	–
5017	511	–	–	–	–	–	–	–	7	–	–
5019	513	–	?4	–	?4	3	1	–	2	–	–
5024	516	–	–	–	–	–	?1	–	9	–	–
5062	524	–	–	–	1	–	–	–	1	–	–
5067	541	–	–	–	–	32	–	–	–	–	–
5073	552, 554, 556	–	–	–	1	–	–	3	1	–	–
5074	557, 561	–	–	–	3	–	–	–	2	–	–
5120	571	–	–	–	14	–	1	–	–	–	–
5122	572	–	?2	–	?2	–	–	–	1	–	–
5137	377	–	–	–	–	–	–	–	?1	–	–
5156	608	–	1	–	–	1	–	–	–	–	–
5100	596	–	–	–	–	3	–	–	2	–	–
5160	609	–	?1	–	1	1	–	–	?1	–	–
5164	611	–	6	–	–	–	–	–	?2	–	–
5163	610	–	–	–	–	–	–	–	4	–	–
5175	614	–	–	?3	–	–	–	–	–	–	–

was sparse and organic material from these contexts could relate to either the Neolithic or the medieval period. The absence of burnt material from other parts of the medieval ditch suggested that the charcoal from the fill of the ring gully 5093 was more likely to relate to the Neolithic period. This sample consisted of a large quantity of charcoal, much of which was too small to identify. Oak (*Quercus*) sapwood and fast-grown heartwood was present, also ash (*Fraxinus*), alder (*Alnus*) and hazel (*Corylus*).

Similar comments apply to samples 552, 554 and 556 and 557 and 561 from contexts 5073 and 5074 at the terminal of the ring ditch 5075 where the charcoal was very sparse. Hazel (*Corylus*), oak (*Quercus*) and blackthorn (*P. spinosa*) were identified.

Middle Bronze Age

Cremation 1160

The charcoal fragments were extremely small and sparse, and many of the identifications could not be verified. The pyre fuel included hazel (*Corylus*), oak (*Quercus*), and possibly *Prunus*, willow or poplar (*Salix/Populus*), and alder (*Alnus*).

Late Bronze Age

Burnt mound 1012 and 1014

The mound was extensive and measured 85 × 25 m. Bulk samples 1012 were taken to assess preservation in the mound, and the entire feature was part-sampled using a grid system 1014. Compared to burnt bone and artefacts, which were sparsely present, the charcoal was relatively abundant though comminuted in the samples examined. Charcoal from alder (*Alnus*) and/or hazel (*Corylus*) was particularly poorly preserved and it was impossible to identify these positively. Some charcoal was slightly vitrified and could indicate exposure to temperatures exceeding 800°C. Cinder-like material was present in context 1014 (sample 62).

The taxa identified from the undifferentiated samples and the grid samples were more or less similar and included oak (*Quercus*) sapwood, hawthorn group (Pomoideae), maple (*Acer*), probable blackthorn (*Prunus*), willow/poplar (*Salix/Populus*), purging buckthorn (*Rhamnus cathartica*), and hazel (*Corylus*) and/or alder (*Alnus*). Some taxa occurred more sporadically than others, such as maple, purging buckthorn and willow/poplar. Those most frequent included oak and members of the Pomoideae (for example, hawthorn). The oak was mainly too fragmented to assess the maturity of the wood but sample 62 included pieces of round-wood measuring from 5–20 mm in diameter (the latter estimated).

The accumulation of burnt flints to form such a massive mound presumably occurred over a considerable span of time and must have consumed large quantities of fuel (probably mainly wood). Oak appears to have formed the greater part of the fuel and the absence of heartwood in the charcoal samples suggested that fairly immature wood was used. The use of coppiced rods seems a strong possibility but without more substantial evidence this remains speculative.

Medieval

Ditches 5082 and 5091

Ditches 5082 (fill 5083) and 5091 (fills 5090 and 5092), and a patch of bone 5150 were assigned to the medieval period although the dating is not certain. Alder (*Alnus*), hazel (*Corylus*), ash (*Fraxinus*), oak (*Quercus*), blackthorn (*P. spinosa*) and hawthorn type (Pomoideae) were identified.

Undated samples

A group of pits and postholes 5016 (fill 5017), 5018 (fill 5019), 5023 (fill 5024) and 5061 (fill 5062) were sited on the gravel terrace and were probably associated with Neolithic activity, although there is no artefactual evidence to support this view. Pit 5061 was close to the Neolithic pit 5010 and pits 5016 and 5018 cut through tree-throw holes. Charcoal was sparse and poorly preserved. Oak (*Quercus*) was common to all pits; other taxa included ash (*Fraxinus*), hawthorn type (Pomoideae*)*, hazel (*Corylus*) and possibly alder (*Alnus*).

Charcoal was also present in a number of pits on the floodplain and, by implication, given this siting

they may be of Bronze Age origin. Although the pits usually contained other rubbish, for example, flints, nutshells and bone, the charcoal was meagre and difficult to identify. Pit 5066 (fill 5067) lay adjacent to ditches and other features on the eastern edge of the site and the fill included ash (*Fraxinus*) charcoal. Charcoal was found in other pits on the floodplain including 5161, 5157 and 5119, and oak (*Quercus*), ash (*Fraxinus*), hazel (*Corylus*) and alder (*Alnus*) were identified. Birch (*Betula*) was tentatively identified from pit 5176.

Woodland environment

Neolithic and Bronze Age settlements were based close to the river on acidic flint gravels. The Neolithic structures were probably built on or close to the floodplain but later on, silt deposits narrowed the river channel leaving the settlement on a gravel terrace. The Bronze Age builders subsequently chose their site on the then exposed floodplain.

The charcoal assessment identified a range of trees and shrubs which was more or less consistent throughout the Neolithic and Bronze Age periods. The taxa identified represent only those used for fuel or other purposes. The presence of at least one other species (not included in the charcoal) is verified by the identification of seeds from elder (*Sambucus*) by Gill Campbell.

The abundance of oak charcoal (*Quercus*) associated with the Neolithic period suggested that oak woodland was probably dominant. Ash (*Fraxinus*) and hazel (*Corylus*) may have grown within the woodland, the latter possibly as understorey or in woodland glades. Hazelnut shells were identified in some contexts and these indicate that the trees grew in areas with sufficient light to enable flowering and fruiting to occur. Members of the Pomoideae were also present. Hawthorn (*Crataegus*) is probably the most likely taxon, and hawthorn trees may have grown in fairly open woodland or as scrub. Blackthorn (*P. spinosa*) forms a tall spiny shrub which can rapidly colonise cleared land. At this site it may have grown with hawthorn as scrub or formed dense thickets. Wetland species included alder (*Alnus*) and almost certainly willow (*Salix*) and/or poplar (*Populus*), although the last two were only identified from Bronze Age contexts. These species may have grown densely along the floodplain; the seasonally wet conditions would have suited them well.

The taxa identified from Bronze Age contexts suggested that the woodland element was similar to that of the Neolithic. Additional taxa from this period included maple (*Acer*), birch (*Betula*) and purging buckthorn (*Rhamnus cathartica*) but these were sparse in the charcoal. Birch is usually common on acidic soils although its paucity at this site suggests that it may not have been particularly so here. Purging buckthorn is more characteristic of neutral or alkaline soils.

115

The vast pile of burnt flints heaped up along the watercourse evinces the use of huge quantities of fuel, which was most probably wood. The time scale during which this heap accumulated is unknown and may have been perhaps slowly over decades or possibly in a short burst of activity. Oak (*Quercus*) appears to have been the most commonly used fuel. Heartwood was not recorded and, although the charcoal was fragmented, roundwood measuring between 5 and 20 mm in diameter was noted. It is likely that fuel requirements were sustained through the use of coppiced or pollarded trees, and although the presence of roundwood tends to support this suggestion, the evidence is inconclusive.

The use of woodland resources

The charcoal from most contexts, for example, that associated with burnt flints, bone and the cremation, can be assigned as fuel residue. Oak (*Quercus*) occurred in more samples than other taxa and was probably the preferred fuel. Oak provides an efficient, high energy fuel (Webster 1919; Porter 1990) and was probably readily available, particularly if coppicing was practiced. Most dense woods make good firewood, for example, ash (*Fraxinus*), hazel (*Corylus*), maple (*Acer*), hawthorn (*Crataegus*), blackthorn (*P. spinosa*) (Porter 1990). Lightweight woods, for example, alder (*Alnus*), willow (*Salix*), and poplar (*Populus*) are less efficient, although birch (*Betula*) burns with an intense but short-lived heat (Edlin 1949). With the exception of blackthorn and poplar, the taxa named above respond well to coppicing (Rackham 1990) and it is likely that woodland resources were sustained through coppicing.

Palaeochannel: soils, sediments and hydrology

by Mark Robinson

The palaeochannel in Area 3000B (Fig. 3.22) was evident as a hollow in the gravel lying to the north of the burnt mound. It probably represented a minor channel which had been working its way southwards across the floodplain at the end of the Devensian, before the gravels were fully stabilised. It was probably at least seasonally dry for much of the Flandrian, and middle Bronze Age boundary ditches ran across the channel bed. Charcoal and burnt stone from late Bronze Age burnt mound activity was seen along the southern bank and extended into the channel. The hollow of the palaeochannel probably provided a winter source of water for the burnt mound activity, but waterlogged sediments were absent. There was no evidence for water flow in the channel in the late Bronze Age, and the Bronze Age deposits were all non-calcareous, unlike the later fluvial sediments.

The Bronze Age soil was non-calcareous, red-brown clay loam, which survived beneath the burnt mound. Badly preserved waterlogged organic remains were recovered from some late Bronze Age pits to the south of the palaeochannel. The state of preservation of the remains suggested a fluctuating water table. A fluvial deposit ran along the southern side of the palaeochannel and cut into the burnt mound deposits. It comprised calcareous, very shelly, sandy clay and a rich flowing-water molluscan fauna had thrived within it as indicated on Table 5.6. Some seeds and insect remains, apparently preserved by waterlogging, were also present, suggesting sedimentation had occurred after a rise in the water table. This deposit probably resulted from a medieval or more recent stream diversion along the hollow of the palaeochannel.

Some alluvial clay had been deposited over the prehistoric features of Area 3000B but it had largely been incorporated into a recent ploughsoil.

Table 5.6 Mollusc species present in palaeochannel

Theodoxus fluviatilis	Gyraulus acronicus
Valvata piscinalis	Planorbis corneus
Bithynia tentaculata	Pisidium amnicum

Chapter 6:   Discussion and Conclusions

by Adam Brossler and Carol Allen

with contributions by Angela Boyle

Introduction

Features of a number of periods were found in Areas 3017 and 3000B of RBP2 (Reading Business Park second phase of excavations in 1995). In Area 3017 (Fig. 2.1 and Chapter 2) Neolithic pits, post-holes and tree-throw holes were identified and there were pits of late Bronze Age date and some medieval agricultural activity. Excavations of Area 3000B (Figs 3.7–3.9 and Chapter 3) uncovered field systems of middle to late Bronze Age date (Fig. 3.1) which were a continuation of ditches found previously in nearby areas during RBP1 (Reading Business Park first phase of excavations in 1986–8). Middle Bronze Age Deverel Rimbury pottery and a cremation burial of this period were also found in Area 3000B. In the late Bronze Age this area was used extensively, and late Bronze Age pottery was found in many features. A number of posthole structures, including roundhouses and other structures of 6-, 4- and 2-posts were identified. Pits and waterholes of the late Bronze Age were found and a burnt mound feature which lay just to the south of a palaeochannel was also partially excavated.

Neolithic

All the evidence for Neolithic activity in the RBP2 excavations lay within Area 3017 (Fig. 1.2), where a segmented ring ditch, a series of pits, tree-throw holes and a number of postholes were uncovered (Fig. 2.1). A total of 27 pits were identified in the area, 19 of which were assigned a late Neolithic date on the basis of the finds recovered, which also dated the postholes and tree-throw holes.

Segmented ring ditch

The ring ditch had an external diameter of 10 m and comprised two segments with an oval pit lying between the ditch terminals on the north-east side of the monument (Fig. 2.2). Radiocarbon dating of an animal bone and an antler, from two separate fills of the ditch, gave dates of 2900–2580 cal BC and 2920–2620 cal BC (Table A1.1) thus placing the ditch into the late Neolithic. The flint assemblage confirmed the late Neolithic date of the segmented ring ditch and of many of the pits and tree-throw holes.

An unaccompanied adult human female crema-tion was contained in the southern area of the ring ditch. A single radiocarbon date from an associated animal bone, a pig humerus from 5095, the fill of 5094 (Fig. 2.2), gave a date of 1700–1440 cal BC

(Table A1.1). This may indicate that the cremation was placed within the ring ditch during the middle Bronze Age and that the ditch was still visible at this time.

Other segmented ring ditches are known in this area as at Barrow Hills, Radley (Barclay and Halpin 1999, 44–7) and at Dorchester-on-Thames (Atkinson *et al.* 1951), both in Oxfordshire. At Dorchester (site II) excavations revealed a sequence of three con-centric segmented ring ditches with cremation burials associated with the final phase. A radio-carbon date obtained from material in the primary fill of the ditch provided a date of 2922–2628 cal BC (Whittle *et al.* 1992, 197), very similar to the date at Reading. The segmented ring ditch at Barrow Hills, comprised four segments, and although more oval in plan, was also about 10 m in external diameter. The upper fills contained small quantities of worked flint, fragmented animal bone and a Beaker sherd. Two funerary deposits were associated with the monument, although it was possible that these related to a phase of Roman activity (Barclay and Halpin 1999, 45).

At Radley and at Dorchester such segmented ditches appear to have formed part of a monument complex but this is not apparent in the RBP2 excavations where this was the only Neolithic ditched feature found. In Area 7000, about 150 m to the north-west of Area 3017, a ditched enclosure was uncovered during the RBP1 excavations (Moore and Jennings 1992, 11–12). The possibility that this enclosure may have been an associated cursus monument has been considered, but the form of the u-shaped enclosure and the late Bronze Age pottery found within the fills suggested that this was an unlikely interpretation of the feature. As at other sites, the segmented ring ditch at Reading may have formed an enclosed area for ceremonies or meetings but no contemporaneous burials were found and the exact function remains unclear.

In the earlier RBP1 excavations a small continuous ring ditch with an external diameter of approxi-mately 4 m was found on the eastern side of Area 3100 (Fig. 3.8). That ditch was undated but could have been Neolithic or early Bronze Age.

Pits and postholes

The 19 Neolithic pits were all circular or oval in plan with scooped sides and rounded bases (Fig. 2.5.1 and 2), or with a slightly more rectangular profile and flatter base (Fig. 2.5.3 and 4). These were similar types to those seen in the nearby Neolithic Area 7000 of the RBP1 excavations. The two types of pits were distributed fairly randomly across the Area 3017 (Fig. 2.1) and therefore no particular spatial arrangement was indicated which might assist with identifying their function.

Eight of the pits were shallow scoops, and most of the remaining 11 pits had gently sloping sides and flat bases. None of the pits had a depth of more than 0.57 m. The shape and size of the pits suggests that they were unlikely to have been intended for long term storage which probably required deeper pits of either straight-sided or of beehive form (Thomas 1999, 64). Neolithic storage pits have been found, for example, at the late Neolithic site of Cassington, Oxfordshire, where steep-sided pits containing apparent domestic refuse may have originally been dug as storage pits (Case 1982, 121–4). At RBP2 some wheat grain was found within pit 5005 but this was not thought to be primarily a storage pit, as described below. However, some grain was present on the Neolithic site which would have required storage either in a pit or elsewhere, but the exact process and location involved was unclear.

Unlike the Neolithic pits found in the RBP1 excavations (Moore and Jennings 1992, 117) only a few of the RBP2 pits were intercutting. Most of the pits have one or two fills, with only 5010 and 5143 having three fills (Figs 2.5.1 and 3), and this may indicate that most pits were deliberately backfilled quite soon after they were dug rather than silting naturally. There were artefactual and environmental remains in many of the pits. Eight contained animal bone and 15 produced worked flint, and therefore it is possible that these particular pits were used for depositing domestic rubbish. Little pottery was apparent within the Neolithic pits, suggesting that pottery was rare and may not have been used domestically but only in socially significant activities (Thomas 1999, 125).

Postholes

A total of 15 postholes dated to the Neolithic were found in Area 3107 of the RBP2 excavations as indicated on Figure 2.1. A small group of five postholes in the northern part of the site may indicate the remains of a small structure, and a core fragment was found in one of these holes, 5058. Within the Neolithic Area 7000 of the earlier RBP1 excavations a number of pairs of posts were recognised (Moore and Jennings 1992, 117–18), although their function was unclear, but no similar pairing was recognisable in the RBP2 excavations. The remaining postholes of Area 3017 were fairly scattered and isolated and did not appear to represent any coherent pattern although some evidence may have been lost in modern times. A notched and serrated flint flake was found in posthole 5207 on the western side of the site.

Similarly at Yarnton, Oxfordshire, an extensive Neolithic landscape has been revealed and a large number of pits were found, some with Peterborough pottery and Grooved Ware. A large number of postholes were also found but no structures could be identified (Hey 1997).

Pits 5005 and 5010 with special deposits and Neolithic pottery

Pit 5005 contained a single fill (Fig. 2.4) and was dug into tree-throw hole 5072 in the north-west of Area 3017. The pit was steep-sided, 0.36 m deep and contained 845 pieces of worked flint, two sherds of middle Neolithic Peterborough pottery, cattle bones and teeth. The flint included debitage, keeled and discoidal cores (Fig. 4.1.4), scrapers (Fig. 4.2.6–9), a polished implement (Fig. 4.2.10) and chisel arrowheads (Fig. 4.2.11–12) but there was little irregular waste. The overall size and composition of the flint collection from this pit is impressively different to the rest of the site with an extensively worked range of artefacts (Bradley, Chapter 4). Also included were 14 pieces of burnt unworked flint, wood charcoal and some charred plant remains including wheat grains. These were similar to deposits noted in other Neolithic pits (Thomas 1999, 64), where the deliberate selection of items for inclusion seems to have taken place. The material within such a pit may have represented a special deposit, that is the burial of certain items carried out at a particular time, to commemorate or ritualise an event or discard (ibid., 70).

In pit 5010 a decorated rim sherd of a late Neolithic vessel of Woodlands Grooved Ware type was found (Fig. 4.5). Grooved Ware is not a common find on sites and in this case was associated with 102 flints including chisel arrowheads. This pottery could have been redeposited but the unusual decorated rim found in association with flint may again suggest a special deposit. Such deposits of Grooved Ware in Neolithic pits often included a vessel fragment such as a rim with complex decoration (Barclay 1999, 14).

Flintworking in the Neolithic

Fifteen pits in Area 3017 contained flint (Table 4.6) and a small, but significant, quantity of flint was recovered from the segmented ring ditch and the tree-throw holes. All the flint from this area was later Neolithic in date indicated by the types and technology of the material found in the pits and tree-throw holes, with less diagnostic material being found in the ring ditch. The large flint assemblage from pit 5005 produced a wide range of artefacts and extensively worked cores. The flint found on this site was similar to that found in the earlier RBP1 excavations, and both have retouched forms such as transverse arrowheads, polished implements and discoidal cores. A wide range of activities were taking place on the site in this period, including knapping, hide preparation, food processing and probably woodworking (Bradley, Chapter 4)

In general, good quality flint was used on this site in the Neolithic, and a wide variety of core types was employed. The Neolithic cores had been prepared and maintained and particular types were being employed for artefacts such as serrated and retouched flakes and chisel arrowheads. Retouch was used on the later Neolithic artefacts to give them shape and also to improve their appearance, as areas larger than required for purely functional needs had been retouched.

Neolithic environment and economy

Within the pits in Area 3017, and particularly from pit 5005, animal bone found indicated use of domesticated animals, particularly pig and cattle. This data also suggested that domesticated animals probably provided the main element of diet for the Neolithic people on this site, as seen also in the RBP1 excavations (Levitan 1992). Auroch, beaver and deer bones were found indicating both woodland and wetland environments. There was only one sheep bone and no horse bone in the Neolithic assemblage.

The animal bone assemblage reflected the later Neolithic trend toward pig and cattle as the main domestic animals (Richards 1991, 21). Neolithic Grooved Ware has been found with pig bones on sites elsewhere and it is thought that this association may reflect feasting activities (Richards and Thomas 1984, 204). However, as only one sherd of Grooved Ware was found on the site it is difficult to estimate the significance of these finds.

Charred plant remains, including hazelnut fragments, wheat grains and the remains of elder, suggested use of both woodland and arable land (Campbell, Chapter 5). The large numbers of hazelnut fragments seen in the Neolithic pits compared to the smaller number of wheat grains may suggest some dependency upon the woodland resources. However, it is possible that the hazelnut shells had several economic uses, perhaps being used for food and for fuel, and this resulted in larger numbers of the charred remains. Wood was also used for fuel, and the wood charcoal found within the pits and in the segmented ring ditch included oak, ash, hazel and alder, which is a wetland species (Gale, Chapter 5). However, the abundance of oak charcoal in this period suggested that oak woodland was probably dominant with ash and hazel as understorey.

A number of tree-throw holes were excavated in this area, and many included flints dated to the late Neolithic (Table 4.3). The holes were located throughout the site with a number seen in the north-west corner, and these indicated that the trees had fallen predominantly to the north and to the east (Fig. 2.4). On the RBP1 excavation of Area 7000 many of the tree-throw holes were undated and also showed that the trees fell in all directions of the compass

(Moore and Jennings 1992, 13). There was no evidence in the RBP2 Neolithic Area 3107 to suggest that there was a deliberate policy of deforestation.

Middle Bronze Age to late Bronze Age

Middle to late Bronze Age features found within Area 3000B of the RBP2 excavations comprised field boundaries, a cremation burial, middle Bronze Age Deverel Rimbury pottery, some pits and a waterhole.

Buried soil and stone axe

A buried soil which survived beneath the burnt mound was considered to be at least of middle Bronze Age date, as it was truncated by ditches of the middle to late Bronze Age field system. However, as a result of bioturbation this buried soil was very contaminated by the burnt mound material and no information was available concerning its nature and use. A damaged stone axe of decomposed dolerite was recovered from this soil (Roe, Chapter 4) but this could not be attributed to a specific source. The axe (Fig. 4.21.2, Plate 6.1) may be of Bronze Age date or could be a residual find of earlier prehistoric date.

Plate 6.1   Polished stone axe from soil beneath burnt mound. Scale 1:1

Plate 6.2   Deverel Rimbury bucket urn 1160 found in pit with cremations

Pits, cremations and Deverel Rimbury pottery

Pit 1159 (Figs 3.1 and 3.4) contained a middle Bronze Age Deverel Rimbury bucket urn (Fig. 4.7.1, Plate 6.2) with lugs and fingertip decoration which contained cremated bone, and some cremated bone was also excavated from the pit fill outside the vessel. Examination suggested that two cremations had been buried within the pit, an adult of unknown sex outside the pot and a sub-adult within the vessel, although the two deposits had been mixed. The largest cremation was found within the protection of the inverted urn. A single radiocarbon date of 1220–890 cal BC (Table A1.1) was obtained from charcoal associated with the cremation deposit found in the pot.

Similar Deverel Rimbury pottery is known from cremation cemeteries at Knight's Farm, Berkshire (Bradley *et al.* 1980, fig. 32) and at cemeteries in Middlesex (Barrett 1973), where dating confirms that these vessels are usually found in the later 2nd millennium BC (Morris, Chapter 4). It has been suggested (ibid.) that larger and middle sized urns were used on middle Bronze Age settlements, while larger urns were used for burial containers. However, elsewhere it has been shown that the size of the Deverel Rimbury urn containing a burial

varied with the age of the deceased, with younger people being placed into smaller pots and older people into larger pots (Allen *et al.* 1987, fig. 20). This concurs with the RBP2 evidence where the large pot contained the remains of a sub-adult cremation.

Wood charcoal found with the cremation in pit 1159 was most likely the remains of fuel used for the pyre. The fragments were small but oak, hazel, alder and willow or poplar were identified. Oak would have been the most suitable fuel (Gale, Chapter 5), but the other wood may also have been used for the pyre.

Pit 1753, lying to the south of 1159, also contained a large number of sherds of Deverel Rimbury pottery (Fig. 3.5) including a fragmentary but almost complete pot (Fig. 4.7.2). There was no associated cremation.

Pit 1390, just north-west of 1753, contained nine fills, with middle Bronze Age pottery in the upper fills. The two lower fills were waterlogged and it was considered that this might have been used as a waterhole. A similar middle Bronze Age waterhole located adjacent to field systems can be seen at Eight Acre Field, Radley, Oxfordshire (Mudd 1995). Such a waterhole may have been used for watering animals kept within the fields.

Field boundaries

A system of field boundaries denoted by ditches was apparent in the RBP2 excavations of Area 3000B. These ditches (Fig. 3.1) were considered to be a continuation of the boundary ditches uncovered in the RBP1 excavations of the adjacent Area 3100 to the west and these had been thought to continue southwards through Area 2000 (Moore and Jennings 1992, fig. 18). The ditches were features established prior to the late Bronze Age settlement of the location and are considered to be of middle to late Bronze Age date. The present excavations recognised three phases of the boundaries (Fig. 3.1) which designated a number of rectangular and square fields of different sizes. Bronze Age Deverel Rimbury pottery was found in the lower fill of ditch 1134, which appears to be part of this field system.

An increasing number of Bronze Age field systems have been identified in southern England. A survey published in 1999 has recorded 44 middle and late Bronze Age field systems in the Middle and Upper Thames Valley alone (Yates 1999). On some of these sites, including the Reading Business Park, an organised field system preceded the settlement. A site at Stanwell on the River Colne on the Heathrow terraces is believed to have been cleared for the first time to create the field systems, so here too the settlement was established *after* the field systems (O'Connell 1990). The late Bronze Age ringwork settlements at Mucking, in Essex, were preceded by a middle Bronze Age field system (Bond 1988).

By contrast, at Yarnton, Oxfordshire the settlement preceded the field systems (Hey and Muir 1997, 73). Other settlements appear to have been contemporary with the field systems; the middle Bronze Age field system and settlement at Eton Rowing Lake, Buckinghamshire is an example of this (Allen and Mitchell 2001; Allen and Welsh 1997). Fengate, Cambridgeshire (Pryor 1980) and Hornchurch, Essex (Guttmann and Last 2000) had co-axial field systems with late Bronze Age structures set within the fields, which suggests that the fields and structures were in existence at the same time. Welland Bank, Lincolnshire also had structures within the fields, but they were organised as a larger settlement rather than as scattered farmsteads (Pryor 1998). At Bluntisham, Cambridgeshire a middle and late Bronze Age field system had roundhouses set along the margins, and a large longhouse was set within an enclosure aligned with and set within the field system (Evans 1995). On the Marlborough Downs, Wiltshire there are a number of settlements which are each associated with contemporary field systems, although these are 'Celtic fields', that is, fields which have developed in a piecemeal fashion, rather than the more organised co-axial type (Gingell 1992).

The presence of a single cremation of Bronze Age date within the boundaries and the occurrence of the Deverel Rimbury pottery within the field ditches suggests that people were living and farming in this area in this period. A similar field system of middle to late Bronze Age date with an associated cremation burial was also found at Weir Bank Stud Farm, Bray, Berkshire (Barnes and Cleal 1995, 18), and other enclosures of similar size and rectilinear form are known elsewhere in southern Britain (Cunliffe 1991, fig. 3.4; Yates 1999). However, as noted in the previous RBP1 excavations, there is no indication at the Reading Business Park of the location of a Bronze Age settlement contemporaneous with the field ditches (Moore and Jennings 1992, 118). It is possible that such occupation may have been seasonal, and that its ephemeral remains left little trace or were removed by later ploughing activity.

These fields could have functioned as stock enclosures with an associated waterhole. It was suggested that the small size of the fields uncovered in the RBP1 excavations would have been suitable for the cultivation of flax (ibid., 120). Flax is poorly represented in the pollen record as it produces small numbers of pollen grains, but a single grain was noted in the basal level of the late Bronze Age waterhole 1015 (Scaife, Chapter 5). It is possible therefore that this was a continuation of a tradition of flax cultivation.

Late Bronze Age

Many features excavated within RBP2 Area 3000B were dated to the late Bronze Age, and these included post-built roundhouses and 6-, 4- and 2-post structures. In addition a number of pits, waterholes, a large burnt mound and part of a palaeochannel were identified and excavated. The distribution of similar structures and occupation within the adjacent Areas 3000B of the RBP2 excavation and 3100 of the earlier RBP1 excavations (Fig. 3.7) must indicate that the features relate to the same settlement areas.

When the two excavated areas are considered together (Fig. 3.7), it becomes apparent that the pits, postholes and structures form an almost circular cluster. This may be an indication that this area of settlement was enclosed. A similar clustering of features was noted at Aldermaston Wharf, Berkshire where the abrupt edge of the feature distribution suggested to the authors that the site had been enclosed, possibly by a hedge (Bradley *et al.* 1980). Although no clear archaeological evidence was recovered from the Reading Business Park which would support this, the environmental evidence nevertheless included a number of potential hedge species. Charcoal of blackthorn (*Prunus spinosa*), purging buckthorn (*Rhamnus cathartica*) and hawthorn type (*Pomoideae*) were recovered, and elder seeds were also identified. Charcoal from maple (*Acer*) may derive from *Acer campestre*, the field maple often found in older hedges. There are a number of references in the Roman literature to hedging, including one which describes an Iron Age tribe in Flanders, where

> They cut into slender trees and bent them over so that many branches came out along their length; they finished these off by inserting brambles and briars, so that these hedges formed a defence like a wall, which could not only not be penetrated but not even be seen through (De bello Gallico II, xvii).

Structures

Roundhouses

Five roundhouses were located within Area 3000B (Fig. 3.9). The post-rings, which formed the basis of these structures, measured between 8.00 and 9.00 m in diameter, and consisted of between 8 and 15 posts (Table 3.2). Two of the roundhouses clearly had porches, one facing east and one south-south-east, and two others may have had porches, facing south-east and north-north-west, but these were not so clearly defined. The postholes of the roundhouses were identified by their location around a central point, although only one house (RH 4) actually had a central post (Fig. 3.11). Unfortunately the depth of truncation of the features on this site was unclear and it was not always possible to ideally form the pairs of posts that might be expected (Guilbert 1982, 67–86).

On the adjacent Area 3100, ten late Bronze Age circular buildings were identified in the RBP1 excavations and a number had porches which also faced to the east and south-east (Moore and Jennings 1992, fig. 31). The roundhouses in Area 3100 appeared to have been built in a more linear arrangement and some of the buildings may have been paired, an arrangement not apparent in the RBP2 excavations of Area 3000B. In Area 5, the south-eastern part of the RBP1 excavations (Fig. 1.2), a further 20 late Bronze Age circular buildings were identified. Eight had postholes indicating porches which faced broadly east (ibid., 14–25). On that site houses seem to have been rebuilt in many cases in almost the same location and a number of phases could be determined. On Area 3000B roundhouses RH1 and RH2 overlapped and there was some evidence of the reuse of locations and postholes for subsequent structures suggesting that at least two phases of use of the site were apparent. Larger quantities of pottery sherds of late Bronze Age date were found within the postholes of the roundhouses RH3 and RH4, but evidence of pottery found in postholes of all the roundhouse structures suggested that they were all of broadly the same date.

The post-rings were identified as circles of posts used to support the roof of the buildings (Avery and Close-Brooks 1969). The exterior of the porch of each roundhouse would have been located on the line of the wall, and the house walls therefore lay outside the rings of posts. The wall diameters were thus between 11.00 and 12.40 m (Table 3.2) and these roundhouses were slightly larger than those on the adjacent excavations (Moore and Jennings 1992, table 6).

Late Bronze Age roundhouses of similar type have also been found on other sites in this region. At Rams Hill, Berkshire (Bradley and Ellison 1975, 52–5) four post-rings with between 8 and 13 postholes were identified measuring approximately 7 m in diameter. During excavations at Yarnton, Oxfordshire, three late Bronze Age roundhouses were identified. The structures were oval in plan and consisted of between 7 and 12 postholes, measuring 4–7 m in width and 5–9 m in length (Hey and Bell 1997). The houses on Area 3000B of the RBP2 excavations are therefore of comparable size and construction to those found on other excavations of similar date in the region.

The function of the roundhouses in Area 3000B is unclear as considerable modern disturbance of the occupation levels within the houses meant that little evidence was recovered. The structures could have functioned as domestic dwellings and as workshops within the settlement. In roundhouse RH2 two pits, 1845 and 1862, contained pottery, animal bone and fired clay, and may have been used as rubbish pits after the structure was abandoned.

East and south-easterly facing doorways were seen in both Area 3000B and Area 3100. It has been noted that many roundhouse doorways faced broadly east and south-east (Parker-Pearson 1996, 119) and that this is the direction of sunrise in the shorter and darker days between September and March, enabling best advantage to be taken of the daylight hours. An east facing doorway would also have been well-placed to avoid northerly winds (Hingley and Miles 1984, 63).

Four- and six-post structures

One 6-post structure and thirteen 4-post structures were identified within Area 3000B (Table 3.3). A number of similar 6- and 4-post structures were noted on the adjacent RBP1 excavations (Moore and Jennings 1992, table 7). The 6-post structure on the RBP2 excavations shared a number of postholes with RH3 and RH4, which it lay between, and must therefore have been a construction of a different period to the roundhouses.

The 4-post structures on RBP2 Area 3000B varied in size from 1.5 × 0.7 m to 2.5 × 2.0 m. Few of the 4-post structures on either the RBP1 or RBP2 excavations were symmetrical, in common with similar structures at other sites of this period, such as Knight's Farm, Burghfield (Bradley *et al.* 1980) and Rams Hill (Bradley and Ellison 1975), both in Berkshire. For suitable storage facilities it has been suggested (Gent 1983, 245) that a structure should have an area of between 3 and 12 m², with sides of between 1.50 and 3.50 m. In RBP2 Area 3000B the areas of the 4-post structures varied between 1.05 and 5.0 m², suggesting limited storage facilities. Four-post structures found on Iron Age sites seem to be larger around 8–9 m² (Williams and Zeepvat 1994, 54). It is possible that the 4-post structures in Area 3000B were only temporary structures, and that the large number of posthole clusters without any discernible pattern could suggest that their posts were reused elsewhere.

The function of the 4-post structures is not certain and it is possible that they had a number of different uses within the settlement (Knight 1984, 154f), or that the use may even have changed over time. With the addition of a roof and a floor these could have been raised granaries for storage of grain, straw, fodder or other food products. Other uses such as huts for cooking or sleeping have been proposed, or their use as small shrines, although there is no evidence from the RBP2 excavations to clarify their function. At Knight's Farm it was thought that similar 4-post structures were used as granaries or for storage of hay (Bradley *et al.* 1980, 291). The storage of grain in post-built structures may have declined in the Iron Age period and there may have been a move towards use of pits (Cunliffe 1978, 164).

Two-post structures and postholes

Eight 2-post structures were identified on Area 3000B, with posts spaced at intervals of 1.30, 1.50 or 1.65 m (Table 3.3). Within the RBP1 excavations of Area 3100, 38 further 2-post structures were identified and another 38 in Area 5, all of late Bronze Age date (Moore and Jennings 1992, 27 and 39). These posts may have been drying racks, hay-racks, skinning and butchery frames, or frames for the curing of hides (ibid., 118). As fired clay loomweights were found in Area 3000B (Barclay, Chapter 5) the possibility that some of the post structures within the roundhouses on the RBP2 excavations could have been parts of looms was considered. Usually a loom comprised two upright posts which supported a beam, onto which the warp was sewn. However, there was no clear evidence that any of the posts were suitable to provide the correct position to work the loom (Hoffman 1964, 24, fig. 2) although this possibility cannot be discounted.

A large number of postholes were identified on Area 3000B, of which 42% were attributed to structures. The purpose of the remaining excavated postholes is unclear but these must have formed part of unidentified features, some of which may have been temporary or short-term structures such as single posts for haystacks.

Waterholes and palaeochannel

Seven waterholes were excavated which were thought to have been dug below the Bronze Age water table and which contained waterlogged material (pale blue on Fig. 3.9). In the Upper Thames Valley it seems likely that the water table was relatively low in the Bronze Age with little flooding and alluviation taking place, and the digging of waterholes would therefore be essential for the occupation of the settlement. A marked rise in the water table is thought to have occurred in the late Bronze Age to early Iron Age period (Lambrick 1992, 217).

Palaeochannel

The palaeochannel which lay just to the north of the burnt mound (Figs 3.9 and 3.22), probably represents a minor channel which was moving southwards across the floodplain at the end of the Late Devensian (Robinson, Chapter 5). Water may have collected in the hollow of the palaeochannel providing a winter source of water for the burnt mound activity, but there was no evidence for water flow in the channel in the late Bronze Age and there were no waterlogged sediments present. The fills of the palaeochannel are detailed on Table 3.7 and illustrated on Figure 3.23.

Waterholes

Several of the waterholes (1015, 1127, 1144 and 2042) were located within the vicinity of the roundhouse structures (Fig. 3.9) and may have been for domestic use. Others lay further from the houses and could have been for watering animals (1118 and 1264). A waterhole (1156) was dug on the edge of the palaeochannel and may have provided a water source for the burnt mound in the summer. This was eventually covered with material from the burnt mound.

The waterholes varied in size, were a maximum of 6 m diameter and 1.08 m deep, and contained between 5 and 18 fills (Table 3.4). The lower fills were predominantly silts or clays, with low frequencies of sand and gravel inclusions. These fills may represent natural silting and slumping which took place while the waterholes were open and in use. The middle fills were of similar composition but appeared to seal the features, which probably indicates a period of disuse when material was dumped into the pits. The upper fills contained charcoal, animal bone, loomweights and a fragment of a possible oven plate (1118, Barclay, Chapter 4), and may also represent dumping of domestic debris into the unused hollows of the waterholes. The waterholes and the sequence of their fills were comparable to others seen on sites of similar date elsewhere. For example, at Watkins Farm, Northmoor (Allen 1990), and Eight Acre Field, Radley (Mudd 1995), both in Oxfordshire, similar patterns of use, abandonment and discard were found with comparable deposits.

Many of the waterholes contained substantial quantities of pottery (1118, 452 sherds, 8.408 kg:

1127, 498 sherds, 9.129 kg: 1144, 268 sherds, 3.257 kg: 1156, 47 sherds, 0.753 kg: 2042, 457 sherds, 6.402 kg: 1015, discussed below). Much of the material in 1144 is of F4 fabric and may therefore have been water-hole lining as described below. Sherds from the same vessels were found within a number of fills of waterhole 1127 suggesting that these layers were dumped into the hole in a single episode as a deliberate backfill, whilst material in waterhole 1118 seems to represent at least two backfills. This pottery appears to represent domestic debris deposited into the waterholes when abandoned, and the range and form of the material suggests the pottery was of the date of the pre-burnt mound assemblage. Also in waterhole 1127, a point made from animal bone was found (Fig. 4.23.1).

Waterhole 2042 lay about 4 m to the west of roundhouses RH3 and RH4 and the forms and fabrics of the vessels found were very similar to the pottery found in the roundhouses, although no joining sherds were found. It seems very likely that the roundhouses and the waterhole were in use at the same time.

Similar waterlogged holes were found in a linear arrangement in the southern part of RBP1 Area 3100

Plate 6.3   Worked human skull fragment from waterhole 1015. Scale 1:1

and were interpreted as a series of flax retting pits. This was a process which required the plant to be submerged in stagnant water for several weeks to loosen the plant fibres (Wild 1988, 22). The holes contained waterlogged samples which included flax remains and associated flint scrapers considered suitable for flax stripping (Moore and Jennings 1992, 122). However, no comparable holes were found on the Area 3000B RBP2 excavations, although a single occurrence of flax pollen was noted in waterhole 1015. Flax produces only a small number of pollen grains making it difficult to confidently assess its presence.

Waterhole lining

Over 650 pieces of a fired clay material tempered with coarse burnt flint were found in the waterholes (F4 fabric, Morris, Chapter 4). Most of the material was in waterholes 1118, 1144 and 2042, which are detailed on Table 3.4 and shown on Figure 3.9, where they are seen to be widely spaced across the excavated Area 3000. All the pieces of this material had wiped interior surfaces but the exterior was roughly made and no base or rim sherds were apparent. It seems likely that this material formed some kind of lining for the waterholes and could be compared with similar fired clay material also thought to be a lining found on the late Bronze Age site of Aldermaston Wharf, Berkshire (Bradley *et al.* 1980). Some of the F4 material on the RBP2 site had a thin, white residue on the interior surface possibly suggesting something like a whitewash had been applied.

Waterhole 1015 and worked human bone

This substantial waterhole measured 4.4 × 4.0 m, was 1.08 m deep and contained 18 fills (detailed on Table 3.4). A pollen sample was taken (Scaife, Chapter 5) and the results from this are examined in the environmental discussion below. A total of 649 sherds (7.627 kg) of late Bronze Age pottery were found, with substantial quantities in the upper levels and smaller amounts in the lower levels (see Tables 3.4 and 4.17). One fine jar found in this feature could have been used to transport water (Morris, Chapter 4). Two pieces of the F4 possible clay lining material discussed above were also found. The upper fills contained a smoothed sarsen fragment which may have been used as a rubbing stone (Roe, Chapter 4), with pieces of clay and loomweights (Barclay, Chapter 4).

An interesting piece of waterlogged wood was also found in a lower fill of the waterhole. This was an oak disc with a central hole (Fig. 4.24) possibly used as part of a press for cheese making (Taylor, Chapter 4). Also in the lower fill (Fig. 3.13) was part of a bone disc with a central hole. This had been worked from a human skull (Fig. 4.23.4, Plate 6.3). It is possible that both these latter items had been dropped by accident into the waterhole during its use.

Pieces of human skull have often been noted on late Bronze Age settlement sites and are particularly common in pits (Brück 1995, figs 2 and 3). It has been suggested that in this period, the presence of human bones was of importance when problems of boundaries, group identity, continuity and renewal needed reassurance or support. This would have been important during disputes over land ownership, when affinities to the status of the dead were vital (ibid., 245–77). A number of similar pieces of human skull, which have been worked and drilled in the same way as this one from Reading, have been found elsewhere, for example, at Ivinghoe Beacon, Buckinghamshire (ibid., 271). These must have been used as pendants and possibly as amulets (ibid., 253), to highlight the symbolic nature of human remains (ibid., 264).

Middle Bronze Age to late Bronze Age pottery continuity

Within the pottery assemblage of the RBP2 excavation it is possible to follow the continuity of potting traditions from the middle Bronze Age to late Bronze Age (Morris, Chapter 4). The single date from charcoal associated with Deverel Rimbury pottery at RBP2 Area 3000B of 1220–890 cal BC (as discussed above) is exactly the same as the single date obtained from material in pit 1518 alongside late Bronze Age pottery (see Table A1.1).

The majority of the middle Bronze Age pottery was made from a well sorted coarse flint-tempered fabric and a similar fabric is also seen in the late Bronze Age pottery. However, new sources for clay and new pottery fabrics were also seen in the late Bronze Age pottery assemblage. The middle Bronze Age bucket-shaped vessels (Fig. 4.7) are similar in size to those of the late Bronze Age and also very alike in shape to the most common late Bronze Age ovoid forms (R11 and R12).

The decorative techniques of the middle Bronze Age, particularly the use of fingertip impressions on the interior edge of rims, were also employed in the later Bronze Age material. Fingertip impressions on shoulders of jars and the exterior edge of rims are seen in both traditions, and were also common in the pottery seen on the RBP1 excavations (Moore and Jennings 1992, eg fig. 45.66–9). The use of lugs does not continue into the late Bronze Age, but embedded flint chips in the base of vessels were apparent in both periods on this site.

Excavations at Pingewood, about 2 km to the west of Reading Business Park, uncovered a similar range of ironised and flint-tempered pottery (Johnston 1983–5). Vessels ranged from the middle Bronze Age Deverel Rimbury pottery to the straight-sided and ovoid jars with hooked and simple rim types of the late Bronze Age. The late Bronze Age decorative techniques of fingertip decoration with pinched protrusions or bosses and splayed or simple bases were also apparent, again comparable with RBP2 vessels (Morris, Chapter 4). This pottery assemblage at Pingewood, directly comparable to that from the RBP2 excavations, indicates that a site of similar date range lay nearby.

Other nearby sites of Bronze Age date (ibid.), for example, Rams Hill (Barrett 1980), show only plainware pottery transitional middle to late Bronze Age phases, and lack the middle Bronze Age Deverel Rimbury material seen on the RBP2 site. At Eynsham, Oxfordshire, the pottery found was a plainware assemblage of late Bronze Age date characterised by straight-sided or barrel-shaped vessels and round-shouldered jars with everted rims. The assemblage was considered to have a date range of between 1200 and 800 cal BC (Barclay *et al.* 2001).

The RBP2 site assemblage is important therefore for contributing information on the pottery traditions seen in the transition from the middle to late Bronze Age assemblages. These were current in the period from the mid to late 2nd millennium to the early 1st millennium BC. More absolute dating is needed to clarify the dates for this clearly indicated transition (Morris, Chapter 4).

Late Bronze Age settlement shift

Middle Bronze Age Deverel Rimbury pottery was clearly apparent in the assemblage from features on the RBP2 Area 3000B excavations. Also, the late Bronze Age pottery from Area 3000B showed affinities to the preceding middle Bronze Age types, suggesting continuity of potting traditions, alongside the development of new fabrics and shapes, such as bowls (Morris, Chapter 4). The late Bronze Age pottery in Area 3000B came from a variety of features, including structures, waterholes and pits, but only 2% showed any decoration. The pottery found in the burnt mound deposits was of similar character to the rest of Area 3000B, and included only a single decorated rim sherd.

Within the assemblage of the RBP1 excavations only a very limited amount of Deverel Rimbury pottery of middle Bronze Age date was recognised (Bradley and Hall 1992a, 79). Again, in contrast to the RBP2 excavations, about 37% of the late Bronze Age pottery assemblage from RBP1 Areas 3100 and 5 was decorated. This strongly suggests (Morris, Chapter 4) that there was a substantial change of emphasis in the character of the occupation in the eastern area of the excavated site. The area was first used for housing and for other structures probably associated with farming and general living activities. Whilst the potting traditions employed were still within the plainwares of the late Bronze Age transitional period, the eastern area was reused as an area for flint burning, probably for domestic and industrial uses. However, by the time the pottery had developed into the decorated late Bronze Age tradition the settlement seems to have shifted to the west, to the RBP1 Area 3100, where far more decorated pottery was being used. The western RBP1 area then continued in use as a settlement as the eastern area was employed as a flint burning area.

Flintworking in the late Bronze Age

Flint was utilised for tools in the Bronze Age, indicating that metalwork was rare, and that flint was still more readily available and preferred to metal for many purposes. The flint from the RBP2 Area 3000B provides a late Bronze Age assemblage for comparison with that described earlier from the Neolithic parts of the site (Bradley, Chapter 4). The Bronze Age assemblage was dominated by debitage. Only a limited number of retouched tools, scrapers, piercing and cutting tools were produced, with unretouched flints also being used. The quality of the gravel flint employed was generally poorer, utilising anything which could be reasonably well flaked. The types of cores were also limited in the Bronze Age, and were poorly maintained and only roughly worked. Retouch was no longer applied to flints to improve their appearance but merely used for functional purposes. The late Bronze Age flint material found on the RBP1 excavations was generally of similar character to that found in these excavations.

Pits

A total of 68 late Bronze Age pits were identified in RBP2 Area 3000B. These were broken down into four types according to the profile of the individual pit to attempt to determine spatial or functional differences between them. The pits were circular or oval in plan and are summarised on Table 3.5. In the RBP1 excavations two profile types were described and these could be seen to be broadly comparable with those of the RBP2 excavations (see Chapter 3).

Pit types 1–4

There were 23 type 1 pits excavated on the site, and these were scooped with gradually sloping sides to a rounded base (Fig. 3.17). All were quite shallow, no more than 0.55 m deep. The dimensions of the pits vary considerably and could represent gravel pits which were reused for deposits of domestic debris. The pits were distributed quite randomly throughout the site (dark blue on Fig. 3.9). Six contained sherds of late Bronze Age pottery and one pit (1892) had part of a saddle quern (Fig. 4.21.1). Pit 1862, which contained 77 sherds of pottery (0.779 kg) and 11 loomweight fragments, lay within roundhouse RH2 (Fig. 3.10) and may have been a small storage pit reused for rubbish.

A total of 15 type 2 pits were found and these had a more rectangular profile and flat base (Fig. 3.18). These were also distributed throughout the excavated area (dark red on Fig. 3.9), with a larger number apparent in the south-east of the excavated area. The profile of these pits was much more like those used in the Iron Age period for storage (Cunliffe 1992, 77–8; Thomas 1999, 64), and then reused for domestic waste. However, the pits tended to be rather shallow varying from 0.25 to 0.93 m in depth. The fills varied but suggested that many of the pits may have silted naturally. Ten pits contained late Bronze Age pottery mainly in the upper fills and two of these also had clay pieces. A loomweight fragment was found with pottery in one pit, and seems to confirm these pits were eventually used for domestic debris. Some worked wood was found in pit 1168.

Seven type 3 pits were more v-shaped in profile (Fig. 3.19). These varied in size and none were deeper than 0.55 m. These were found throughout the site (dark green on Fig. 3.9), and contained few fills but appeared to have silted naturally. Only one pit 1845 contained late Bronze Age pottery (73 sherds, 0.82 kg) and this lay close to pit 1862 (type 1) within roundhouse RH2 (Fig. 3.10). These may have been small storage pits reused for rubbish.

Type 4 pits (pale green on Fig. 3.9) were scoops with sloping sides and rounded bases (Fig. 3.20). These 14 pits were generally larger than other types, up to 2.5 m in length and between 0.4 and 0.8 m in depth. Pit 1518 was sealed by the burnt mound feature (Figs 3.9 and 3.22). Two sherds of late Bronze Age pottery and part of a quernstone were recovered from a lower fill 1695 (Fig. 3.20). An animal bone found in the same context was dated to 1220–890 cal BC (see Table A1.1), placing the pit into the later Bronze Age. The large pit 1551 cut through the postholes of roundhouse RH3, which it must have superseded (Fig. 3.11) and contained 52 sherds of late Bronze Age pottery, 55 pieces of fired clay and part of a cylindrical loomweight of late Bronze Age type (Fig. 4.20.1). Some waterlogged split oak was also found in this pit (Plate 6.4). At the late Bronze Age settlement of Aldermaston Wharf, Berkshire, it was concluded that smaller pits found on the site may have contained food stored for immediate consumption, whilst larger pits were used for storage of surplus produce (Bradley *et al.* 1980, 248–56). It is possible therefore, that these larger pits were used for storage and later were filled with deposits of discarded domestic items.

In addition, nine more irregular pits (Fig. 3.21) were found in RBP2 Area 3000B, and these are detailed in Table 3.6. Only one pit contained sherds of late Bronze Age pottery and another contained animal bone, but there is no clear indication of their function.

Distribution and analysis of pits

Most of the pits, shown in Figure 3.9, were randomly distributed across the site, and in general no clusters of the different types were apparent. There is also a considerable variation in size

Plate 6.4   Waterlogged wood from pit 1551

amongst the types. Only the type 2 pits appear to be more numerous on the south-eastern side of the excavated area away from the roundhouses, and their shape suggests these may at first have been intended for storage. It is possible that the pits lying to the south of roundhouse RH1 formed a north-west to south-east group which was used to create a boundary, as at Butler's Field, Lechlade (Jennings 1998, 28–9). All four pits contained late Bronze Age pottery, and three contained animal bone, and formed a line composed of similar sized pits of types 1 to 4. If these pits were used at the same time for the same purpose this suggests that the appearance of different profiles in the pits may have had no functional meaning. These pits and a number of others lay close to 4-post structure FP7, and there may have been some connection.

In general it is not possible to tell whether there was any chronological divide between the pits, as the pottery deposited within them was very similar: a late Bronze Age date was obtained for animal bone associated with similar pottery. No grain deposits were found which might be indicative of storage pits, and if the pits were used for storage of other food produce this was removed for use and left no trace. A small cluster of pits was found,

partially linear, close to waterhole 1156, and all these features were sealed by the burnt mound (Fig. 3.15). These included two type 2 pits (1168 and 1172) and two type 3 (1623 and 1690) and one type 4 (1170) pit. The sizes of the pits varied and it is difficult to see a common use. Their proximity may be coincidental, and each may have been dug and refilled at slightly different times being employed for different or changing purposes.

Numbers of pits were clustered in the areas of the 4-post structures FP13, FP14 and FP15, and FP16, FP17 and FP18 (Fig. 3.9). The clusters of pits were not equally spaced and were of mixed types. Pottery was recovered from some of these pits; one had charcoal inclusions and several contained animal bones. These pits therefore seem to be connected with the domestic activity on the site but again the exact function is unclear. It may be that the use was constantly changing with pits being dug, used and infilled as requirements changed, and it is therefore not possible to discern how the pits relate to the different parts of the occupation area. Similar difficulties of interpretation of the function and association of pits and structures were seen on the preceding RBP1 excavations of the adjacent Area 3100 (Moore and Jennings 1992, 41).

Burnt mound

The burnt mound excavated on Area 3000B was aligned north-west to south-east. It was located to the north-east of the settlement and extended outside the eastern edge of the excavation. Parts of the mound are thought to have been truncated by modern ploughing, and therefore the full extent could not be investigated, and the south-eastern edge of the mound could not be fully recorded due to flooding of the site. Two quadrants and six slots were excavated across the mound (Fig. 3.22), which was dated to the late Bronze Age by the presence of over 250 sherds of pottery found within the deposit. The part of the mound revealed by the present excavations was approximately 85 m in length, and up to 25 m wide and 0.2 m in depth (Fig. 3.9). The large size of the mound suggests it represented a long period of activity which resulted in numerous separate depositions of burnt material.

The mound comprised about 70% burnt flint in a black silt and sand soil, with about 10% gravel inclusions and much charcoal. The charcoal included hawthorn, willow, hazel, alder and other species, but oak sapwood formed the greater part of the fuel (Gale, Chapter 5). The absence of heartwood suggested that immature wood was used and this may have been coppiced. Oak would have provided an ideal and efficient fuel for heating flint.

The burnt mound sealed a number of features, including middle to late Bronze Age field boundaries, a number of late Bronze Age pits and a late Bronze Age waterhole, all discussed above. These late Bronze Age features could have been in use whilst the burnt mound was being built up but they eventually went out of use when covered with burnt mound material.

Within the mound deposits, eight sherds of pottery were found in layer 1012 together with a loomweight fragment and some fired clay. In layer 1014, 180 sherds of late Bronze Age pottery were found and part of a D-shaped shale bracelet (Fig. 4.22). Such bracelets were common on late Bronze Age sites (Boyle, Chapter 4). The material for the bracelet may have come from the Kimmeridge area of Dorset. A bone point was also found in this layer (Fig. 4.23.2).

Burnt mounds have been located throughout Britain and Ireland (Buckley 1990; Hodder and Barfield 1991). These comprise a mound of fire-cracked pebbles, or mainly burnt flints in southern England, found with ash and charcoal. The mounds are frequently associated with a hearth and a water source, and usually also with a trough for holding water (Raymond 1987). Most have been clearly dated to the Bronze Age period and many continued in use into the late Bronze Age (Barfield and Hodder 1987; Welch 1994–5, 5; Elliott and Knight 1998).

A typology of burnt mounds has been suggested (Barber 1990), but the RBP2 burnt mound is unusual. The large size of the mound is exceptional, and the spread of the material although extensive may even have been larger. Also, the mound lay alongside a number of settlement structures, features not always found in conjunction with burnt mounds. The elongated shape seems to have been determined by the location, as material was deposited to the north-east of the occupation areas and to the south of the palaeochannel. There is no evidence for a water flow in the channel, but its hollow could have provided a water source in the winter, as could the waterhole 1156, until this too was covered with mound material. Also, the mound lies less than 150 m from the Foudry Brook where water could have been obtained. There is no evidence within the areas excavated for troughs or pits to hold the water.

Whilst in use, the mound activity and its remains would have produced smoke, hot ash and probably steam, and the occupation area moved away and kept away from the burnt mound, as discussed above and seen in the RBP1 excavations of Area 3100. Even after it went out of use the mound presented an obstacle to settlement in that locality. Spreads of dense flint and charcoal, but less extensive in character, are known from other areas in southern England, for example, at Anslow's Cottages Burghfield, Berkshire, where a mound covering 25 m² was found. The mound lay adjacent to a river channel and was considered to be the remains of a sauna (Butterworth and Lobb 1992, 90). At Duffield House, Woodley, Berkshire, a mound of burnt flint and pebbles measured 6 × 4 × 0.3 m and lay close to a rectangular pit with a similar fill (Hardy 1999). An irregular mound of burnt flint and charcoal was excavated at Phoenix Wharf, London. Due to the location and shape of the associated pit it was suggested that this might have been used for roasting meat (Bowsher 1991, 17). Other interpretations for the function of the mounds and troughs include brewing and leather working (Ó Drisceoil 1988, 671),

Documentary records from areas such as Ireland and the use of mounds and troughs (or *fulachta fiadh*) within folk memory, suggest that many were employed for cooking. The stones were heated and dropped into water within a trough which was used for the boiling of meat (Hedges 1975), and modern experiments have proved this to be feasible (O'Kelly 1954). Extraction of grease from animal bone could also be carried out in the same manner (Barfield 1991). The presence of structures around some of the troughs as at Liddle in Orkney (Hedges 1975) would make a cooking process very hot and steamy and in such instances the use as a sauna may seem more likely (Barfield and Hodder 1987, 376). Other uses have been suggested such as processing of wool (Jeffrey 1991). The warm water in tanks could have been used for fulling or cleansing and for dyeing of wool, or the steam could have been employed for felting.

In Area 3000B of RBP2 sheep bones were found, and parts of loomweights were also apparent, some being found within the burnt mound, so processing of wool is very likely to have taken place. Cattle bones too were present on site, although little animal bone was recovered from the mound itself, so cooking or roasting was also a possible use of the heated flint. Some of the material in the mound may be the remains of domestic hearths from the occupation areas, or from some other process not yet defined, but the lack of a hearth or trough close to the burnt mound makes interpretation more difficult. Nevertheless the presence of such large quantities of burnt material beside the settlement indicates that a number of processes were likely to have taken place over a considerable period of time.

Late Bronze Age environment and economy

Cattle bones predominated in the RBP2 assemblage, and sheep were also present along with a few pig and deer bones. Most of the cattle appear to have been killed before they reached maturity, possibly reflecting lack of winter fodder or milk production. Grass and pasture must have been available in the vicinity of the settlement for these animals, which provided both food and valuable resources of hides, wool and bone.

Charred plant remains of this period included emmer wheat rachis and barley rachis fragments, which must be waste from threshing and winnowing (Campbell, Chapter 5). In the RBP1 excavations it was suggested that processed cereals were being transported to the site, and this may indicate a change in emphasis as time progressed, as pottery evidence suggests that the western area of the excavations was later in date. Parts of saddle querns found on the site indicate that grain was being processed. Four-post structures were apparent on the site and these may have been used for storage of grain or hay. Pits may have been used for more long term storage if they were sealed. Waterholes within and on the periphery of the settlement areas would have been necessary for the occupants and their animals if brought in from the fields at night or during the winter.

Pollen was analysed only from one small feature, and it is considered that the results were indicative of pollen either on or very near to the site. The dominance of herbs and lack of trees in the vicinity of the site in the late Bronze Age was noted. Woodland nearby may have been cleared, and herbs of arable cultivation were present. A single occurrence of flax was seen, but as this produces only very small numbers of pollen grains, it seems likely that this was being grown near the site. More evidence for flax was seen in the waterlogged plant remains from the RBP1 excavations (Campbell 1992, table 26).

Wood charcoal from the burnt mound showed that oak woodland predominated with some haw-thorn, blackthorn, willow, hazel and alder present. The accumulation of the extensive burnt mound deposits consumed large quantities of fuel, probably mainly wood, and therefore woodland must have been available nearby. Roundwood was present in the remains but no heartwood, suggesting that the local woodland was managed, probably at a little distance from the site, and that coppiced rods or pollarded trees would have been used for heating of the flint.

The evidence thus suggests a mixed economy providing cereals, meat and animal by-products for the settlement. The presence of loomweights indicates that weaving was taking place on the site, probably using both wool and flax. The function of the 2-post structures apparent on the site is unclear, but one possible use is to dry or stretch fabrics. The small wooden object with a central hole may have been a cheese-press (Plate 6.5) which suggests that milk may have been processed into cheese on the site. This provides rare evidence for cheese making in prehistory (Ryder 1981). The evidence for mixed farming on the RBP2 site concurs well with the evidence of the RBP1 excavations, as it was concluded that the inhabitants of the western Area 3100 were pursuing mixed farming rather than specialising in arable or pastoral farming (Campbell 1992, 110).

No bronze tools or evidence of metalworking were found on this site. Flint was still in use for tools, although the preparation and finishing were poor. This suggests that the flint was not for display but was merely functional. Bone points were being used perhaps for sewing leather or for use in making baskets or wattle, particularly as suitably flexible wood, alder, willow and poplar was found on the site and may have been coppiced nearby.

Waterlogged worked wood, mainly oak, was found on the site, and there was evidence of some pieces being trimmed and split (Taylor, Chapter 4). However, no wood chips were found within the worked wood, suggesting that woodworking was not taking place in the settlement and it seems likely that this was taking place in the woodland areas. The landscape around the settlement must have been carefully managed with areas reserved for grassland, cultivation and woodland. Crops such as flax require rotation and careful management.

There is no indication that this site was occupied only seasonally, as proposed for sites of similar date such as Knight's Farm and Pingewood. As suggested for the RBP1 excavations, the RBP2 Area 3000B seems most likely to have been a permanent late Bronze Age settlement, although the use of parts of the occupation area may have altered and shifted with time. The location around the round-houses on RBP2 Area 3000B seems most likely to represent the domestic area of the settlement. The 4-post structures mainly lie in the south away from this area (Fig. 3.9), thus not associating any structure

Plate 6.5   Disc of split oak (130 × 126 mm) from waterhole 1015, possibly part of a cheese press

of this type with any particular roundhouse. Many pits also lie in the same area, and so if the 4-post structures and the pits were used for storage they must have been used communally.

Conclusions

The second stage of excavations at Reading Business Park in 1995 uncovered two localities with prehistoric occupation, Areas 3017 and 3000B. The latter lay adjacent to Area 3100, which was investigated in the first stage of excavations at this location. Area

3017 contained mainly Neolithic remains and Area 3000B middle and later Bronze Age evidence.

Interesting comparisons can be drawn between the different periods, indicating changes both in the environment and farming on the site. In the Neolithic woodland and wetland oak, ash, hazel and alder were apparent close to the site. Large numbers of hazelnut shells were found, probably indicating use of the nuts for food and the shells for fuel. Cattle and pig bones were common, as were beaver and deer. Some cereal grains were found, but there was no evidence of settled occupation in this period. A number of pits were found which might have been used for storage, but two pits appeared to have retained special deposits. Sherds of Peterborough Ware were found together with a large quantity of flints and animal bones in one pit. A decorated Grooved Ware rim was found with over 100 flints in another pit. These deposits may commemorate or signify events for the community, bringing a special meaning to a locality (Thomas 1999, 72). The people would have recognised this and accepted the actions as part of the cultural life of the society (Barrett 1994, 145–6). In addition, a segmented ring ditch was found of late Neolithic date. There were no burials associated with the ring ditch and no clear function but its existence within this area at this time suggests a shared meeting place suitable for a dispersed farming community (Bradley 1998, 108).

In the middle to late Bronze Age there is evidence, in Area 3000B, of more organisation of the landscape with the laying out of a series of field boundaries. Cremations were buried within these boundaries, and some middle Bronze Age Deverel Rimbury pottery was placed in pits. In common with many sites of this period, fields and burials are not associated with any evidence of occupation.

In the late Bronze Age the character of settlement at RBP2 changed completely, and there is much evidence for roundhouses and other posthole structures on the site. Numerous pits containing domestic debris were found and a number of waterholes accompanied the houses. Pottery of the late Bronze Age is abundant on the site, and this shows an unusual continuity of fabric, form and decoration from the middle Bronze Age types. This strongly suggests that the occupation in this area could have been continuous from the middle to the later Bronze Age, and it remains to be seen whether subsequent excavations will unearth any occupation evidence to clarify this further. Further dating is required to define the period when this was taking place.

Artefactual remains are common and include flints, worked wood and worked bone. Baskets and pottery were probably being produced locally. The late Bronze Age flint industry still flourished but was restricted to producing more functional items than in the previous Neolithic period when care had been taken both in preparation and finish. No metal was found on the site and there was no evidence for metalworking or for clay moulds.

Arable cultivation was taking place nearby, and the cereals grown were threshed and winnowed on site, with saddle querns being used for grinding. Cattle and sheep bones predominated, with few pig and deer bones. There was a predominance of young animals and milk was probably being made into cheese. Hides were probably being utilised, and the remains of cylindrical late Bronze Age loomweights on the site indicate that wool was being used for textile production. Flax may also have been used to produce linen cloth. The activity of the burnt mound,

which produced an exceptionally large area of burnt deposits, necessitated the heating of flint, presumably for both domestic and more communal industrial activities. These could have varied from cooking and processing of materials to taking saunas.

Roundwood oak was found in the burnt mound remains and suggests that woodland around the site was being coppiced. The late Bronze Age landscape was therefore occupied and carefully managed by the occupants of this village. Areas of open land were required as pasture for cattle and sheep, areas of woodland were required for fuel and building materials and areas of cultivation were required for growing cereals, with flax cultivation in particular demanding careful management of the land resources.

The Bronze Age pottery on the RBP2 Area 3000B excavations, including the material within and below the burnt mound, exhibited only 2% decoration and was mainly limited to the plainwares of the middle to late Bronze Age tradition. In the adjacent Area 3100 to the west, previously excavated, 37% of the pottery was of the later Bronze Age decorated wares tradition. As time went by in the later Bronze Age, people seemed to have moved away from the roundhouses and structures of the eastern area towards the western side. The burnt mound was not attractive for settlement, even when out of use, and this area was avoided.

There is some evidence that these farmers were trading outside the settlement. A shale bracelet found within the burnt mound is thought to have originated in Dorset and a quernstone of Lower Greensand found in a pit probably came from Culham, Oxfordshire, about 35 km from the site. The occupation levels of the site had been severely disturbed by ploughing in the past, but no metalwork was found, or any evidence of prestige items or artefacts of high status. Presumably farming produce or textiles could have been exchanged for other materials not readily available. In all other aspects the people were self-sufficient pastoral and arable farmers.

The site at Reading Business Park was being intensively used by a small community of farmers. The occupation of this area and surrounding sites such as Pingewood in the late Bronze Age is widespread, and the late Bronze Age does appear to be a period of settlement expansion. Numerous Bronze Age sites are already known in the area of Reading Business Park (Moore and Jennings 1992, fig. 58), and excavations have also been completed within the south-western Green Park area (A on Fig. 1.2) of the Business Park. Further investigations have also uncovered a late Bronze Age settlement at Moore's Farm to the south of the M4. With this and other evidence coming to light in the locality, it will be possible to gain a better understanding of the character and scope of the settlements in this area and to set the results within a framework of the regional landscape.

Appendix

Table A1.1: Radiocarbon dating

Laboratory number	Context number	Sample ID	δ ^{13} C (‰)	Uncalibrated date (BP)	Calibrated date range, 1 sigma	Calibrated date range, 2 sigma	Context type
Area 3017							
R244443/5 NZA 9411	5076	animal humerus	−22.0%	4183 ± 58	2820–2670 BC (56.4%) 2880–2840 BC (11.8%)	2900–2580 BC (95.4%)	segmented ring ditch fill
R24443/4 NZA 9478	5092	antler	−22.4%	4212 ± 57	2820–2680 BC (51.7%) 2900–2850 BC (16.5%)	2920–2620 BC (95.4%)	segmented ring ditch fill
R24443/3 NZA 9508	5095	pig humerus	−20.5%	3300 ± 57	1640–1510 BC (61.7%) 1680–1670 BC (4.3%) 1660–1650 BC (2.2%)	1700–1440 BC (93.1%) 1740–1710 BC (2.3%)	segmented ring ditch fill
Area 3000B							
R24443/2 NZA 9422	1160	charcoal	−27.5%	2857 ± 60	1130–920 BC (68.2%)	1220–890 BC (92.0%) 1260–1240 BC (1.3%) 880–840 BC (2.1%)	cremation
R24443/10 NZA 9412	1695	animal bone	−21.2%	2859±58	1130–920 BC (68.2%)	1220–890 BC (93.0%) 1260–1230 BC (1.3%) 880–860 BC (1.0%)	fill of pit 1518

From Bronk Ramsay 2000 OxCalv3.5 www.rlaha.ox.ac.uk

Bibliography

Adkins, L and Needham, S, 1985 New research on a late Bronze Age enclosure at Queen Mary's Hospital, Carshalton, *Surrey Archaeol Collect* **76**, 11–50

Allen, C S M, Harman, M and Wheeler, H, 1987 Bronze Age cremation cemeteries in the east Midlands, *Proc Prehist Soc* **53**, 187–221

Allen, T, 1990 *An Iron Age and Romano-British enclosed settlement at Watkins Farm, Northmoor, Oxon.* OA Thames Valley Landscapes Monograph: The Windrush Valley **1**, Oxford

Allen, T and Mitchell, N, 2001 Dorney, Eton Rowing Lake: fifth interim report, *South Midlands Archaeol* **31**, 26–30

Allen, T and Welsh, K, 1997 Eton Rowing Lake, Dorney, Buckinghamshire. Second interim report, *South Midlands Archaeol* **27**, 25–34

Atkinson, R J C, Piggott, C M and Sanders, N K, 1951 *Excavations at Dorchester, Oxon*, Oxford

Avery, M and Close-Brooks, J, 1969 Shearplace Hill, Sydling St. Nicholas, Dorset house A: a suggested reinterpretation, *Proc Prehist Soc* **35**, 345–51

Barber, J, 1990 Scottish burnt mounds: variations on a theme, in Buckley 1990, 98–103

Barclay, A, 1999 Grooved Ware from the Upper Thames region, in *Grooved Ware in Britain and Ireland* (R Cleal and A MacSween), Neolithic Group Seminar Papers **3**, 9–22, Oxford

Barclay, A and Halpin, C, 1999 *Excavations at Barrow Hills, Radley, Oxfordshire. Volume 1. The Neolithic and Bronze Age monument complex*, OA Thames Valley Landscapes Monograph **11**, Oxford

Barclay, A and Roe, F, forthcoming Worked stone, in Cromarty *et al.* forthcoming

Barclay, A, Boyle, A and Keevill, G D, 2001 A prehistoric enclosure at Eynsham Abbey, Oxfordshire, *Oxoniensia* **66**, 105–62

Barfield, L, 1991 Hot stones: hot food or hot baths?, in Hodder and Barfield 1991, 59–67

Barfield, L and Hodder, M A, 1987 Burnt mounds as saunas and the prehistory of bathing, *Antiquity* **61**, 370–9

Barnes, I and Cleal, R M J, 1995 Neolithic and Bronze Age settlement at Weir Bank Stud Farm, Bray, in Barnes *et al.* 1995, 1–51

Barnes, I, Boismier, W A, Cleal, R M J, Fitzpatrick, A P and Roberts, M R, 1995 *Early settlement in Berkshire: mesolithic-Roman occupation sites in the Thames and Kennet Valleys*, Wessex Archaeol Rep **6**, Salisbury

Barrett, J C, 1973 Four Bronze Age cremation cemeteries from Middlesex, *Trans London Middlesex Archaeol Soc* **24**, 111–34

Barrett, J C, 1980 The pottery of the later Bronze Age in lowland England, *Proc Prehist Soc* **46**, 297–319

Barrett, J C, 1994 *Fragments from antiquity*, Oxford

Barrett, J C and Bradley, R (eds), 1980 *Settlement and society in the British later Bronze Age*, BAR Ser **83** (2 vols), Oxford

Bennett, K D, Whittington, G and Edwards, K J, 1994 Recent plant nomenclatural changes and pollen morphology in the British Isles, *Quaternary Newsletter* **73**,1–6

Blake, J H, 1903 *The geology of the country around Reading*. Memoir of the Geological Survey for Sheet **268**

Blinkhorn, P, in press The pottery, in *Excavations at Eynsham Abbey 1989–92* (A Hardy, A Dodd and G Keevil), OA Thames Valley Landscapes Monograph

Bond, D, 1988 Excavation at the North Ring, Mucking, Essex: a late Bronze Age enclosure. *EAA* **43**

Bowsher, M C, 1991 A burnt mound at Phoenix Wharf, south-east London: a preliminary report, in Hodder and Barfield 1991, 11–19

Boyle, A, 1992 An analysis of the human remains, in Moore and Jennings 1992, 89–98

Boyle, A, 2001 Shale, in Barclay *et al.* 2001, 144

Bradley, P, 1994 Struck flint, in The excavation of a later Bronze Age site at Coldharbour Road, Gravesend (A Mudd), *Archaeol Cantiana* **114**, 394–9

Bradley, P, 1997 The worked flint, in *Excavations at the former Jewsons yard, Harefield Road, Uxbridge, Middlesex* (A Barclay, A Boyle, P Bradley and M R Roberts), *Trans London Middlesex Archaeol Soc* **46**, 13–18

Bradley, P, 1999 Worked flint, in Barclay and Halpin 1999, various

Bradley, R, 1983–5 Prehistoric pottery, in Johnston 1983–5, 26–31

Bradley, R, 1986 The Bronze Age in the Oxford area – its local and regional significance, in *The archaeology of the Oxford region* (G Briggs, J Cook and T Rowley), 38–48, Oxford

Bradley, R, 1992 Worked flint – Neolithic, in Moore and Jennings 1992, 89–93

Bradley, R, 1998 *The significance of monuments*, London

Bradley, R and Brown, A, 1992 Flint artefacts, in Moore and Jennings 1992, 89–93

Bradley, R and Ellison, A, 1975 *Rams Hill: a defended enclosure and its landscape*, BAR Ser **19**, Oxford

Bradley, R and Hall, M, 1992a Contexts, chronology and wider associations, in Moore and Jennings 1992, 71–82

Bradley, R and Hall, M, 1992b Oven fragments or pit liner, in Moore and Jennings 1992, 87–9

Bradley, R, Lobb, S, Richards, J and Robinson, M, 1980 Two late Bronze Age settlements on the Kennet gravels: excavations at Aldermaston Wharf and Knight's Farm, Burghfield, Berkshire, *Proc Prehist Soc* **46**, 217–95

Brown, A, 1991 Structured deposition and technological change among the flaked stone artefacts from Cranborne Chase, in *Papers on the prehistoric archaeology of Cranborne Chase* (eds J Barrett, R Bradley and M Hall), 101–33

Brown, A, 1992 Worked flint, late Bronze Age, in Moore and Jennings 1992, 90–3

Brown, A and Bradley, P, forthcoming Worked flint, in Cromarty *et al.* forthcoming

Brown, G, Field, D and McOrmish, D, 1994 East Chisenbury midden complex, in *The Iron Age in Wessex: recent work* (eds A Fitzpatrick and E Morris), Salisbury

Brück, J, 1995 A place for the dead: the role of human remains in late Bronze Age Britain, *Proc Prehist Soc* **61**, 245–77

Buckley, V, 1990 *Burnt offerings: international contributions to burnt mound archaeology*, Dublin

Butterworth, C A and Hawkes, J W, 1997 Floodplain excavations and observations (W244), 1988, in *Excavations at the Thames Valley Park, Reading, 1986–88: prehistoric and Romano-British occupation of the floodplain and a terrace of the River Thames* (I Barnes, C A Butterworth, J W Hawkes and L Smith), Wessex Archaeol Rep **14**, 78–110, Salisbury

Butterworth, C A and Lobb, S J, 1992 *Excavations in the Burghfield area, Berkshire: developments in the Bronze Age and Saxon landscapes*, Wessex Archaeol Rep **1**, Salisbury

Calkin, J B, 1953 Kimmeridge coal-money: the Romano-British shale armulet industry, *Proc Dorset Natur Hist Archaeol Soc* **75**, 45–71

Campbell, G V, 1992 Bronze Age plant remains, in Moore and Jennings 1992, 103–10

Case, H J, 1982 Cassington 1950–2: late Neolithic pits and the big enclosure, in *Settlement patterns in the Oxford region: excavations at the Abingdon causewayed enclosure and other sites* (eds H J Case and A W R Whittle), CBA Res Rep **44**, 118–51, London

Champion, T, 1980 Settlement and environment in later Bronze Age Kent, in Barrett and Bradley 1980, 223–46

Clapham, A J, 1995 Plant remains, in Barnes *et al.* 1995, 35–45

Clapham, A R, Tutin, T G and Moore, D M, 1989 *Flora of the British Isles*, Cambridge

Cleal, R M J, 1991–3 Pottery, in The excavation of a ring ditch at Englefield by John Wymer and Paul Ashbee, 1963, *Berkshire Archaeol J* **74**, 18–21

Cleal, R M J, 1999 Prehistoric pottery, in Barclay and Halpin 1999, various

Cleal, R M J and Gingell, C, 1992 Discussion, in *The Marlborough Downs: a late Bronze Age landscape and its origins* (C Gingell), 99–103, Devizes

Coe, D and Newman, R, 1992 Excavations of an early Iron Age building and Romano-British enclosure at Brighton Hill South, Hampshire, *Proc Hampshire Field Club Archaeol Soc* **48**, 5–21

Collins, A E P, 1947 Excavations on Blewburton Hill, 1947, *Berkshire Archaeol J* **50**, 4–29

Collins, A E P, 1953 Excavations on Blewburton Hill, 1948 and 1949, *Berkshire Archaeol J* **56**, 21–59

Cromarty, A M, Barclay, A and Lambrick, G, forthcoming *Settlement and landscape: the archaeology of the Wallingford Bypass*, OA Thames Valley Landscapes Monograph

Cunliffe, B, 1978 *Iron Age societies in Britain: an account of England, Scotland and Wales from the 7th century BC until the Roman conquest*, 2 edn, London

Cunliffe, B, 1991 *Iron Age communities in Britain*, London

Cunliffe, B, 1992 Pits, preconceptions and propitiation in the British Iron Age, *Oxford J Archaeol* **11(1)**, 69–83

Dacre, M and Ellison, A, 1981 A Bronze Age urn cemetery at Kimpton, Hampshire, *Proc Prehist Soc* **47**, 147–203

De bello Gallico II, xvii, cited in *The history of the countryside: the classic history of Britain's landscape, flora and fauna* (O Rackham), London

Earwood, C, 1993 *Domestic wooden artefacts*, Exeter

Edlin, H L, 1949 *Woodland crafts in Britain*, London

Elliott, L and Knight, D, 1998 A burnt mound at Holme Dyke, Gonalston, Nottinghamshire, *Trans Thoroton Soc Nottinghamshire* **102**, 15–22

Evans, C, 1995 Investigations at Barleycroft Farm, Cambridgeshire, 1994, unpubl. report Cambridge Archaeological Unit

Fasham, P J and Ross, J, 1978 A Bronze Age flint industry from a barrow in Micheldever Wood, Hampshire, *Proc Prehist Soc* **44**, 47–67

Ford, S, Bradley, R, Hawkes, J and Fisher, P, 1984 Flint-working in the Metal Age, *Oxford J Archaeol* **3(1)**, 157–72

Foreman, S and Bradley, P, 1998 *Maidenhead, Windsor and Eaton flood alleviation scheme tranche 2, post-excavation assessment and updated project design*, Oxford

Foxon, A, 1991 Worked skeletal material, in Needham 1991, 148–9

Gent, H, 1983 Centralised storage in later Prehistoric Britain, *Proc Prehist Soc* **49**, 243–67

Gingell, C J, 1980 The Marlborough Downs in the Bronze Age: the first results of current research, in Barrett and Bradley 1980, 209–22

Gingell, C, 1992 *The Marlborough Downs: a later Bronze Age landscape and its origins*, Wiltshire Archaeol Natur Hist Soc, Devizes.

Gingell, C J and Lawson, A J, 1984 The Potterne project: excavation and research at a major settlement of the late Bronze Age, *Wiltshire Archaeol Natur Hist Mag* **78**, 31–4

Gingell, C J and Lawson, A J, 1985 Excavations at Potterne 1984, *Wiltshire Archaeol Natur Hist Mag* **79**, 101–8

Grant, A, 1982 The use of tooth wear as a guide to the age of domestic ungulates, in *Ageing and sexing animal bones from archaeological sites* (eds R Wilson, C Grigson and S Payne), BAR Ser **109**, 91–108, Oxford

Green, H S, 1980 *The flint arrowheads of the British Isles*, BAR Ser **75**, Oxford

Greig, J R A, 1991 The botanical remains, in Needham 1991, 234–6

Guilbert, G, 1982 Post-ring symmetry in roundhouses at Moel Y Gaer and some sites in prehistoric Britain, in *Structural reconstruction: approaches to the inter-*

pretation of the excavated remains of buildings (ed P J Drury), BAR Ser **110**, 67–86, Oxford

Guttmann, E B A and Last, J, 2000 A late Bronze Age landscape at South Hornchurch, Essex, *Proc Prehist Soc* **66**, 319–59

Hall, M, 1992 The prehistoric pottery, in Moore and Jennings 1992, 63–71

Harding, P, 1992a Flint, in Excavations at Field Farm, Burghfield, Berkshire, in Butterworth and Lobb 1992, 38–9

Harding, P A, 1992b Flint, in Archaeological investigations at Anslow's Cottages, Burghfield, in Butterworth and Lobb 1992, 106–8

Harding, P A, 1996 Worked flint, in *Three excavations along the Thames and its tributaries, 1994. Neolithic to Saxon settlement and burial in the Thames, Colne and Kennet Valleys* (P Andrews and A Crockett), Wessex Archaeol Rep **10**, 141–2, Salisbury

Hardy, A, 1999 Excavations at Duffield House, Woodley, Berkshire, *OAU Occas Pap* **4**, Oxford

Healy, F, 1981 Description and analysis (flint industry), in *The excavation of a Bronze Age cemetery on Knighton Heath, Dorset* (F Peterson), BAR Ser **98**, 150–66, Oxford

Healy, F, 1985 The struck flint, in The excavation of a ring ditch at the Tye Field, Lawford, Essex (S J Shennan, F Healy and I F Smith), *Archaeol J* **142**, 177–207

Healy, F, 1991–3 The excavation of a ring ditch at Engelfield by J Wymer and P Ashbee, 1963, *Berkshire Archaeol J* **74**, 9–25

Hedges, J, 1975 Excavation of two Orcadian burnt mounds at Liddle and Beaquoy, *Proc Soc Antiq Scot* **106**, 39–98

Hey, G, 1997 Neolithic settlement at Yarnton, Oxfordshire, in *Neolithic Landscapes, Neolithic Studies Group* 2 (ed P Topping), Oxbow Monograph **86**, 99–111, Oxford

Hey, G, in preparation *Yarnton: Neolithic and Bronze Age settlement and landscape*, OA Thames Valley Landscapes Monograph

Hey, G and Bell, C, 1997 Yarnton floodplain 1996 (SP 469 107), *South Midlands Archaeol* **27**, 62–4

Hey, G and Muir, J, 1997 Yarnton Cassington project post excavation assessment, unpubl. OAU

Hillman, G, 1981 Reconstructing crop husbandry practices from charred remains of crops, in *Farming practice in British prehistory* (ed R Mercer), 123–62, Edinburgh

Hingley, R and Miles, D, 1984 Aspects of Iron Age settlement in the Upper Thames Valley, in *Aspects of the Iron Age in central southern Britain* (eds B Cunliffe and D Miles), University of Oxford: Committee for Archaeology Monograph **2**, 52–71, Oxford

Hodder, M A and Barfield, L H, 1991 *Burnt mounds and hot stone technology: papers from the second international conference 1990*, Sandwell

Hoffman, M, 1964 *The warp-weighted loom: studies in the history and technology of an ancient implement*, Norway

Jarvis, R, 1968 *The soils of Reading district*, Harpenden

Jeffrey, P, 1991 Burnt mounds, fulling and early textiles, in Hodder and Barfield 1991, 97–107

Jennings, D, 1998 Prehistoric and Roman activity, in *The Anglo-Saxon cemetery at Butler's Field, Lechlade, Gloucestershire* (A Boyle, D Jennings, D Miles and S Palmer), Thames Valley Monograph **10**, 9–34, Oxford

Johnston, J, 1983–5 Excavations at Pingewood, ed M Bowden, *Berkshire Archaeol J* **72**, 17–52

King, J E, 1962 Report on animal bones, in Excavations at the Maglemosian site in Thatcham, Berks (J Wymer), *Proc Prehist Soc* **28**, 355–61

Knight, D, 1984 Late Bronze Age and Iron settlement in the Nene and Great Ouse Basins, BAR Ser **130(i)**, Oxford

Lambrick, G, 1992 Alluvial archaeology of the Holocene in the Upper Thames Basin 1971–1991: a review, in *Alluvial archaeology in Britain* (eds S Needham and M G Macklin), Oxbow Monograph **27**, 209–26, Oxford

Lamdin-Whymark, H, in preparation The flint, in *Opening the wood: making the land – Mesolithic to earlier Bronze Age* (T Allen, A Barclay and H Lamdin-Whymark), OA Thames Valley Landscapes Monograph

Lawson, A J, 2000 *Potterne 1982–5: animal husbandry in later prehistoric Wiltshire*, Wessex Archaeol Rep **17**, Salisbury

Legge, T, Payne, S and Rowley-Conwy, P, 1998 The study of food evidence in prehistoric Britain, in *Science in archaeology* (ed J Bayley), 89–94, London

Levitan, B, 1992 Vertebrate remains, in Moore and Jennings 1992, 98–103

Lobb, S J, 1986–90 Excavations and observations of Bronze Age and Saxon deposits at Brimpton, 1978–9, *Berkshire Archaeol J* **73**, 43–53

Lobb, S J, 1992, Excavation at Shortheath Lane, Abbotts Farm, Sulhamstead, in Butterworth and Lobb 1992, 73–8

Longley, D, 1980 *Runnymede Bridge 1976: excavation on the site of a late Bronze Age settlement*, Surrey Archaeol Res Vol **6**, Guildford

Longley, D, 1991 The late Bronze Age pottery, in Needham 1991, 162–212

McCarthy, M R and Brooks, C M, 1988 *Medieval pottery in Britain c AD900–1600*, Leicester

McOrmish, D, 1996 East Chisenbury: ritual and rubbish at the British Bronze Age-Iron Age transition, *Antiquity* **267**, 68–76

Mellor, M, 1994 Oxford pottery: a synthesis of middle and late Saxon, medieval and early post-medieval pottery in the Oxford region, *Oxoniensia* **59**, 17–217

Miller, T, 1987 Systematics and evolution, in *Wheat breeding: its scientific basis* (F G H Lupton), 1–30, London

Moffett, L, Robinson, M A and Straker, V, 1989 Cereals, fruits and nuts: charred plant remains from Neolithic sites in England and Wales and the Neolithic economy, in *The beginnings of agriculture* (eds N Gardner, A Milles and D Williams), BAR Int Ser **496**, 243–61

Monckton, H W, 1893 On the occurrence of boulders and

pebbles from the Glacial Drift in gravels south of the Thames, *Quarterly J Geol Soc* **49**, 308–19

Montague, R, 1995 Flint, in Barnes and Cleal 1995, 24–5

Moore, J and Jennings, D, 1992 *Reading Business Park: a Bronze Age landscape*, OA Thames Valley Landscapes Monograph: the Kennet Valley **1**, Oxford

Moore, J and Miles, D, 1988 *Reading Business Park (axiom 4) proposals for archaeological investigations*, Oxford

Moore, P D and Webb, J A, 1978 *An illustrated guide to pollen analysis*, London

Moore, P D, Webb, J A and Collinson, M E, 1991 *Pollen analysis*, Oxford

Morris, E L, 1991 Ceramic analysis and the pottery from Potterne, in *Recent developments in ceramic petrology* (eds A Middleton and I Freestone), British Museum Occasional Paper **81**, 277–87, London

Morris, E L, 1992 The pottery, in Coe and Newman 1992, 5–21

Morris, E L, 1994 Production and distribution of pottery and salt in Iron Age Britain: a review, *Proc Prehist Soc* **60**, 371–94

Morris, E L, 2000 Pottery, summary, in Lawson 2000, 166–77

Mudd, A, 1995 A late Bronze Age/early Iron Age site at Eight Acre Field, Radley, *Oxoniensia* **60**, 21–66

Murphy, P, 1983 Studies of the environment and economy of a Bronze Age fen-edge site at West Row, Mildenhall, Suffolk: a preliminary report, *Circaea* **1**, 49–60

Needham, S P, 1991 *Excavation and salvage at Runnymede Bridge 1978. The late Bronze Age waterfront site*, London

Needham, S and Burgess, C, 1980 The later Bronze Age in the Lower Thames Valley: the metalwork evidence, in Barrett and Bradley 1980, 437–69

Needham, S and Longley, D, 1980 Runnymede Bridge, Egham: a late Bronze Age riverside settlement, in Barrett and Bradley 1980, 397–436

Needham, S P and Spence, T, 1996 *Refuse and disposal at area 16 East Runnymede*, Runnymede Bridge Research Excavations **2**, London

Northover, P, 1992 Clay mould fragment, in Moore and Jennings 1992, 87–9

Oakley, K P, Rankine, W F and Lowther, A W G, 1939 *A survey of the prehistory of the Farnham district (Surrey)*, Surrey Archaeol Soc, Guildford

O'Connell, M, 1986 *Petters Sports Field, Egham: excavation of a late Bronze Age/early Iron Age site*, Surrey Archaeol Soc Res Vol **10**, Guildford

O'Connell, M, 1990 Excavations during 1979–1985 of a multi-period site at Stanwell, *Surrey Archaeol Collect* **80**, 1–62

Ó Drisceoil, D A, 1988 Burnt mounds: cooking or bathing?, *Antiquity* **62**, 671–80

O'Kelly, M J, 1954 Excavations and experiments in ancient Irish cooking-places, *J Roy Soc Antiq Ir* **84**, 105–55

Parker-Pearson, M, 1996 Food, fertility and front doors in the first millennium BC, in *The Iron Age in Britain: recent trends* (eds T Champion and J R Collis), 117–32, Sheffield

PCRG, 1997 *The study of later prehistoric pottery: general policies and guidelines for analysis and publication*, Prehistoric Ceramics Research Group Occasional Papers 1 and 2

Peacock, D P S, 1982 *Pottery in the Roman world; an ethnoarchaeological approach*, London

Porter, V, 1990 *Small woods and hedgerows*, London

Pryor, F M M, 1980 *Excavation at Fengate, Peterborough, England: the third report*, Northants Archaeol Soc Monogr 1/Royal Ontario Museum Archaeol Monogr **6**

Pryor, F 1998 *Farmers in prehistoric Britain*, Stroud

Rackham, O, 1990 *Trees and woodland*, London

Raymond, F, 1987 *Monuments protection programme single monument class description: burnt mounds*, London

Raymond, F, 1994 The pottery, in *Prehistoric land divisions on Salisbury Plain* (R J Bradley, R Entwhistle and F Raymond), English Heritage Archaeol Rep **2**, 69–90, London

Richards, C C and Thomas, J S, 1984 Ritual activity and structured deposition in later Neolithic Wessex, in *Neolithic studies* (eds R J Bradley and J Gardiner), BAR Ser **133**, 189–218, Oxford

Richards, J, 1990 *Stonehenge environs project*, English Heritage Archaeol Rep **16**, London

Richards, J, 1991 *Stonehenge*, London

Robertson-Mackay, R 1987 The Neolithic causewayed enclosures at Staines, Surrey: excavations 1961–3, *Proc Prehist Soc* **53**, 23–128

Robinson, M A, 1992 Soils, sediments and hydrology, in Moore and Jennings 1992, 5, 112–16

Robinson, M, 2000 Further considerations of Neolithic charred cereals, fruits and nuts, in *Plants in Neolithic Britain and beyond*, Neolithic Studies Group Seminar Papers 5 (ed. A S Fairbairn), Oxford, 85–90

Robinson, M and Hubbard, R N L B, 1977 The transport of pollen in bracts of hulled cereals, *J Archaeol Sci* **4**, 197–9

Robinson, M and Wilson, R, 1987 A survey of environmental archaeology in the south Midlands, in *Environmental archaeology: a regional review* (H Keeley), Dir Anc Monu Hist Build Occas Pap **6(2)**, 16–100, London

Roe, F, in preparation Worked stone, in Hey in preparation

Ryder, M J, 1981 Livestock products: skins and fleeces, in *Farming practice in British prehistory* (ed R Mercer), 182–209, Edinburgh

Seager Smith, R and Cleal, R M J, 1997 Earlier prehistoric pottery, in Butterworth and Hawkes 1997, 89–91

Serjeantson, D, 1996 The animal bones, in Needham and Spence 1996, 194–253

Shepherd, W, 1972 *Flint. Its origins, properties and uses*, London

Stace, C, 1991 *New flora of the British Isles*, Cambridge

Stockmarr, J, 1971 Tablets with spores used in absolute pollen analysis, *Pollen et Spores* **13**, 614–21

Taylor, M, 1992 Wood from Flag Fen and Fengate, *Antiquity* **66**, 476–98

Taylor, M, 2001 The wood, in *The Flag Fen Basin: archaeology and environment of a fenland landscape* (ed F Pryor), 167–228, Swindon

Thomas, J, 1991 *Rethinking the Neolithic*, Cambridge

Thomas, J, 1999 *Understanding the Neolithic*, London

Thomas, R, Robinson, M, Barrett, J and Wilson, B, 1986 A late Bronze Age riverside settlement at Wallingford, *Archaeol J* **143**, 174–200

Underwood-Keevil, C, 1997 Pottery, in *Excavations on Reading waterfront sites, 1979–1988* (J W Hawkes and P J Fasham), Wessex Archaeol Rep **5**, 142–61, Salisbury

Wainwright, G and Longworth, I H, 1971 *Durrington Walls: excavations 1966–1968*, Rep Res Comm Soc Antiq London **29**, London

Webster, A D, 1919 *Firewoods: their production and fuel values*, London

Welch, C M, 1994–5 A Bronze Age burnt mound at Milwich, *Trans Staffordshire Archaeol Hist Soc* **36**, 1–5

Whittle, A, 1991 Wayland's Smithy, Oxfordshire: excavations at the Neolithic tomb in 1962 by R J C Atkinson and S Piggott, *Proc Prehist Soc* **57(2)**, 61–101

Whittle, A, Atkinson, R J C, Chambers, R and Thomas, N, 1992 Excavations in the Neolithic and Bronze Age complex at Dorchester-on-Thames, Oxfordshire, 1947–1952 and 1981, *Proc Prehist Soc* **58**, 143–201

Wild, J P, 1988 *Textiles in archaeology*, Aylesbury

Wilkinson, D, 1992 *Oxford Archaeological Unit field manual*, Oxford

Williams, R J and Zeepvat, R J, 1994 *Bancroft: a late Bronze Age and Iron Age settlement, Roman villa and temple mausoleum, excavations and building materials*, Buckingham Archaeol Soc Monogr Ser 7, **1**

Wilson, R, 1985 Degraded bones, feature type and spatial patterning on an Iron Age occupation site in Oxfordshire, England, in *Palaeobotanical investigations: research design, methods and data analysis* (eds N R J Fieller, D D Gilbertson and N G A Ralph), BAR Int Ser **266**, 81–94

Wilson, R, 1990 The animal bones, in Allen 1990, 57–61 and 94–8

Wilson, R, 1993 Reports on the bones and oyster shell, in *The prehistoric landscape and Iron Age enclosed settlement at Mingies Ditch, Hardwick with Yelford, Oxon* (T G Allen and M A Robinson), OA Thames Valley Landscapes Monograph: The Windrush Valley **2**, 123–34 and 168–204, Oxford

Wilson, R, 1996 *Spatial patterning among animal bones in settlement archaeology*, BAR Ser **251**

Yates, D, 1999 Bronze Age field systems in the Thames Valley, *Oxford J Archaeol* **18(2)**, 157–70

Zohary, D and Hopf, M, 1994 *Domestication of plants in the Old World*, Oxford

Index

Note: Page references in *italics* denote Figures and Plates. There may also be textual references on these pages.